Land of the Free, Home of the Brave

Our Founding Documents & Concise History of the USA

Declaration of Independence · US Constitution · Bill of Rights
National Anthem · US Presidents · The 50 States
A Concise History of the United States of America
The Flag Code · Monuments · Military History
Sports Champions of the Past Century

Mark Zimmerman
Author of God, Guns, Guitars & Whiskey

Also by Mark Zimmerman
and available from Zimco Publications LLC:

Mud, Blood & Cold Steel:
The Retreat From Nashville, December 1864

Iron Maidens and the Devil's Daughters:
U.S. Navy Gunboats versus Confederate Gunners and Cavalry
on the Tennessee and Cumberland Rivers, 1861-65

Guide to Civil War Nashville, 2nd Edition

God, Guns, Guitars & Whiskey:
An Illustrated Guide to Historic Nashville, Tennessee, 2nd Edition

Gone Under:
Historic Cemeteries and Burial Grounds
of Nashville, Tennessee, 2nd Edition

Zimco Publications LLC
zimcopubs.com

―――― *Land of the Free, Home of the Brave* ――――

*We, the People, hold these truths to be self-evident,
that all men are created equal,
that they are endowed by their Creator
with certain unalienable Rights,
that among these are
Life, Liberty and the pursuit of Happiness.*

―――― ❖ ❖ ❖ ――――

Dedicated to the men and women who created and built the United States of America, especially those who made the supreme sacrifice.

―――― ❖ ❖ ❖ ――――

*The author would like to acknowledge the assistance of the National Archives and Records Administration for much of the content of this publication, used with permission. To access much more information about our founding documents, go to
https://www.archives.gov/founding-docs*

The Honor Wall in Wilson County, Tennessee, displays the names of at least 130 former students of nearby Wilson Central High School who serve or have served in the US armed forces, including Army Spc. Michael L. Stansbery, 1st Battalion, 320th Field Artillery Regiment, 2nd Brigade Combat Team, 101st Airborne Division (Air Assault), who died July 30, 2010 near Kandahar, Afghanistan, of injuries sustained when insurgents attacked his unit with an improvised explosive device. He was 21 years old. He is buried at Arlington National Cemetery. The Honor Wall is maintained by WCHS teachers and students.

―――― ❖ ❖ ❖ ――――

On the Cover: The Bennington Flag, associated with the 1777 Battle of Bennington, Vermont, a Patriot victory. The '76' refers to the 1776 Declaration of Independence.

Land of the Free, Home of the Brave
Our Founding Documents & Concise History of the USA

Copyright © 2020 Mark Zimmerman
Zimco Publications LLC
Website: zimcopubs.com
Email: info@zimcopubs.com

ISBN Paperback 978-0-9858692-8-1

All rights reserved.

No part of this book may be reproduced or transmitted in any form or by any means — electronic or manual, including photocopy, scanner, email, CD or other information storage and retreival system — without written permission from the author, except for personal use or as provided to the news media and book sellers.

Printed in the United States of America.

The text in this book, which is published to inform and entertain, should be used for general information and not as the ultimate source of educational or travel information. Every effort has been made to ensure the accuracy and relevence of information in this book but the author and publisher do not assume responsibility for any errors, inaccuracies, omissions or inconsistencies within. Any slights of people, places, or organizations are strictly unintentional.

The names of organizations and destinations mentioned in this book may be trade names or trademarks of their owners. The author and publisher disclaims any connection with, sponsorship by or endorsement of such owners.
Content related to this publication can be found on the publisher's website at: zimcopubs.com

Table of Contents

Declaration of Independence 3
History of the Declaration of Independence 6
US Constitution 19
The Bill of Rights and Amendments 28
A More Perfect Union –
   The Creation of the U.S. Constitution 37
Our Founding Fathers 47
National Anthem 60
Gettysburg Address 61
Oath of Allegiance 62
Oaths of Office 62
U.S. Citizenship 63
Pledge of Allegiance 64
National Holidays 64
US Flag and Flag Code 65
Flag Myths 66
USA Third Largest Country in the World 67
US Territories 67
Time Zones, Currency, Federal Reserve, Fort Knox 68
Constitutional Republic Form of Government 69
Concise History of the USA 72
Presidents of the United States of America 83
Presidential Factoids 91
Presidential Elections 92
The White House 95
National Statuary Hall Collection 96
Lain in State or Honor at US Capitol Rotunda 98
The 50 States: State by State Data 101
Largest Cities by Population 103
US Armed Forces 105
US Army Bases and Facilities 106
US Navy Bases and Facilities 108
US Air Force Bases and Facilities 109
US Marine Corps Bases and Facilities 110

Table of Contents

Highest Ranking Military Officers 111
US Medals and Honors 113
Wars Ranked by Military Combat Deaths 114
US Military Casualties by War 115
Arlington National Cemetery 116
American Battle Monuments Commission 116
National Cemeteries 117
Big Battles, Minor Wars, Old Forts, Military Museums 121
History of US Space Program 127
Monuments, Engineering Marvels of the USA 131
Disasters and Catastrophes 134
Top USA Tourist Attractions 137
National Park System Properties 138
Historic Sites in the USA 144

Sports Champions of the Past Century:
MLB World Series 148
NFL Super Bowl 151
NHL Stanley Cup 153
NBA Finals 154
Golf Major Tournaments 155
Indianapolis 500 158
NASCAR Cup Champions 159
Kentucky Derby 160
College NCAA Football Champions 164
Largest Football Stadiums in US 167
College NCAA Basketball Champions 168
College NCAA Women's Basketball Champions 170
Olympic Games in USA 171

Learning More:
Suggested Readings 172

Declaration of Independence

In Congress, July 4, 1776.

The unanimous Declaration of the thirteen united States of America, When in the Course of human events, it becomes necessary for one people to dissolve the political bands which have connected them with another, and to assume among the powers of the earth, the separate and equal station to which the Laws of Nature and of Nature's God entitle them, a decent respect to the opinions of mankind requires that they should declare the causes which impel them to the separation.

We hold these truths to be self-evident, that all men are created equal, that they are endowed by their Creator with certain unalienable Rights, that among these are Life, Liberty and the pursuit of Happiness.–That to secure these rights, Governments are instituted among Men, deriving their just powers from the consent of the governed, –That whenever any Form of Government becomes destructive of these ends, it is the Right of the People to alter or to abolish it, and to institute new Government, laying its foundation on such principles and organizing its powers in such form, as to them shall seem most likely to effect their Safety and Happiness. Prudence, indeed, will dictate that Governments long established should not be changed for light and transient causes; and accordingly all experience hath shewn, that mankind are more disposed to suffer, while evils are sufferable, than to right themselves by abolishing the forms to which they are accustomed. But when a long train of abuses and usurpations, pursuing invariably the same Object evinces a design to reduce them under absolute Despotism, it is their right, it is their duty, to throw off such Government, and to provide new Guards for their future security.– Such has been the patient sufferance of these Colonies; and such is now the necessity which constrains them to alter their former Systems of Government. The history of the present King of Great Britain is a history of repeated injuries and usurpations, all having in direct object the establishment of an absolute Tyranny over these States. To prove this, let Facts be submitted to a candid world.

He has refused his Assent to Laws, the most wholesome and necessary for the public good.

He has forbidden his Governors to pass Laws of immediate and pressing importance, unless suspended in their operation till his Assent should be obtained; and when so suspended, he has utterly neglected to attend to them.

He has refused to pass other Laws for the accommodation of large districts of people, unless those people would relinquish the right of Representation in the Legislature, a right inestimable to them and formidable to tyrants only.

He has called together legislative bodies at places unusual, uncomfortable, and distant from the depository of their public Records, for the sole purpose of fatiguing them into compliance with his measures.

He has dissolved Representative Houses repeatedly, for opposing with manly firmness his invasions on the rights of the people.

He has refused for a long time, after such dissolutions, to cause others to be elected; whereby the Legislative powers, incapable of Annihilation, have returned to the People at large for their exercise; the State remaining in the mean time exposed to all the dangers of invasion from without, and convulsions within.

He has endeavoured to prevent the population of these States; for that purpose obstructing the Laws for Naturalization of Foreigners; refusing to pass others to encourage their migrations hither, and raising the conditions of new Appropriations of Lands.

Declaration of Independence

He has obstructed the Administration of Justice, by refusing his Assent to Laws for establishing Judiciary powers.

He has made Judges dependent on his Will alone, for the tenure of their offices, and the amount and payment of their salaries.

He has erected a multitude of New Offices, and sent hither swarms of Officers to harrass our people, and eat out their substance.

He has kept among us, in times of peace, Standing Armies without the Consent of our legislatures.

He has affected to render the Military independent of and superior to the Civil power.

He has combined with others to subject us to a jurisdiction foreign to our constitution, and unacknowledged by our laws; giving his Assent to their Acts of pretended Legislation:

For Quartering large bodies of armed troops among us:

For protecting them, by a mock Trial, from punishment for any Murders which they should commit on the Inhabitants of these States:

For cutting off our Trade with all parts of the world:

For imposing Taxes on us without our Consent:

For depriving us in many cases, of the benefits of Trial by Jury:

For transporting us beyond Seas to be tried for pretended offences

For abolishing the free System of English Laws in a neighbouring Province, establishing therein an Arbitrary government, and enlarging its Boundaries so as to render it at once an example and fit instrument for introducing the same absolute rule into these Colonies:

For taking away our Charters, abolishing our most valuable Laws, and altering fundamentally the Forms of our Governments:

For suspending our own Legislatures, and declaring themselves invested with power to legislate for us in all cases whatsoever.

He has abdicated Government here, by declaring us out of his Protection and waging War against us.

He has plundered our seas, ravaged our Coasts, burnt our towns, and destroyed the lives of our people.

He is at this time transporting large Armies of foreign Mercenaries to compleat the works of death, desolation and tyranny, already begun with circumstances of Cruelty & perfidy scarcely paralleled in the most barbarous ages, and totally unworthy the Head of a civilized nation.

He has constrained our fellow Citizens taken Captive on the high Seas to bear Arms against their Country, to become the executioners of their friends and Brethren, or to fall themselves by their Hands.

He has excited domestic insurrections amongst us, and has endeavoured to bring on the inhabitants of our frontiers, the merciless Indian Savages, whose known rule of warfare, is an undistinguished destruction of all ages, sexes and conditions.

In every stage of these Oppressions We have Petitioned for Redress in the most humble terms: Our repeated Petitions have been answered only by repeated injury. A Prince whose character is thus marked by every act which may define a Tyrant, is unfit to be the ruler of a free people.

Nor have We been wanting in attentions to our Brittish brethren. We have warned them from time to time of attempts by their legislature to extend an unwarrantable jurisdiction over us. We have reminded them of the circumstances of our emigration and settlement here. We have appealed to their native

Declaration of Independence

justice and magnanimity, and we have conjured them by the ties of our common kindred to disavow these usurpations, which, would inevitably interrupt our connections and correspondence. They too have been deaf to the voice of justice and of consanguinity. We must, therefore, acquiesce in the necessity, which denounces our Separation, and hold them, as we hold the rest of mankind, Enemies in War, in Peace Friends.

We, therefore, the Representatives of the united States of America, in General Congress, Assembled, appealing to the Supreme Judge of the world for the rectitude of our intentions, do, in the Name, and by Authority of the good People of these Colonies, solemnly publish and declare, That these United Colonies are, and of Right ought to be Free and Independent States; that they are Absolved from all Allegiance to the British Crown, and that all political connection between them and the State of Great Britain, is and ought to be totally dissolved; and that as Free and Independent States, they have full Power to levy War, conclude Peace, contract Alliances, establish Commerce, and to do all other Acts and Things which Independent States may of right do. And for the support of this Declaration, with a firm reliance on the protection of divine Providence, we mutually pledge to each other our Lives, our Fortunes and our sacred Honor.

Georgia
Button Gwinnett
Lyman Hall
George Walton
North Carolina
William Hooper
Joseph Hewes
John Penn
South Carolina
Edward Rutledge
Thomas Heyward, Jr.
Thomas Lynch, Jr.
Arthur Middleton
Massachusetts
John Hancock
Maryland
Samuel Chase
William Paca

Thomas Stone
Charles Carroll
of Carrollton
Virginia
George Wythe
Richard Henry Lee
Thomas Jefferson
Benjamin Harrison
Thomas Nelson, Jr.
Francis Lightfoot Lee
Carter Braxton
Pennsylvania
Robert Morris
Benjamin Rush
Benjamin Franklin
John Morton
George Clymer
James Smith

George Taylor
James Wilson
George Ross
Delaware
Caesar Rodney
George Read
Thomas McKean
New York
William Floyd
Philip Livingston
Francis Lewis
Lewis Morris
New Jersey
Richard Stockton
John Witherspoon
Francis Hopkinson
John Hart
Abraham Clark

New Hampshire
Josiah Bartlett
William Whipple
Massachusetts
Samuel Adams
John Adams
Robert Treat Paine
Elbridge Gerry
Rhode Island
Stephen Hopkins
William Ellery
Connecticut
Roger Sherman
Samuel Huntington
William Williams
Oliver Wolcott
New Hampshire
Matthew Thornton

Note: The text is a transcription of the Stone Engraving of the parchment Declaration of Independence (the document on display in the Rotunda at the National Archives Museum). The spelling and punctuation reflect the original.

A History of the Declaration of Independence

The clearest call for independence up to the summer of 1776 came in Philadelphia on June 7. On that date in session in the Pennsylvania State House (later Independence Hall), the Continental Congress heard Richard Henry Lee of Virginia read his resolution beginning: "Resolved: That these United Colonies are, and of right ought to be, free and independent States, that they are absolved from all allegiance to the British Crown, and that all political connection between them and the State of Great Britain is, and ought to be, totally dissolved."

The Lee Resolution was an expression of what was already beginning to happen throughout the colonies. When the Second Continental Congress, which was essentially the government of the United States from 1775 to 1788, first met in May 1775, King George III had not replied to the petition for redress of grievances that he had been sent by the First Continental Congress. The Congress gradually took on the responsibilities of a national government. In June 1775 the Congress established the Continental Army as well as a continental currency. By the end of July of that year, it created a post office for the "United Colonies."

In August 1775 a royal proclamation declared that the King's American subjects were "engaged in open and avowed rebellion." Later that year, Parliament passed the American Prohibitory Act, which made all American vessels and cargoes forfeit to the Crown. And in May 1776 the Congress learned that the King had negotiated treaties with German states to hire mercenaries to fight in America. The weight of these actions combined to convince many Americans that the mother country was treating the colonies as a foreign entity.

One by one, the Continental Congress continued to cut the colonies' ties to Britain. The Privateering Resolution, passed in March 1776, allowed the colonists "to fit out armed vessels to cruize [sic] on the enemies of these United Colonies." On April 6, 1776, American ports were opened to commerce with other nations, an action that severed the economic ties fostered by the Navigation Acts. A "Resolution for the Formation of Local Governments" was passed on May 10, 1776.

At the same time, more of the colonists themselves were becoming convinced of the inevitability of independence. Thomas Paine's *Common Sense*,

Source: US National Archives. Used with permission.

published in January 1776, was sold by the thousands. By the middle of May 1776, eight colonies had decided that they would support independence. On May 15, 1776, the Virginia Convention passed a resolution that "the delegates appointed to represent this colony in General Congress be instructed to propose to that respectable body to declare the United Colonies free and independent states."

It was in keeping with these instructions that Richard Henry Lee, on June 7, 1776, presented his resolution. There were still some delegates, however, including those bound by earlier instructions, who wished to pursue the path of reconciliation with Britain. On June 11 consideration of the Lee Resolution was postponed by a vote of seven colonies to five, with New York abstaining. Congress then recessed for three weeks. The tone of the debate indicated that at the end of that time the Lee Resolution would be adopted. Before Congress recessed, therefore, a Committee of Five was appointed to draft a statement presenting to the world the colonies' case for independence.

The Committee of Five

The committee consisted of two New England men, John Adams of Massachusetts and Roger Sherman of Connecticut; two men from the Middle Colonies, Benjamin Franklin of Pennsylvania and Robert R. Livingston of New York; and one southerner, Thomas Jefferson of Virginia. In 1823 Jefferson wrote that the other members of the committee "unanimously pressed on myself alone to undertake the draught [sic]. I consented; I drew it; but before I reported it to the committee I communicated it separately to Dr. Franklin and Mr. Adams requesting their corrections…I then wrote a fair copy, reported it to the committee, and from them, unaltered to the Congress." (If Jefferson did make a "fair copy," incorporating the changes made by Franklin and Adams, it has not been preserved. It may have been the copy that was amended by the Congress and used for printing, but in any case, it has not survived. Jefferson's rough draft, however, with changes made by Franklin and Adams, as well as Jefferson's own notes of changes by the Congress, is housed at the Library of Congress.)

Jefferson's account reflects three stages in the life of

A History of the Declaration of Independence

the Declaration: the document originally written by Jefferson; the changes to that document made by Franklin and Adams, resulting in the version that was submitted by the Committee of Five to the Congress; and the version that was eventually adopted.

On July 1, 1776, Congress reconvened. The following day, the Lee Resolution for independence was adopted by 12 of the 13 colonies, New York not voting. Immediately afterward, the Congress began to consider the Declaration. Adams and Franklin had made only a few changes before the committee submitted the document. The discussion in Congress resulted in some alterations and deletions, but the basic document remained Jefferson's. The process of revision continued through all of July 3 and into the late morning of July 4. The Declaration had been officially adopted.

The Declaration of Independence is made up of five distinct parts: the introduction; the preamble; the body, which can be divided into two sections; and a conclusion. The introduction states that this document will "declare" the "causes" that have made it necessary for the American colonies to leave the British Empire. Having stated in the introduction that independence is unavoidable, even necessary, the preamble sets out principles that were already recognized to be "self-evident" by most 18th-century Englishmen, closing with the statement that "a long train of abuses and usurpations... evinces a design to reduce [a people] under absolute Despotism, it is their right, it is their duty, to throw off such Government, and to provide new Guards for their future security." The first section of the body of the Declaration gives evidence of the "long train of abuses and usurpations" heaped upon the colonists by King George III. The second section of the body states that the colonists had appealed in vain to their "British brethren" for a redress of their grievances. Having stated the conditions that made independence necessary and having shown that those conditions existed in British North America, the Declaration concludes that "these United Colonies are, and of Right ought to be Free and Independent States; that they are Absolved from all Allegiance to the British Crown, and that all political connection between them and the State of Great Britain, is and ought to be totally dissolved."

Although Congress had adopted the Declaration submitted by the Committee of Five, the committee's task was not yet completed. Congress had also directed that the committee supervise the printing of the adopted document. The first printed copies of the Declaration of Independence were turned out from the shop of John Dunlap, official printer to the Congress. After the Declaration had been adopted, the committee took to Dunlap the manuscript document, possibly Jefferson's "fair copy" of his rough draft. On the morning of July 5, copies were dispatched by members of Congress to various assemblies, conventions, and committees of safety as well as to the commanders of Continental troops. Also on July 5, a copy of the printed version of the approved Declaration was inserted into the "rough journal" of the Continental Congress for July 4. The text was followed by the words "Signed by Order and in Behalf of the Congress, John Hancock, President. Attest. Charles Thomson, Secretary." It is not known how many copies John Dunlap printed on his busy night of July 4. There are 26 copies known to exist of what is commonly referred to as "the Dunlap broadside," 21 owned by American institutions, two by British institutions, and three by private owners.

The Engrossed Declaration

On July 9 the action of Congress was officially approved by the New York Convention. All 13 colonies had now signified their approval. On July 19, therefore, Congress was able to order that the Declaration be "fairly engrossed on parchment, with the title and stile [sic] of 'The unanimous declaration of the thirteen United States of America,' and that the same, when engrossed, be signed by every member of Congress."

Engrossing is the process of preparing an official document in a large, clear hand. Timothy Matlack was probably the engrosser of the Declaration. He was a Pennsylvanian who had assisted the Secretary of the Congress, Charles Thomson, in his duties for over a year and who had written out George Washington's commission as commanding general of the Continental Army. Matlack set to work with pen, ink, parchment, and practiced hand, and finally, on August 2, the journal of the Continental Congress records that "The declaration of independence being engrossed and compared at the table was signed." One of the most widely held misconceptions about the Declaration is that it was signed on July 4, 1776, by all

A History of the Declaration of Independence

the delegates in attendance.

John Hancock, the President of the Congress, was the first to sign the sheet of parchment measuring 24¼ by 29¾ inches. He used a bold signature centered below the text. In accordance with prevailing custom, the other delegates began to sign at the right below the text, their signatures arranged according to the geographic location of the states they represented. New Hampshire, the northernmost state, began the list, and Georgia, the southernmost, ended it. Eventually 56 delegates signed, although all were not present on August 2. Among the later signers were Elbridge Gerry, Oliver Wolcott, Lewis Morris, Thomas McKean, and Matthew Thornton, who found that he had no room to sign with the other New Hampshire delegates. A few delegates who voted for adoption of the Declaration on July 4 were never to sign in spite of the July 19 order of Congress that the engrossed document "be signed by every member of Congress." Nonsigners included John Dickinson, who clung to the idea of reconciliation with Britain, and Robert R. Livingston, one of the Committee of Five, who thought the Declaration was premature.

Parchment and Ink

Over the next 200 years, the nation whose birth was announced with a Declaration "fairly engrossed on parchment" was to show immense growth in area, population, economic power, and social complexity and a lasting commitment to a testing and strengthening of its democracy. But what of the parchment itself? How was it to fare over the course of two centuries?

In the chronicle of the Declaration as a physical object, three themes necessarily entwine themselves: the relationship between the physical aging of the parchment and the steps taken to preserve it from deterioration; the relationship between the parchment and the copies that were made from it; and finally, the often dramatic story of the travels of the parchment during wartime and to its various homes.

Chronologically, it is helpful to divide the history of the Declaration after its signing into five main periods, some more distinct than others. The first period consists of the early travels of the parchment and lasts until 1814. The second period relates to the long sojourn of the Declaration in Washington, DC, from 1814 until its brief return to Philadelphia for the 1876 Centennial. The third period covers the years 1877-1921, a period marked by increasing concern for the deterioration of the document and the need for a fitting and permanent Washington home. Except for an interlude during World War II, the fourth and fifth periods cover the time the Declaration rested in the Library of Congress from 1921 to 1952 and in the National Archives from 1952 to the present.

Early Travels, 1776-1814

Once the Declaration was signed, the document probably accompanied the Continental Congress as that body traveled during the uncertain months and years of the Revolution. Initially, like other parchment documents of the time, the Declaration was probably stored in a rolled format. Each time the document was used, it would have been unrolled and re-rolled. This action, as well as holding the curled parchment flat, doubtless took its toll on the ink and on the parchment surface through abrasion and flexing. The acidity inherent in the iron gall ink used by Timothy Matlack allowed the ink to "bite" into the surface of the parchment, thus contributing to the ink's longevity, but the rolling and unrolling of the parchment still presented many hazards.

After the signing ceremony on Aug. 2, 1776, the Declaration was most likely filed in Philadelphia in the office of Charles Thomson, who served as the Secretary of the Continental Congress from 1774 to 1789. On December 12, threatened by the British, Congress adjourned and reconvened eight days later in Baltimore, Md. A light wagon carried the Declaration to its new home, where it remained until its return to Philadelphia in March of 1777.

On Jan. 18, 1777, while the Declaration was still in Baltimore, Congress, bolstered by military successes at Trenton and Princeton, ordered the second official printing of the document. The July 4 printing had included only the names of John Hancock and Charles Thomson, and even though the first printing had been promptly circulated to the states, the names of subsequent signers were kept secret for a time because of fear of British reprisals. By its order of January 18, however, Congress required that "an authentic copy of the Declaration of Independency, with the names of the members of Congress subscribing to the same, be sent to each of the United States, and that they be desired to

A History of the Declaration of Independence

have the same put upon record." The "authentic copy" was duly printed, complete with signers' names, by Mary Katherine Goddard in Baltimore.

Assuming that the Declaration moved with the Congress, it would have been back in Philadelphia from March to September 1777. On September 27, it would have moved to Lancaster, Pa., for one day only. From Sept. 30, 1777, through June 1778, the Declaration would have been kept in the courthouse at York, Pa. From July 1778 to June 1783, it would have had a long stay back in Philadelphia. In 1783, it would have been at Princeton, NJ, from June to November, and then, after the signing of the Treaty of Paris, the Declaration would have been moved to Annapolis, Md., where it stayed until October 1784. For the months of November and December 1784, it would have been at Trenton, NJ. Then in 1785, when Congress met in New York, the Declaration was housed in the old New York City Hall, where it probably remained until 1790 (although when Pierre L'Enfant was remodeling the building for the convening of the First Federal Congress, it might have been temporarily removed).

In July 1789 the First Congress under the new Constitution created the Department of Foreign Affairs and directed that its Secretary should have "the custody and charge of all records, books and papers" kept by the department of the same name under the old government. On July 24 Charles Thomson retired as Secretary of the Congress and, upon the order of President George Washington, surrendered the Declaration to Roger Alden, Deputy Secretary of Foreign Affairs. In September 1789 the name of the department was changed to the Department of State. Thomas Jefferson, the drafter of the Declaration, returned from France to assume his duties as the first Secretary of State in March of 1790. Appropriately, those duties now included custody of the Declaration.

In July 1790 Congress provided for a permanent capital to be built among the woodlands and swamps bordering the Potomac River. Meanwhile, the temporary seat of government was to return to Philadelphia. Congress also provided that "prior to the first Monday in December next, all offices attached to the seat of the government of the United States" should be removed to Philadelphia. The Declaration was therefore back in Philadelphia by the close of 1790.

It was housed in various buildings — on Market Street, at Arch and Sixth, and at Fifth and Chestnut.

In 1800, by direction of President John Adams, the Declaration and other government records were moved from Philadelphia to the new federal capital now rising in the District of Columbia. To reach its new home, the Declaration traveled down the Delaware River and Bay, out into the ocean, into the Chesapeake Bay, and up the Potomac to Washington, completing its longest water journey.

For about two months the Declaration was housed in buildings built for the use of the Treasury Department. For the next year it was housed in one of the "Seven Buildings" then standing at Nineteenth Street and Pennsylvania Avenue. Its third home before 1814 was in the old War Office Building on Seventeenth Street.

In August 1814, the United States being again at war with Great Britain, a British fleet appeared in the Chesapeake Bay. Secretary of State James Monroe rode out to observe the landing of British forces along the Patuxent River in Maryland. A message from Monroe alerted State Department officials, in particular a clerk named Stephen Pleasonton, of the imminent threat to the capital city and, of course, the government's official records. Pleasonton "proceeded to purchase coarse linen, and cause it to be made into bags of convenient size, in which the gentlemen of the office" packed the precious books and records including the Declaration.

A cartload of records was then taken up the Potomac River to an unused gristmill belonging to Edgar Patterson. The structure was located on the Virginia side of the Potomac, about two miles upstream from Georgetown. Here the Declaration and the other records remained, probably overnight. Pleasonton, meanwhile, asked neighboring farmers for the use of their wagons. On August 24, the day of the British attack on Washington, the Declaration was on its way to Leesburg, Va. That evening, while the White House and other government buildings were burning, the Declaration was stored 35 miles away at Leesburg.

The Declaration remained safe at a private home in Leesburg for an interval of several weeks — in fact, until the British had withdrawn their troops from Washington and their fleet from the Chesapeake Bay. In September 1814 the Declaration was returned

A History of the Declaration of Independence

to the national capital. With the exception of a trip to Philadelphia for the Centennial and to Fort Knox during World War II, it has remained there ever since.

Washington, 1814-76

The Declaration remained in Washington from September 1814 to May 1841. It was housed in four locations. From 1814 to 1841, it was kept in three different locations as the State Department records were shifted about the growing city. The last of these locations was a brick building that, it was later observed, "offered no security against fire."

One factor that had no small effect on the physical condition of the Declaration was recognized as interest in reproductions of the Declaration increased as the nation grew. Two early facsimile printings of the Declaration were made during the second decade of the 19th century: those of Benjamin Owen Tyler (1818) and John Binns (1819). Both facsimiles used decorative and ornamental elements to enhance the text of the Declaration. Richard Rush, who was Acting Secretary of State in 1817, remarked on September 10 of that year about the Tyler copy: "The foregoing copy of the Declaration of Independence has been collated with the original instrument and found correct. I have myself examined the signatures to each. Those executed by Mr. Tyler, are curiously exact imitations, so much so, that it would be difficult, if not impossible, for the closest scrutiny to distinguish them, were it not for the hand of time, from the originals." Rush's reference to "the hand of time" suggests that the signatures were already fading in 1817, only 40 years after they were first affixed to the parchment.

One later theory as to why the Declaration was aging so soon after its creation stems from the common 18th-century practice of taking "press copies." Press copies were made by placing a damp sheet of thin paper on a manuscript and pressing it until a portion of the ink was transferred. The thin paper copy was retained in the same manner as a modern carbon copy. The ink was reimposed on a copper plate, which was then etched so that copies could be run off the plate on a press. This "wet transfer" method may have been used by William J. Stone when in 1820 he was commissioned by Secretary of State John Quincy Adams to make a facsimile of the entire Declaration, signatures as well as text. By June 5, 1823, almost exactly 47 years after Jefferson's first draft of the Declaration, the (Washington) *National Intelligencer* was able to report "that Mr. William J. Stone, a respectable and enterprising Engraver of this City, has, after a labor of three years, completed a fac simile of the original of the Declaration of Independence, now in the archives of the government; that it is executed with the greatest exactness and fidelity; and that the Department of State has become the purchaser of the plate."

As the *Intelligencer* went on to observe: "We are very glad to hear this, for the original of that paper which ought to be immortal and imperishable, by being so much handled by copyists and curious visitors, might receive serious injury. The facility of multiplying copies of it now possessed by the Department of State will render further exposure of the original unnecessary." The language of the newspaper report, like that of Rush's earlier comment, would seem to indicate some fear of the deterioration of the Declaration even prior to Stone's work.

The copies made from Stone's copperplate established the clear visual image of the Declaration for generations of Americans. The 200 official parchment copies struck from the Stone plate carry the identification "Engraved by W. J. Stone for the Department of State, by order" in the upper left corner followed by "of J. Q. Adams, Sec. of State July 4th 1823." in the upper right corner. "Unofficial" copies that were struck later do not have the identification at the top of the document. Instead the engraver identified his work by engraving "W. J. Stone SC. Washn." near the lower left corner and burnishing out the earlier identification.

The longest of the early sojourns of the Declaration was from 1841 to 1876. Daniel Webster was Secretary of State in 1841. On June 11 he wrote to Commissioner of Patents Henry L. Ellsworth, who was then occupying a new building (now the National Portrait Gallery), that "having learned that there is in the new building appropriated to the Patent Office suitable accommodations for the safe-keeping, as well as the exhibition of the various articles now deposited in this Department, and usually, exhibited to visitors... I have directed them to be transmitted to you." An inventory accompanied the letter. Item 6 was the Declaration.

The "new building" was a white stone structure at Seventh and F Streets. The Declaration and

A History of the Declaration of Independence

Washington's commission as commander in chief were mounted together in a single frame and hung in a white painted hall opposite a window offering exposure to sunlight. There they were to remain on exhibit for 35 years, even after the Patent Office separated from the State Department to become administratively a part of the Interior Department. This prolonged exposure to sunlight accelerated the deterioration of the ink and parchment of the Declaration, which was approaching 100 years of age toward the end of this period.

During the years that the Declaration was exhibited in the Patent Office, the combined effects of aging, sunlight, and fluctuating temperature and relative humidity took their toll on the document. Occasionally, writers made somewhat negative comments on the appearance of the Declaration. An observer in the *United States Magazine* (October 1856) went so far as to refer to "that old looking paper with the fading ink." John B. Ellis remarked in *The Sights and Secrets of the National Capital* (Chicago, 1869) that "it is old and yellow, and the ink is fading from the paper." An anonymous writer in the *Historical Magazine* (October 1870) wrote: "The original manuscript of the Declaration of Independence and of Washington's Commission, now in the United States Patent Office at Washington, D.C., are said to be rapidly fading out so that in a few years, only the naked parchment will remain. Already, nearly all the signatures attached to the Declaration of Independence are entirely effaced." In May 1873 the *Historical Magazine* published an official statement by Mortimer Dormer Leggett, Commissioner of Patents, who admitted that "many of the names to the Declaration are already illegible."

The technology of a new age and the interest in historical roots engendered by the approaching Centennial focused new interest on the Declaration in the 1870s and brought about a brief change of home.

The Centennial and the Debate Over Preservation, 1876-1921

In 1876 the Declaration traveled to Philadelphia, where it was on exhibit for the Centennial National Exposition from May to October. Philadelphia's Mayor William S. Stokley was entrusted by President Ulysses S. Grant with temporary custody of the Declaration. *The Public Ledger* for May 8, 1876, noted that it was in Independence Hall "framed and glazed for protection, and…deposited in a fireproof safe especially designed for both preservation and convenient display. [When the outer doors of the safe were opened, the parchment was visible behind a heavy plate-glass inner door; the doors were closed at night.] Its aspect is of course faded and time-worn. The text is fully legible, but the major part of the signatures are so pale as to be only dimly discernible in the strongest light, a few remain wholly readable, and some are wholly invisible, the spaces which contained them presenting only a blank."

Other descriptions made at Philadelphia were equally unflattering: "scarce bears trace of the signatures the execution of which made fifty-six names imperishable," "aged-dimmed." But on the Fourth of July, after the text was read aloud to a throng on Independence Square by Richard Henry Lee of Virginia (grandson of the signer Richard Henry Lee), "The faded and crumbling manuscript, held together by a simple frame was then exhibited to the crowd and was greeted with cheer after cheer."

By late summer the Declaration's physical condition had become a matter of public concern. On Aug. 3, 1876, Congress adopted a joint resolution providing "that a commission, consisting of the Secretary of the Interior, the Secretary of the Smithsonian Institution, and the Librarian of Congress be empowered to have resort to such means as will most effectually restore the writing of the original manuscript of the Declaration of Independence, with the signatures appended thereto." This resolution had actually been introduced as early as Jan. 5, 1876. One candidate for the task of restoration was William J. Canby, an employee of the Washington Gas Light Company. On April 13 Canby had written to the Librarian of Congress: "I have had over thirty years experience in handling the pen upon parchment and in that time, as an expert, have engrossed hundreds of ornamental, special documents." Canby went on to suggest that "the only feasible plan is to replenish the original with a supply of ink, which has been destroyed by the action of light and time, with an ink well known to be, for all practical purposes, imperishable."

The commission did not, however, take any action at that time. After the conclusion of the Centennial exposition, attempts were made to secure possession of the Declaration for Philadelphia, but these failed and the parchment was returned to the Patent Office

A History of the Declaration of Independence

in Washington, where it had been since 1841, even though that office had become a part of the Interior Department. On April 11, 1876, Robert H. Duell, Commissioner of Patents, had written to Zachariah Chandler, Secretary of the Interior, suggesting that "the Declaration of Independence, and the commission of General Washington, associated with it in the same frame, belong to your Department as heirlooms."

Chandler appears to have ignored this claim, for in an exchange of letters with Secretary of State Hamilton Fish, it was agreed — with the approval of President Grant — to move the Declaration into the new, fireproof building that the State Department shared with the War and Navy Departments (now the Old Executive Office Building).

On March 3, 1877, the Declaration was placed in a cabinet on the eastern side of the State Department library, where it was to be exhibited for 17 years. It may be noted that not only was smoking permitted in the library, but the room contained an open fireplace. Nevertheless this location turned out to be safer than the premises just vacated; much of the Patent Office was gutted in a fire that occurred a few months later.

On May 5, 1880, the commission that had been appointed almost four years earlier came to life again in response to a call from the Secretary of the Interior. It requested that William B. Rogers, president of the National Academy of Sciences, appoint a committee of experts to consider "whether such restoration [of the Declaration] be expedient or practicable and if so in what way the object can best be accomplished."

The duly appointed committee reported on Jan. 7, 1881, that Stone used the "wet transfer" method in the creation of his facsimile printing of 1823, that the process had probably removed some of the original ink, and that chemical restoration methods were "at best imperfect and uncertain in their results." The committee concluded, therefore, that "it is not expedient to attempt to restore the manuscript by chemical means." The group of experts then recommended that "it will be best either to cover the present receptacle of the manuscript with an opaque lid or to remove the manuscript from its frame and place it in a portfolio, where it may be protected from the action of light." Finally, the committee recommended that "no press copies of any part of it should in future be permitted."

Recent study of the Declaration by conservators at the National Archives has raised doubts that a "wet transfer" took place. Proof of this occurrence, however, cannot be verified or denied strictly by modern examination methods. No documentation prior to the 1881 reference has been found to support the theory; therefore, we may never know if Stone actually performed the procedure.

Little, if any, action was taken as a result of the 1881 report. It was not until 1894 that the State Department announced: "The rapid fading of the text of the original Declaration of Independence and the deterioration of the parchment upon which it is engrossed, from exposure to light and lapse of time, render it impracticable for the Department longer to exhibit it or to handle it. For the secure preservation of its present condition, so far as may be possible, it has been carefully wrapped and placed flat in a steel case."

A new plate for engravings was made by the Coast and Geodetic Survey in 1895, and in 1898 a photograph was made for the *Ladies' Home Journal*. On this latter occasion, the parchment was noted as "still in good legible condition" although "some of the signatures" were "necessarily blurred."

On April 14, 1903, Secretary of State John Hay solicited again the help of the National Academy of Sciences in providing "such recommendations as may seem practicable...touching [the Declaration's] preservation." Hay went on to explain: "It is now kept out of the light, sealed between two sheets of glass, presumably proof against air, and locked in a steel safe. I am unable to say, however, that, in spite of these precautions, observed for the past ten years, the text is not continuing to fade and the parchment to wrinkle and perhaps to break."

On April 24 a committee of the academy reported its findings. Summarizing the physical history of the Declaration, the report stated: "The instrument has suffered very seriously from the very harsh treatment to which it was exposed in the early years of the Republic. Folding and rolling have creased the parchment. The wet press-copying operation to which it was exposed about 1820, for the purpose of producing a facsimile copy, removed a large portion of the ink. Subsequent exposure to the action of light for more than thirty

A History of the Declaration of Independence

years, while the instrument was placed on exhibition, has resulted in the fading of the ink, particularly in the signatures. The present method of caring for the instrument seems to be the best that can be suggested."

The committee added its own "opinion that the present method of protecting the instrument should be continued; that it should be kept in the dark and dry as possible, and never placed on exhibition." Secretary Hay seems to have accepted the committee's recommendation; in the following year, William H. Michael, author of *The Declaration of Independence* (Washington, 1904), recorded that the Declaration was "locked and sealed, by order of Secretary Hay, and is no longer shown to anyone except by his direction."

World War I came and went. Then, on April 21, 1920, Secretary of State Bainbridge Colby issued an order creating yet another committee: "A Committee is hereby appointed to study the proper steps that should be taken for the permanent and effective preservation from deterioration and from danger from fire, or other form of destruction, of those documents of supreme value which under the law are deposited with the Secretary of State. The inquiry will include the question of display of certain of these documents for the benefit of the patriotic public."

On May 5, 1920, the new committee reported on the physical condition of the safes that housed the Declaration and the Constitution. It declared: "The safes are constructed of thin sheets of steel. They are not fireproof nor would they offer much obstruction to an evil-disposed person who wished to break into them." About the physical condition of the Declaration, the committee stated: "We believe the fading can go no further. We see no reason why the original document should not be exhibited if the parchment be laid between two sheets of glass, hermetically sealed at the edges and exposed only to diffused light."

The committee also made some important "supplementary recommendations." It noted that on March 3, 1903, President Theodore Roosevelt had directed that certain records relating to the Continental Congress be turned over by the Department of State to the Library of Congress: "This transfer was made under a provision of an Act of Feb. 25, 1903, that any Executive Department may turn over to the Library of Congress books, maps, or other material no longer needed for the use of the Department." The committee recommended that the remaining papers, including the Declaration and the Constitution, be similarly given over to the custody of the Library of Congress. For the Declaration, therefore, two important changes were in the offing: a new home and the possibility of exhibition to "the patriotic public."

The Library of Congress … and Fort Knox, 1921-52

There was no action on the recommendations of 1920 until after the Harding administration took office. On Sept. 28, 1921, Secretary of State Charles Evans Hughes addressed the new President: "I enclose an executive order for your signature, if you approve, transferring to the custody of the Library of Congress the original Declaration of Independence and Constitution of the United States which are now in the custody of this Department…I make this recommendation because in the Library of Congress these muniments will be in the custody of experts skilled in archival preservation, in a building of modern fireproof construction, where they can safely be exhibited to the many visitors who now desire to see them."

President Warren G. Harding agreed. On Sept. 29, 1921, he issued the Executive order authorizing the transfer. The following day Secretary Hughes sent a copy of the order to Librarian of Congress Herbert Putnam, stating that he was "prepared to turn the documents over to you when you are ready to receive them."

Putnam was both ready and eager. He presented himself forthwith at the State Department. The safes were opened, and the Declaration and the Constitution were carried off to the Library of Congress on Capitol Hill in the Library's "mail wagon," cushioned by a pile of leather U.S. mail sacks. Upon arrival, the two national treasures were placed in a safe in Putnam's office.

On October 3, Putnam took up the matter of a permanent location. In a memorandum to the superintendent of the Library building and grounds, Putnam proceeded from the premise that "in the Library" the documents "might be treated in such a way as, while fully safe-guarding them and giving them distinction, they should be open to inspection by the public at large." The memorandum discussed the need for a setting "safe, dignified, adequate, and in every way suitable…Material less than bronze would

A History of the Declaration of Independence

be unworthy. The cost must be considerable."

The Librarian then requested the sum of $12,000 for his purpose. The need was urgent because the new Bureau of the Budget was about to print forthcoming fiscal year estimates. There was therefore no time to make detailed architectural plans. Putnam told an appropriations committee on Jan. 16, 1922, just what he had in mind. "There is a way…we could construct, say, on the second floor on the western side in that long open gallery a railed inclosure, material of bronze, where these documents, with one or two auxiliary documents leading up to them, could be placed, where they need not be touched by anybody but where a mere passer-by could see them, where they could be set in permanent bronze frames and where they could be protected from the natural light, lighted only by soft incandescent lamps. The result could be achieved and you would have something every visitor to Washington would wish to tell about when he returned and who would regard it, as the newspapermen are saying, with keen interest as a sort of 'shrine.'" The Librarian's imaginative presentation was successful: The sum of $12,000 was appropriated and approved on March 20, 1922.

Before long, the "sort of shrine" was being designed by Francis H. Bacon, whose brother Henry was the architect of the Lincoln Memorial. Materials used included different kinds of marble from New York, Vermont, Tennessee, the Greek island of Tinos, and Italy. The marbles surrounding the manuscripts were American; the floor and balustrade were made of foreign marbles to correspond with the material used in the rest of the Library. The Declaration was to be housed in a frame of gold-plated bronze doors and covered with double panes of plate glass with specially prepared gelatin films between the plates to exclude the harmful rays of light. A 24-hour guard would provide protection.

On Feb. 28, 1924, the shrine was dedicated in the presence of President and Mrs. Calvin Coolidge, Secretary Hughes, and other distinguished guests. Not a word was spoken during a moving ceremony in which Putnam fitted the Declaration into its frame. There were no speeches. Two stanzas of "America" were sung. In Putnam's words: "The impression on the audience proved the emotional potency of documents animate with a great tradition."

With only one interruption, the Declaration hung on the wall of the second floor of the Great Hall of the Library of Congress until December 1952. During the prosperity of the 1920s and the Depression of the 1930s, millions of people visited the shrine. But the threat of war and then war itself caused a prolonged interruption in the steady stream of visitors.

On April 30, 1941, worried that the war raging in Europe might engulf the United States, the newly appointed Librarian of Congress, Archibald MacLeish, wrote to the Secretary of the Treasury, Henry Morgenthau, Jr. The Librarian was concerned for the most precious of the many objects in his charge. He wrote "to enquire whether space might perhaps be found" at the Bullion Depository in Fort Knox for his most valuable materials, including the Declaration, "in the unlikely event that it becomes necessary to remove them from Washington." Secretary Morgenthau replied that space would indeed be made available as necessary for the "storage of such of the more important papers as you might designate."

On Dec. 7, 1941, the Japanese attacked Pearl Harbor. On December 23, the Declaration and the Constitution were removed from the shrine and placed between two sheets of acid-free manilla paper. The documents were then carefully wrapped in a container of all-rag neutral millboard and placed in a specially designed bronze container. It was late at night when the container was finally secured with padlocks on each side. Preparations were resumed on the day after Christmas, when the Attorney General ruled that the Librarian needed no "further authority from the Congress or the President" to take such action as he deemed necessary for the "proper protection and preservation" of the documents in his charge.

The packing process continued under constant armed guard. The container was finally sealed with lead and packed in a heavy box; the whole weighed some 150 pounds. It was a far cry from the simple linen bag of the summer of 1814.

At about 5 p.m. the box, along with other boxes containing vital records, was loaded into an armed and escorted truck, taken to Union Station, and loaded into a compartment of the Pullman sleeper *Eastlake*. Armed Secret Service agents occupied the neighboring

A History of the Declaration of Independence

compartments. After departing from Washington at 6:30 p.m., the Declaration traveled to Louisville, Ky., arriving at 10:30 a.m., Dec. 27, 1941. More Secret Service agents and a cavalry troop of the 13th Armored Division met the train, convoyed its precious contents to the Bullion Depository at Fort Knox, and placed the Declaration in compartment 24 in the outer tier on the ground level.

The Declaration was periodically examined during its sojourn at Fort Knox. One such examination in 1942 found that the Declaration had become detached in part from its mount, including the upper right corner, which had been stuck down with copious amounts of glue. In his journal for May 14, 1942, Verner W. Clapp, a Library of Congress official, noted: "At one time also (about January 12, 1940) an attempt had been made to reunite the detached upper right hand corner to the main portion by means of a strip of 'scotch' cellulose tape which was still in place, discolored to a molasses color. In the various mending efforts glue had been splattered in two places on the obverse of the document."

The opportunity was taken to perform conservation treatment in order to stabilize and rejoin the upper right corner. Under great secrecy, George Stout and Evelyn Erlich, both of the Fogg Museum at Harvard University, traveled to Fort Knox. Over a period of two days, they performed mending of small tears, removed excess adhesive and the "scotch" tape, and rejoined the detached upper right corner.

Finally, in 1944, the military authorities assured the Library of Congress that all danger of enemy attack had passed. On September 19, the documents were withdrawn from Fort Knox. On Sun., Oct. 1, at 11:30 a.m., the doors of the Library were opened. The Declaration was back in its shrine.

With the return of peace, the keepers of the Declaration were mindful of the increasing technological expertise available to them relating to the preservation of the parchment. In this they were readily assisted by the National Bureau of Standards, which even before World War II, had researched the preservation of the Declaration. The problem of shielding it from harsh light, for example, had in 1924 led to the insertion of a sheet of yellow gelatin between the protective plates of glass. Yet this procedure lessened the visibility of an already faded parchment. Could not some improvement be made?

Following reports of May 5, 1949, on studies in which the Library staff, members of the National Bureau of Standards, and representatives of a glass manufacturer had participated, new recommendations were made. In 1951 the Declaration was sealed in a thermopane enclosure filled with properly humidified helium. The exhibit case was equipped with a filter to screen out damaging light. The new enclosure also had the effect of preventing harm from air pollution, a growing peril. Soon after, however, the Declaration was to make one more move, the one to its present home.

The National Archives, 1952 to the Present

In 1933, while the Depression gripped the nation, President Hoover laid the cornerstone for the National Archives Building in Washington, DC. He announced that the Declaration of Independence and the Constitution would eventually be kept in the impressive structure that was to occupy the site. Indeed, it was for their keeping and display that the exhibition hall in the National Archives had been designed. Two large murals were painted for its walls. In one, Thomas Jefferson is depicted presenting the Declaration to John Hancock, President of the Continental Congress, while members of that Revolutionary body look on. In the second, James Madison is portrayed submitting the Constitution to George Washington.

The final transfer of these special documents did not, however, take place until almost 20 years later. In October 1934 President Franklin D. Roosevelt appointed the first Archivist of the United States, Robert Digges Wimberly Connor. The President told Connor that "valuable historic documents," such as the Declaration of Independence and the U.S. Constitution, would reside in the National Archives Building. The Library of Congress, especially Librarian Herbert Putnam, objected. In a meeting with the President two months after his appointment, Connor explained to Roosevelt how the documents came to be in the Library and that Putnam felt another Act of Congress was necessary in order for them to be transferred to the Archives. Connor eventually told the President that it would be better to leave the matter alone until Putnam retired.

When Herbert Putnam retired on April 5, 1939,

A History of the Declaration of Independence

Archibald MacLeish was nominated to replace him. MacLeish agreed with Roosevelt and Connor that the two important documents belonged in the National Archives. Because of World War II, during much of which the Declaration was stored at Fort Knox, and Connor's resignation in 1941, MacLeish was unable to enact the transfer. By 1944, when the Declaration and Constitution returned to Washington from Fort Knox, MacLeish had been appointed Assistant Secretary of State.

Solon J. Buck, Connor's successor as Archivist of the United States (1941-48), felt that the documents were in good hands at the Library of Congress. His successor, Wayne Grover, disagreed. Luther Evans, the Librarian of Congress appointed by President Truman in June 1945, shared Grover's opinion that the documents should be transferred to the Archives.

In 1951 the two men began working with their staff members and legal advisers to have the documents transferred. The Archives position was that the documents were federal records and therefore covered by the Federal Records Act of 1950, which was "paramount to and took precedence over" the 1922 act that had appropriated money for the shrine at the Library of Congress. Luther Evans agreed with this line of reasoning, but he emphasized getting the approval of the President and the Joint Committee on the Library.

Senator Theodore H. Green, Chairman of the Joint Committee on the Library, agreed that the transfer should take place but stipulated that it would be necessary to have his committee act on the matter. Evans went to the April 30, 1952, committee meeting alone. There is no formal record of what was said at the meeting, except that the Joint Committee on the Library ordered that the documents be transferred to the National Archives. Not only was the Archives the official depository of the government's records, it was also, in the judgment of the committee, the most nearly bombproof building in Washington.

At 11 a.m., Dec. 13, 1952, Brigadier General Stoyte O. Ross, commanding general of the Air Force Headquarters Command, formally received the documents at the Library of Congress. Twelve members of the Armed Forces Special Police carried the six pieces of parchment in their helium-filled glass cases, enclosed in wooden crates, down the Library steps through a line of 88 servicewomen. An armored Marine Corps personnel carrier awaited the documents. Once they had been placed on mattresses inside the vehicle, they were accompanied by a color guard, ceremonial troops, the Army Band, the Air Force Drum and Bugle Corps, two light tanks, four servicemen carrying submachine guns, and a motorcycle escort in a parade down Pennsylvania and Constitution Avenues to the Archives Building. Both sides of the parade route were lined by Army, Navy, Coast Guard, Marine, and Air Force personnel. At 11:35 a.m. General Ross and the 12 special policemen arrived at the National Archives Building, carried the crates up the steps, and formally delivered them into the custody of Archivist of the United States Wayne Grover. (Already at the National Archives was the Bill of Rights, protectively sealed according to the modern techniques used a year earlier for the Declaration and Constitution.)

The formal enshrining ceremony on Dec. 15, 1952, was equally impressive. Chief Justice of the United States Fred M. Vinson presided over the ceremony, which was attended by officials of more than 100 national civic, patriotic, religious, veterans, educational, business, and labor groups. After the invocation by the Reverend Frederick Brown Harris, chaplain of the Senate, Governor Elbert N. Carvel of Delaware, the first state to ratify the Constitution, called the roll of states in the order in which they ratified the Constitution or were admitted to the Union. As each state was called, a servicewoman carrying the state flag entered the Exhibition Hall and remained at attention in front of the display cases circling the hall. President Harry S. Truman, the featured speaker, said:

"The Declaration of Independence, the Constitution, and the Bill of Rights are now assembled in one place for display and safekeeping...We are engaged here today in a symbolic act. We are enshrining these documents for future ages...This magnificent hall has been constructed to exhibit them, and the vault beneath, that we have built to protect them, is as safe from destruction as anything that the wit of modern man can devise. All this is an honorable effort, based upon reverence for the great past, and our generation can take just pride in it."

A History of the Declaration of Independence

Senator Green briefly traced the history of the three documents, and then the Librarian of Congress and the Archivist of the United States jointly unveiled the shrine. Finally, Justice Vinson spoke briefly, the Reverend Bernard Braskamp, chaplain of the House of Representatives, gave the benediction, the U.S. Marine Corps Band played the "Star Spangled Banner," the President was escorted from the hall, the 48 flagbearers marched out, and the ceremony was over. (The story of the transfer of the documents is found in Milton O. Gustafson, " The Empty Shrine: The Transfer of the Declaration of Independence and the Constitution to the National Archives," *The American Archivist* 39 (July 1976): 271-285.)

The present shrine provides an imposing home. The priceless documents stand at the center of a semicircle of display cases showing other important records of the growth of the United States. The Declaration, the Constitution, and the Bill of Rights stand slightly elevated, under armed guard, in their bronze and marble shrine. The Bill of Rights and two of the five leaves of the Constitution are displayed flat. Above them the Declaration of Independence is held impressively in an upright case constructed of ballistically tested glass and plastic laminate. Ultraviolet-light filters in the laminate give the inner layer a slightly greenish hue. At night, the documents are stored in an underground vault.

In 1987 the National Archives and Records Administration installed a $3 million camera and computerized system to monitor the condition of the three documents. The Charters Monitoring System was designed by the Jet Propulsion Laboratory to assess the state of preservation of the Constitution, the Declaration of Independence, and the Bill of Rights. It can detect any changes in readability due to ink flaking, off-setting of ink to glass, changes in document dimensions, and ink fading. The system is capable of recording in very fine detail 1-inch square areas of documents and later retaking the pictures in exactly the same places and under the same conditions of lighting and charge-coupled device (CCD) sensitivity. (The CCD measures reflectivity.) Periodic measurements are compared to the baseline image to determine if changes or deterioration invisible to the human eye have taken place.

Locations of Dunlap Broadside

The 26 copies of the Dunlap broadside known to exist are dispersed among American and British institutions and private owners. The following are the current locations of the copies.

National Archives, Washington, DC

Library of Congress, Washington, DC (two copies)

Maryland Historical Society, Baltimore, MD

University of Virginia, Charlottesville, VA (two copies)

Independence National Historic Park, Philadelphia, PA

American Philosophical Society, Philadelphia, PA

Historical Society of Pennsylvania, Philadelphia, PA

Scheide Library, Princeton University, Princeton, NJ

New York Public Library, New York

Morgan Library, New York

Massachusetts Historical Society, Boston, MA

Harvard University, Cambridge, MA

Chapin Library, Williams College, Williamstown, MA

Yale University, New Haven, CT

American Independence Museum, Exeter, NH

Maine Historical Society, Portland, ME

Indiana University, Bloomington, IN

Chicago Historical Society, Chicago, IL

J. Erik Jonsson Central Library, Dallas, TX Public Library

Declaration of Independence Road Trip [Norman Lear and David Hayden]

Private collector

National Archives, United Kingdom (three copies)

Locations of Declaration, 1776-1789

The locations given for the Declaration from 1776 to 1789 are based on the locations for meetings of the Continental and Confederation Congresses:

Philadelphia: August-December 1776

Baltimore: December 1776-March 1777

Philadelphia: March-September 1777

Lancaster, PA: September 27, 1777

York, PA: September 30, 1777-June 1778

Philadelphia: July 1778-June 1783

Princeton, NJ: June-November 1783

A History of the Declaration of Independence

Locations of Declaration, 1776-1789 (continued)

Annapolis, MD: November 1783-October 1784

Trenton, NJ: November-December 1784

New York: 1785-1790

Philadelphia: 1790-1800

Washington, DC (three locations): 1800-1814

Leesburg, VA: August-September 1814

Washington, DC (three locations): 1814-1841

Washington, DC (Patent Office Building): 1841-1876

Philadelphia: May-November 1876

Washington, DC (State, War, and Navy Building): 1877-1921

Washington, DC (Library of Congress): 1921-1941

Fort Knox:* 1941-1944

Washington, DC (Library of Congress): 1944-1952

Washington, DC (National Archives): 1952-present

*Except that the document was displayed on April 13, 1943, at the dedication of the Thomas Jefferson Memorial in Washington, D.C.

Constitution of the United States of America

We the People of the United States, in Order to form a more perfect Union, establish Justice, insure domestic Tranquility, provide for the common defence, promote the general Welfare, and secure the Blessings of Liberty to ourselves and our Posterity, do ordain and establish this Constitution for the United States of America.

Article. I.

Section. 1.

All legislative Powers herein granted shall be vested in a Congress of the United States, which shall consist of a Senate and House of Representatives.

Section. 2.

The House of Representatives shall be composed of Members chosen every second Year by the People of the several States, and the Electors in each State shall have the Qualifications requisite for Electors of the most numerous Branch of the State Legislature.

No Person shall be a Representative who shall not have attained to the Age of twenty five Years, and been seven Years a Citizen of the United States, and who shall not, when elected, be an Inhabitant of that State in which he shall be chosen.

Representatives and direct Taxes shall be apportioned among the several States which may be included within this Union, according to their respective Numbers, which shall be determined by adding to the whole Number of free Persons, including those bound to Service for a Term of Years, and excluding Indians not taxed, three fifths of all other Persons. The actual Enumeration shall be made within three Years after the first Meeting of the Congress of the United States, and within every subsequent Term of ten Years, in such Manner as they shall by Law direct. The Number of Representatives shall not exceed one for every thirty Thousand, but each State shall have at Least one Representative; and until such enumeration shall be made, the State of New Hampshire shall be entitled to chuse three, Massachusetts eight, Rhode-Island and Providence Plantations one, Connecticut five, New-York six, New Jersey four, Pennsylvania eight, Delaware one, Maryland six, Virginia ten, North Carolina five, South Carolina five, and Georgia three.

When vacancies happen in the Representation from any State, the Executive Authority thereof shall issue Writs of Election to fill such Vacancies.

The House of Representatives shall chuse their Speaker and other Officers; and shall have the sole Power of Impeachment.

Section. 3.

The Senate of the United States shall be composed of two Senators from each State, chosen by the Legislature thereof, for six Years; and each Senator shall have one Vote.

Immediately after they shall be assembled in Consequence of the first Election, they shall be divided as equally as may be into three Classes. The Seats of the Senators of the first Class shall be vacated at the Expiration of the second Year, of the second Class at the Expiration of the fourth Year, and of the third Class at the Expiration of the sixth Year, so that one third may be chosen every second Year; and if Vacancies happen by Resignation, or otherwise, during the Recess of the Legislature of any State, the Executive thereof may make temporary Appointments until the next Meeting of the Legislature, which shall then fill such Vacancies.

No Person shall be a Senator who shall not have attained to the Age of thirty Years, and been nine Years a Citizen of the United States, and who shall not, when elected, be an Inhabitant of that State for which he shall be chosen.

Constitution of the United States of America

The Vice President of the United States shall be President of the Senate, but shall have no Vote, unless they be equally divided.

The Senate shall chuse their other Officers, and also a President pro tempore, in the Absence of the Vice President, or when he shall exercise the Office of President of the United States.

The Senate shall have the sole Power to try all Impeachments. When sitting for that Purpose, they shall be on Oath or Affirmation. When the President of the United States is tried, the Chief Justice shall preside: And no Person shall be convicted without the Concurrence of two thirds of the Members present.

Judgment in Cases of Impeachment shall not extend further than to removal from Office, and disqualification to hold and enjoy any Office of honor, Trust or Profit under the United States: but the Party convicted shall nevertheless be liable and subject to Indictment, Trial, Judgment and Punishment, according to Law.

Section. 4.

The Times, Places and Manner of holding Elections for Senators and Representatives, shall be prescribed in each State by the Legislature thereof; but the Congress may at any time by Law make or alter such Regulations, except as to the Places of chusing Senators.

The Congress shall assemble at least once in every Year, and such Meeting shall be on the first Monday in December, unless they shall by Law appoint a different Day.

Section. 5.

Each House shall be the Judge of the Elections, Returns and Qualifications of its own Members, and a Majority of each shall constitute a Quorum to do Business; but a smaller Number may adjourn from day to day, and may be authorized to compel the Attendance of absent Members, in such Manner, and under such Penalties as each House may provide.

Each House may determine the Rules of its Proceedings, punish its Members for disorderly Behaviour, and, with the Concurrence of two thirds, expel a Member.

Each House shall keep a Journal of its Proceedings, and from time to time publish the same, excepting such Parts as may in their Judgment require Secrecy; and the Yeas and Nays of the Members of either House on any question shall, at the Desire of one fifth of those Present, be entered on the Journal.

Neither House, during the Session of Congress, shall, without the Consent of the other, adjourn for more than three days, nor to any other Place than that in which the two Houses shall be sitting.

Section. 6.

The Senators and Representatives shall receive a Compensation for their Services, to be ascertained by Law, and paid out of the Treasury of the United States. They shall in all Cases, except Treason, Felony and Breach of the Peace, be privileged from Arrest during their Attendance at the Session of their respective Houses, and in going to and returning from the same; and for any Speech or Debate in either House, they shall not be questioned in any other Place.

No Senator or Representative shall, during the Time for which he was elected, be appointed to any civil Office under the Authority of the United States, which shall have been created, or the Emoluments whereof shall have been encreased during such time; and no Person holding any

Constitution of the United States of America

Office under the United States, shall be a Member of either House during his Continuance in Office.

Section. 7.

All Bills for raising Revenue shall originate in the House of Representatives; but the Senate may propose or concur with Amendments as on other Bills.

Every Bill which shall have passed the House of Representatives and the Senate, shall, before it become a Law, be presented to the President of the United States; If he approve he shall sign it, but if not he shall return it, with his Objections to that House in which it shall have originated, who shall enter the Objections at large on their Journal, and proceed to reconsider it. If after such Reconsideration two thirds of that House shall agree to pass the Bill, it shall be sent, together with the Objections, to the other House, by which it shall likewise be reconsidered, and if approved by two thirds of that House, it shall become a Law. But in all such Cases the Votes of both Houses shall be determined by yeas and Nays, and the Names of the Persons voting for and against the Bill shall be entered on the Journal of each House respectively. If any Bill shall not be returned by the President within ten Days (Sundays excepted) after it shall have been presented to him, the Same shall be a Law, in like Manner as if he had signed it, unless the Congress by their Adjournment prevent its Return, in which Case it shall not be a Law.

Every Order, Resolution, or Vote to which the Concurrence of the Senate and House of Representatives may be necessary (except on a question of Adjournment) shall be presented to the President of the United States; and before the Same shall take Effect, shall be approved by him, or being disapproved by him, shall be repassed by two thirds of the Senate and House of Representatives, according to the Rules and Limitations prescribed in the Case of a Bill.

Section. 8.

The Congress shall have Power To lay and collect Taxes, Duties, Imposts and Excises, to pay the Debts and provide for the common Defence and general Welfare of the United States; but all Duties, Imposts and Excises shall be uniform throughout the United States;

To borrow Money on the credit of the United States;

To regulate Commerce with foreign Nations, and among the several States, and with the Indian Tribes;

To establish an uniform Rule of Naturalization, and uniform Laws on the subject of Bankruptcies throughout the United States;

To coin Money, regulate the Value thereof, and of foreign Coin, and fix the Standard of Weights and Measures;

To provide for the Punishment of counterfeiting the Securities and current Coin of the United States;

To establish Post Offices and post Roads;

To promote the Progress of Science and useful Arts, by securing for limited Times to Authors and Inventors the exclusive Right to their respective Writings and Discoveries;

To constitute Tribunals inferior to the supreme Court;

To define and punish Piracies and Felonies committed on the high Seas, and Offences against the Law of Nations;

To declare War, grant Letters of Marque and Reprisal, and make Rules concerning Captures on

Constitution of the United States of America

Land and Water;

To raise and support Armies, but no Appropriation of Money to that Use shall be for a longer Term than two Years;

To provide and maintain a Navy;

To make Rules for the Government and Regulation of the land and naval Forces;

To provide for calling forth the Militia to execute the Laws of the Union, suppress Insurrections and repel Invasions;

To provide for organizing, arming, and disciplining, the Militia, and for governing such Part of them as may be employed in the Service of the United States, reserving to the States respectively, the Appointment of the Officers, and the Authority of training the Militia according to the discipline prescribed by Congress;

To exercise exclusive Legislation in all Cases whatsoever, over such District (not exceeding ten Miles square) as may, by Cession of particular States, and the Acceptance of Congress, become the Seat of the Government of the United States, and to exercise like Authority over all Places purchased by the Consent of the Legislature of the State in which the Same shall be, for the Erection of Forts, Magazines, Arsenals, dock-Yards, and other needful Buildings;—And

To make all Laws which shall be necessary and proper for carrying into Execution the foregoing Powers, and all other Powers vested by this Constitution in the Government of the United States, or in any Department or Officer thereof.

Section. 9.

The Migration or Importation of such Persons as any of the States now existing shall think proper to admit, shall not be prohibited by the Congress prior to the Year one thousand eight hundred and eight, but a Tax or duty may be imposed on such Importation, not exceeding ten dollars for each Person.

The Privilege of the Writ of Habeas Corpus shall not be suspended, unless when in Cases of Rebellion or Invasion the public Safety may require it.

No Bill of Attainder or ex post facto Law shall be passed.

No Capitation, or other direct, Tax shall be laid, unless in Proportion to the Census or enumeration herein before directed to be taken.

No Tax or Duty shall be laid on Articles exported from any State.

No Preference shall be given by any Regulation of Commerce or Revenue to the Ports of one State over those of another: nor shall Vessels bound to, or from, one State, be obliged to enter, clear, or pay Duties in another.

No Money shall be drawn from the Treasury, but in Consequence of Appropriations made by Law; and a regular Statement and Account of the Receipts and Expenditures of all public Money shall be published from time to time.

No Title of Nobility shall be granted by the United States: And no Person holding any Office of Profit or Trust under them, shall, without the Consent of the Congress, accept of any present, Emolument, Office, or Title, of any kind whatever, from any King, Prince, or foreign State.

Section. 10.

No State shall enter into any Treaty, Alliance, or Confederation; grant Letters of Marque and

Constitution of the United States of America

Reprisal; coin Money; emit Bills of Credit; make any Thing but gold and silver Coin a Tender in Payment of Debts; pass any Bill of Attainder, ex post facto Law, or Law impairing the Obligation of Contracts, or grant any Title of Nobility.

No State shall, without the Consent of the Congress, lay any Imposts or Duties on Imports or Exports, except what may be absolutely necessary for executing its inspection Laws: and the net Produce of all Duties and Imposts, laid by any State on Imports or Exports, shall be for the Use of the Treasury of the United States; and all such Laws shall be subject to the Revision and Controul of the Congress.

No State shall, without the Consent of Congress, lay any Duty of Tonnage, keep Troops, or Ships of War in time of Peace, enter into any Agreement or Compact with another State, or with a foreign Power, or engage in War, unless actually invaded, or in such imminent Danger as will not admit of delay.

Article. II.

Section. 1.

The executive Power shall be vested in a President of the United States of America. He shall hold his Office during the Term of four Years, and, together with the Vice President, chosen for the same Term, be elected, as follows

Each State shall appoint, in such Manner as the Legislature thereof may direct, a Number of Electors, equal to the whole Number of Senators and Representatives to which the State may be entitled in the Congress: but no Senator or Representative, or Person holding an Office of Trust or Profit under the United States, shall be appointed an Elector.

The Electors shall meet in their respective States, and vote by Ballot for two Persons, of whom one at least shall not be an Inhabitant of the same State with themselves. And they shall make a List of all the Persons voted for, and of the Number of Votes for each; which List they shall sign and certify, and transmit sealed to the Seat of the Government of the United States, directed to the President of the Senate. The President of the Senate shall, in the Presence of the Senate and House of Representatives, open all the Certificates, and the Votes shall then be counted. The Person having the greatest Number of Votes shall be the President, if such Number be a Majority of the whole Number of Electors appointed; and if there be more than one who have such Majority, and have an equal Number of Votes, then the House of Representatives shall immediately chuse by Ballot one of them for President; and if no Person have a Majority, then from the five highest on the List the said House shall in like Manner chuse the President. But in chusing the President, the Votes shall be taken by States, the Representation from each State having one Vote; A quorum for this Purpose shall consist of a Member or Members from two thirds of the States, and a Majority of all the States shall be necessary to a Choice. In every Case, after the Choice of the President, the Person having the greatest Number of Votes of the Electors shall be the Vice President. But if there should remain two or more who have equal Votes, the Senate shall chuse from them by Ballot the Vice President.

The Congress may determine the Time of chusing the Electors, and the Day on which they shall give their Votes; which Day shall be the same throughout the United States.

No Person except a natural born Citizen, or a Citizen of the United States, at the time of the Adoption of this Constitution, shall be eligible to the Office of President; neither shall any Person be eligible to that Office who shall not have attained to the Age of thirty five Years, and been fourteen Years a Resident within the United States.

Constitution of the United States of America

In Case of the Removal of the President from Office, or of his Death, Resignation, or Inability to discharge the Powers and Duties of the said Office, the Same shall devolve on the Vice President, and the Congress may by Law provide for the Case of Removal, Death, Resignation or Inability, both of the President and Vice President, declaring what Officer shall then act as President, and such Officer shall act accordingly, until the Disability be removed, or a President shall be elected.

The President shall, at stated Times, receive for his Services, a Compensation, which shall neither be encreased nor diminished during the Period for which he shall have been elected, and he shall not receive within that Period any other Emolument from the United States, or any of them.

Before he enter on the Execution of his Office, he shall take the following Oath or Affirmation: —"I do solemnly swear (or affirm) that I will faithfully execute the Office of President of the United States, and will to the best of my Ability, preserve, protect and defend the Constitution of the United States."

Section. 2.

The President shall be Commander in Chief of the Army and Navy of the United States, and of the Militia of the several States, when called into the actual Service of the United States; he may require the Opinion, in writing, of the principal Officer in each of the executive Departments, upon any Subject relating to the Duties of their respective Offices, and he shall have Power to grant Reprieves and Pardons for Offences against the United States, except in Cases of Impeachment.

He shall have Power, by and with the Advice and Consent of the Senate, to make Treaties, provided two thirds of the Senators present concur; and he shall nominate, and by and with the Advice and Consent of the Senate, shall appoint Ambassadors, other public Ministers and Consuls, Judges of the supreme Court, and all other Officers of the United States, whose Appointments are not herein otherwise provided for, and which shall be established by Law: but the Congress may by Law vest the Appointment of such inferior Officers, as they think proper, in the President alone, in the Courts of Law, or in the Heads of Departments.

The President shall have Power to fill up all Vacancies that may happen during the Recess of the Senate, by granting Commissions which shall expire at the End of their next Session.

Section. 3.

He shall from time to time give to the Congress Information of the State of the Union, and recommend to their Consideration such Measures as he shall judge necessary and expedient; he may, on extraordinary Occasions, convene both Houses, or either of them, and in Case of Disagreement between them, with Respect to the Time of Adjournment, he may adjourn them to such Time as he shall think proper; he shall receive Ambassadors and other public Ministers; he shall take Care that the Laws be faithfully executed, and shall Commission all the Officers of the United States.

Section. 4.

The President, Vice President and all civil Officers of the United States, shall be removed from Office on Impeachment for, and Conviction of, Treason, Bribery, or other high Crimes and Misdemeanors.

Constitution of the United States of America

Article III.

Section. 1.

The judicial Power of the United States, shall be vested in one supreme Court, and in such inferior Courts as the Congress may from time to time ordain and establish. The Judges, both of the supreme and inferior Courts, shall hold their Offices during good Behaviour, and shall, at stated Times, receive for their Services, a Compensation, which shall not be diminished during their Continuance in Office.

Section. 2.

The judicial Power shall extend to all Cases, in Law and Equity, arising under this Constitution, the Laws of the United States, and Treaties made, or which shall be made, under their Authority;—to all Cases affecting Ambassadors, other public Ministers and Consuls;—to all Cases of admiralty and maritime Jurisdiction;—to Controversies to which the United States shall be a Party;—to Controversies between two or more States;— between a State and Citizens of another State,—between Citizens of different States,—between Citizens of the same State claiming Lands under Grants of different States, and between a State, or the Citizens thereof, and foreign States, Citizens or Subjects.

In all Cases affecting Ambassadors, other public Ministers and Consuls, and those in which a State shall be Party, the supreme Court shall have original Jurisdiction. In all the other Cases before mentioned, the supreme Court shall have appellate Jurisdiction, both as to Law and Fact, with such Exceptions, and under such Regulations as the Congress shall make.

The Trial of all Crimes, except in Cases of Impeachment, shall be by Jury; and such Trial shall be held in the State where the said Crimes shall have been committed; but when not committed within any State, the Trial shall be at such Place or Places as the Congress may by Law have directed.

Section. 3.

Treason against the United States, shall consist only in levying War against them, or in adhering to their Enemies, giving them Aid and Comfort. No Person shall be convicted of Treason unless on the Testimony of two Witnesses to the same overt Act, or on Confession in open Court.

The Congress shall have Power to declare the Punishment of Treason, but no Attainder of Treason shall work Corruption of Blood, or Forfeiture except during the Life of the Person attainted.

Article. IV.

Section. 1.

Full Faith and Credit shall be given in each State to the public Acts, Records, and judicial Proceedings of every other State. And the Congress may by general Laws prescribe the Manner in which such Acts, Records and Proceedings shall be proved, and the Effect thereof.

Section. 2.

The Citizens of each State shall be entitled to all Privileges and Immunities of Citizens in the several States.

A Person charged in any State with Treason, Felony, or other Crime, who shall flee from Justice, and be found in another State, shall on Demand of the executive Authority of the State from which he fled, be delivered up, to be removed to the State having Jurisdiction of the Crime.

Constitution of the United States of America

No Person held to Service or Labour in one State, under the Laws thereof, escaping into another, shall, in Consequence of any Law or Regulation therein, be discharged from such Service or Labour, but shall be delivered up on Claim of the Party to whom such Service or Labour may be due.

Section. 3.

New States may be admitted by the Congress into this Union; but no new State shall be formed or erected within the Jurisdiction of any other State; nor any State be formed by the Junction of two or more States, or Parts of States, without the Consent of the Legislatures of the States concerned as well as of the Congress.

The Congress shall have Power to dispose of and make all needful Rules and Regulations respecting the Territory or other Property belonging to the United States; and nothing in this Constitution shall be so construed as to Prejudice any Claims of the United States, or of any particular State.

Section. 4.

The United States shall guarantee to every State in this Union a Republican Form of Government, and shall protect each of them against Invasion; and on Application of the Legislature, or of the Executive (when the Legislature cannot be convened) against domestic Violence.

Article. V.

The Congress, whenever two thirds of both Houses shall deem it necessary, shall propose Amendments to this Constitution, or, on the Application of the Legislatures of two thirds of the several States, shall call a Convention for proposing Amendments, which, in either Case, shall be valid to all Intents and Purposes, as Part of this Constitution, when ratified by the Legislatures of three fourths of the several States, or by Conventions in three fourths thereof, as the one or the other Mode of Ratification may be proposed by the Congress; Provided that no Amendment which may be made prior to the Year One thousand eight hundred and eight shall in any Manner affect the first and fourth Clauses in the Ninth Section of the first Article; and that no State, without its Consent, shall be deprived of its equal Suffrage in the Senate.

Article. VI.

All Debts contracted and Engagements entered into, before the Adoption of this Constitution, shall be as valid against the United States under this Constitution, as under the Confederation.

This Constitution, and the Laws of the United States which shall be made in Pursuance thereof; and all Treaties made, or which shall be made, under the Authority of the United States, shall be the supreme Law of the Land; and the Judges in every State shall be bound thereby, any Thing in the Constitution or Laws of any State to the Contrary notwithstanding.

The Senators and Representatives before mentioned, and the Members of the several State Legislatures, and all executive and judicial Officers, both of the United States and of the several States, shall be bound by Oath or Affirmation, to support this Constitution; but no religious Test shall ever be required as a Qualification to any Office or public Trust under the United States.

Article. VII.

The Ratification of the Conventions of nine States, shall be sufficient for the Establishment of

Constitution of the United States of America

this Constitution between the States so ratifying the Same.

The Word, "the," being interlined between the seventh and eighth Lines of the first Page, The Word "Thirty" being partly written on an Erazure in the fifteenth Line of the first Page, The Words "is tried" being interlined between the thirty second and thirty third Lines of the first Page and the Word "the" being interlined between the forty third and forty fourth Lines of the second Page.

Attest William Jackson Secretary

done in Convention by the Unanimous Consent of the States present the Seventeenth Day of September in the Year of our Lord one thousand seven hundred and Eighty seven and of the Independance of the United States of America the Twelfth In witness whereof We have hereunto subscribed our Names

G°. Washington
Presidt and deputy from Virginia
Delaware
Geo: Read
Gunning Bedford jun
John Dickinson
Richard Bassett
Jaco: Broom
Maryland
James McHenry
Dan of St Thos. Jenifer
Danl. Carroll
Virginia
John Blair
James Madison Jr.
North Carolina
Wm. Blount
Richd. Dobbs Spaight

Hu Williamson
South Carolina
J. Rutledge
Charles Cotesworth Pinckney
Charles Pinckney
Pierce Butler
Georgia
William Few
Abr Baldwin
New Hampshire
John Langdon
Nicholas Gilman
Massachusetts
Nathaniel Gorham
Rufus King
Connecticut
Wm. Saml. Johnson
Roger Sherman

New York
Alexander Hamilton
New Jersey
Wil: Livingston
David Brearley
Wm. Paterson
Jona: Dayton
Pennsylvania
B Franklin
Thomas Mifflin
Robt. Morris
Geo. Clymer
Thos. FitzSimons
Jared Ingersoll
James Wilson
Gouv Morris

Note: The text is a transcription of the Constitution as it was inscribed by Jacob Shallus on parchment (the document on display in the Rotunda at the National Archives Museum). The spelling and punctuation reflect the original.

The Bill of Rights

The Preamble to The Bill of Rights

Congress of the United States begun and held at the City of New-York, on Wednesday the fourth of March, one thousand seven hundred and eighty nine.

THE Conventions of a number of the States, having at the time of their adopting the Constitution, expressed a desire, in order to prevent misconstruction or abuse of its powers, that further declaratory and restrictive clauses should be added: And as extending the ground of public confidence in the Government, will best ensure the beneficent ends of its institution.

RESOLVED by the Senate and House of Representatives of the United States of America, in Congress assembled, two thirds of both Houses concurring, that the following Articles be proposed to the Legislatures of the several States, as amendments to the Constitution of the United States, all, or any of which Articles, when ratified by three fourths of the said Legislatures, to be valid to all intents and purposes, as part of the said Constitution; viz.

ARTICLES in addition to, and Amendment of the Constitution of the United States of America, proposed by Congress, and ratified by the Legislatures of the several States, pursuant to the fifth Article of the original Constitution.

Amendment I

Congress shall make no law respecting an establishment of religion, or prohibiting the free exercise thereof; or abridging the freedom of speech, or of the press; or the right of the people peaceably to assemble, and to petition the Government for a redress of grievances.

Amendment II

A well regulated Militia, being necessary to the security of a free State, the right of the people to keep and bear Arms, shall not be infringed.

Amendment III

No Soldier shall, in time of peace be quartered in any house, without the consent of the Owner, nor in time of war, but in a manner to be prescribed by law.

Amendment IV

The right of the people to be secure in their persons, houses, papers, and effects, against unreasonable searches and seizures, shall not be violated, and no Warrants shall issue, but upon probable cause, supported by Oath or affirmation, and particularly describing the place to be searched, and the persons or things to be seized.

Amendment V

No person shall be held to answer for a capital, or otherwise infamous crime, unless on a presentment or indictment of a Grand Jury, except in cases arising in the land or naval forces, or in the Militia, when in actual service in time of War or public danger; nor shall any person be subject for the same offence to be twice put in jeopardy of life or limb; nor shall be compelled in any criminal case to be a witness against himself, nor be deprived of life, liberty, or property, without due process of law; nor shall private property be taken for public use, without just compensation.

The Bill of Rights

Amendment VI

In all criminal prosecutions, the accused shall enjoy the right to a speedy and public trial, by an impartial jury of the State and district wherein the crime shall have been committed, which district shall have been previously ascertained by law, and to be informed of the nature and cause of the accusation; to be confronted with the witnesses against him; to have compulsory process for obtaining witnesses in his favor, and to have the Assistance of Counsel for his defence.

Amendment VII

In Suits at common law, where the value in controversy shall exceed twenty dollars, the right of trial by jury shall be preserved, and no fact tried by a jury, shall be otherwise re-examined in any Court of the United States, than according to the rules of the common law.

Amendment VIII

Excessive bail shall not be required, nor excessive fines imposed, nor cruel and unusual punishments inflicted.

Amendment IX

The enumeration in the Constitution, of certain rights, shall not be construed to deny or disparage others retained by the people.

Note: The text is a transcription of the first ten amendments to the Constitution in their original form. These amendments were ratified December 15, 1791, and form what is known as the "Bill of Rights."

Amendments to US Constitution

Amendment XI

Passed by Congress March 4, 1794. Ratified February 7, 1795.

Note: Article III, section 2, of the Constitution was modified by amendment 11.

The Judicial power of the United States shall not be construed to extend to any suit in law or equity, commenced or prosecuted against one of the United States by Citizens of another State, or by Citizens or Subjects of any Foreign State.

Amendment XII

Passed by Congress December 9, 1803. Ratified June 15, 1804.

Note: A portion of Article II, section 1 of the Constitution was superseded by the 12th amendment.

The Electors shall meet in their respective states and vote by ballot for President and Vice-President, one of whom, at least, shall not be an inhabitant of the same state with themselves; they shall name in their ballots the person voted for as President, and in distinct ballots the person voted for as Vice-President, and they shall make distinct lists of all persons voted for as President, and of all persons voted for as Vice-President, and of the number of votes for each, which lists they shall sign and certify, and transmit sealed to the seat of the government of the United States, directed to the President of the Senate; — the President of the Senate shall, in the presence of the Senate and House of Representatives, open all the certificates and the votes shall then be counted; — The person having the greatest number of votes for President, shall be the President, if such number be a majority of the whole number of Electors appointed; and if no person have such majority, then from the persons having the highest numbers not exceeding three on the list of those voted for as President, the House of Representatives shall choose immediately, by ballot, the President. But in choosing the President, the votes shall be taken by states, the representation from each state having one vote; a quorum for this purpose shall consist of a member or members from two-thirds of the states, and a majority of all the states shall be necessary to a choice. [And if the House of Representatives shall not choose a President whenever the right of choice shall devolve upon them, before the fourth day of March next following, then the Vice-President shall act as President, as in case of the death or other constitutional disability of the President.]* The person having the greatest number of votes as Vice-President, shall be the Vice-President, if such number be a majority of the whole number of Electors appointed, and if no person have a majority, then from the two highest numbers on the list, the Senate shall choose the Vice-President; a quorum for the purpose shall consist of two-thirds of the whole number of Senators, and a majority of the whole number shall be necessary to a choice. But no person constitutionally ineligible to the office of President shall be eligible to that of Vice-President of the United States.
*Superseded by section 3 of the 20th amendment.

Amendment XIII

Passed by Congress January 31, 1865. Ratified December 6, 1865.

Note: A portion of Article IV, section 2, of the Constitution was superseded by the 13th amendment.

Section 1.

Neither slavery nor involuntary servitude, except as a punishment for crime whereof the party shall have been duly convicted, shall exist within the United States, or any place subject to their jurisdiction.

Amendments to US Constitution

Section 2.

Congress shall have power to enforce this article by appropriate legislation.

Amendment XIV

Passed by Congress June 13, 1866. Ratified July 9, 1868.

Note: Article I, section 2, of the Constitution was modified by section 2 of the 14th amendment.

Section 1.

All persons born or naturalized in the United States, and subject to the jurisdiction thereof, are citizens of the United States and of the State wherein they reside. No State shall make or enforce any law which shall abridge the privileges or immunities of citizens of the United States; nor shall any State deprive any person of life, liberty, or property, without due process of law; nor deny to any person within its jurisdiction the equal protection of the laws.

Section 2.

Representatives shall be apportioned among the several States according to their respective numbers, counting the whole number of persons in each State, excluding Indians not taxed. But when the right to vote at any election for the choice of electors for President and Vice-President of the United States, Representatives in Congress, the Executive and Judicial officers of a State, or the members of the Legislature thereof, is denied to any of the male inhabitants of such State, being twenty-one years of age,* and citizens of the United States, or in any way abridged, except for participation in rebellion, or other crime, the basis of representation therein shall be reduced in the proportion which the number of such male citizens shall bear to the whole number of male citizens twenty-one years of age in such State.

Section 3.

No person shall be a Senator or Representative in Congress, or elector of President and Vice-President, or hold any office, civil or military, under the United States, or under any State, who, having previously taken an oath, as a member of Congress, or as an officer of the United States, or as a member of any State legislature, or as an executive or judicial officer of any State, to support the Constitution of the United States, shall have engaged in insurrection or rebellion against the same, or given aid or comfort to the enemies thereof. But Congress may by a vote of two-thirds of each House, remove such disability.

Section 4.

The validity of the public debt of the United States, authorized by law, including debts incurred for payment of pensions and bounties for services in suppressing insurrection or rebellion, shall not be questioned. But neither the United States nor any State shall assume or pay any debt or obligation incurred in aid of insurrection or rebellion against the United States, or any claim for the loss or emancipation of any slave; but all such debts, obligations and claims shall be held illegal and void.

Section 5.

The Congress shall have the power to enforce, by appropriate legislation, the provisions of this article.

*Changed by section 1 of the 26th amendment.

Amendments to US Constitution

Amendment XV

Passed by Congress February 26, 1869. Ratified February 3, 1870.

Section 1.

The right of citizens of the United States to vote shall not be denied or abridged by the United States or by any State on account of race, color, or previous condition of servitude--

Section 2.

The Congress shall have the power to enforce this article by appropriate legislation.

Amendment XVI

Passed by Congress July 2, 1909. Ratified February 3, 1913.

Note: Article I, section 9, of the Constitution was modified by amendment 16.

The Congress shall have power to lay and collect taxes on incomes, from whatever source derived, without apportionment among the several States, and without regard to any census or enumeration.

Amendment XVII

Passed by Congress May 13, 1912. Ratified April 8, 1913.

Note: Article I, section 3, of the Constitution was modified by the 17th amendment.

The Senate of the United States shall be composed of two Senators from each State, elected by the people thereof, for six years; and each Senator shall have one vote. The electors in each State shall have the qualifications requisite for electors of the most numerous branch of the State legislatures.

When vacancies happen in the representation of any State in the Senate, the executive authority of such State shall issue writs of election to fill such vacancies: Provided, That the legislature of any State may empower the executive thereof to make temporary appointments until the people fill the vacancies by election as the legislature may direct.

This amendment shall not be so construed as to affect the election or term of any Senator chosen before it becomes valid as part of the Constitution.

Amendment XVIII

Passed by Congress December 18, 1917. Ratified January 16, 1919. Repealed by amendment 21.

Section 1.

After one year from the ratification of this article the manufacture, sale, or transportation of intoxicating liquors within, the importation thereof into, or the exportation thereof from the United States and all territory subject to the jurisdiction thereof for beverage purposes is hereby prohibited.

Section 2.

The Congress and the several States shall have concurrent power to enforce this article by appropriate legislation.

Section 3.

This article shall be inoperative unless it shall have been ratified as an amendment to the Constitution by the legislatures of the several States, as provided in the Constitution, within seven years from the date of the submission hereof to the States by the Congress.

Amendments to US Constitution

Amendment XIX

Passed by Congress June 4, 1919. Ratified August 18, 1920.

The right of citizens of the United States to vote shall not be denied or abridged by the United States or by any State on account of sex.

Congress shall have power to enforce this article by appropriate legislation.

Amendment XX

Passed by Congress March 2, 1932. Ratified January 23, 1933.

Note: Article I, section 4, of the Constitution was modified by section 2 of this amendment. In addition, a portion of the 12th amendment was superseded by section 3.

Section 1.

The terms of the President and the Vice President shall end at noon on the 20th day of January, and the terms of Senators and Representatives at noon on the 3d day of January, of the years in which such terms would have ended if this article had not been ratified; and the terms of their successors shall then begin.

Section 2.

The Congress shall assemble at least once in every year, and such meeting shall begin at noon on the 3d day of January, unless they shall by law appoint a different day.

Section 3.

If, at the time fixed for the beginning of the term of the President, the President elect shall have died, the Vice President elect shall become President. If a President shall not have been chosen before the time fixed for the beginning of his term, or if the President elect shall have failed to qualify, then the Vice President elect shall act as President until a President shall have qualified; and the Congress may by law provide for the case wherein neither a President elect nor a Vice President elect shall have qualified, declaring who shall then act as President, or the manner in which one who is to act shall be selected, and such person shall act accordingly until a President or Vice President shall have qualified.

Section 4.

The Congress may by law provide for the case of the death of any of the persons from whom the House of Representatives may choose a President whenever the right of choice shall have devolved upon them, and for the case of the death of any of the persons from whom the Senate may choose a Vice President whenever the right of choice shall have devolved upon them.

Section 5.

Sections 1 and 2 shall take effect on the 15th day of October following the ratification of this article.

Section 6.

This article shall be inoperative unless it shall have been ratified as an amendment to the Constitution by the legislatures of three-fourths of the several States within seven years from the date of its submission.

Amendment XXI

Passed by Congress February 20, 1933. Ratified December 5, 1933.

Amendments to US Constitution

Section 1.

The eighteenth article of amendment to the Constitution of the United States is hereby repealed.

Section 2.

The transportation or importation into any State, Territory, or possession of the United States for delivery or use therein of intoxicating liquors, in violation of the laws thereof, is hereby prohibited.

Section 3.

This article shall be inoperative unless it shall have been ratified as an amendment to the Constitution by conventions in the several States, as provided in the Constitution, within seven years from the date of the submission hereof to the States by the Congress.

Amendment XXII

Passed by Congress March 21, 1947. Ratified February 27, 1951.

Section 1.

No person shall be elected to the office of the President more than twice, and no person who has held the office of President, or acted as President, for more than two years of a term to which some other person was elected President shall be elected to the office of the President more than once. But this Article shall not apply to any person holding the office of President when this Article was proposed by the Congress, and shall not prevent any person who may be holding the office of President, or acting as President, during the term within which this Article becomes operative from holding the office of President or acting as President during the remainder of such term.

Section 2.

This article shall be inoperative unless it shall have been ratified as an amendment to the Constitution by the legislatures of three-fourths of the several States within seven years from the date of its submission to the States by the Congress.

Amendment XXIII

Passed by Congress June 16, 1960. Ratified March 29, 1961.

Section 1.

The District constituting the seat of Government of the United States shall appoint in such manner as the Congress may direct:

A number of electors of President and Vice President equal to the whole number of Senators and Representatives in Congress to which the District would be entitled if it were a State, but in no event more than the least populous State; they shall be in addition to those appointed by the States, but they shall be considered, for the purposes of the election of President and Vice President, to be electors appointed by a State; and they shall meet in the District and perform such duties as provided by the twelfth article of amendment.

Section 2.

The Congress shall have power to enforce this article by appropriate legislation.

Amendment XXIV

Passed by Congress August 27, 1962. Ratified January 23, 1964.

Section 1.

The right of citizens of the United States to vote in any primary or other election for President or

Amendments to US Constitution

Vice President, for electors for President or Vice President, or for Senator or Representative in Congress, shall not be denied or abridged by the United States or any State by reason of failure to pay any poll tax or other tax.

Section 2.

The Congress shall have power to enforce this article by appropriate legislation.

Amendment XXV

Passed by Congress July 6, 1965. Ratified February 10, 1967.

Note: Article II, section 1, of the Constitution was affected by the 25th amendment.

Section 1.

In case of the removal of the President from office or of his death or resignation, the Vice President shall become President.

Section 2.

Whenever there is a vacancy in the office of the Vice President, the President shall nominate a Vice President who shall take office upon confirmation by a majority vote of both Houses of Congress.

Section 3.

Whenever the President transmits to the President pro tempore of the Senate and the Speaker of the House of Representatives his written declaration that he is unable to discharge the powers and duties of his office, and until he transmits to them a written declaration to the contrary, such powers and duties shall be discharged by the Vice President as Acting President.

Section 4.

Whenever the Vice President and a majority of either the principal officers of the executive departments or of such other body as Congress may by law provide, transmit to the President pro tempore of the Senate and the Speaker of the House of Representatives their written declaration that the President is unable to discharge the powers and duties of his office, the Vice President shall immediately assume the powers and duties of the office as Acting President.

Thereafter, when the President transmits to the President pro tempore of the Senate and the Speaker of the House of Representatives his written declaration that no inability exists, he shall resume the powers and duties of his office unless the Vice President and a majority of either the principal officers of the executive department or of such other body as Congress may by law provide, transmit within four days to the President pro tempore of the Senate and the Speaker of the House of Representatives their written declaration that the President is unable to discharge the powers and duties of his office. Thereupon Congress shall decide the issue, assembling within forty-eight hours for that purpose if not in session. If the Congress, within twenty-one days after receipt of the latter written declaration, or, if Congress is not in session, within twenty-one days after Congress is required to assemble, determines by two-thirds vote of both Houses that the President is unable to discharge the powers and duties of his office, the Vice President shall continue to discharge the same as Acting President; otherwise, the President shall resume the powers and duties of his office.

Amendment XXVI

Passed by Congress March 23, 1971. Ratified July 1, 1971.

Note: Amendment 14, section 2, of the Constitution was modified by section 1 of the 26th amendment.

Amendments to US Constitution

Section 1.

The right of citizens of the United States, who are eighteen years of age or older, to vote shall not be denied or abridged by the United States or by any State on account of age.

Section 2.

The Congress shall have power to enforce this article by appropriate legislation.

Amendment XXVII

Originally proposed Sept. 25, 1789. Ratified May 7, 1992.

No law, varying the compensation for the services of the Senators and Representatives, shall take effect, until an election of Representatives shall have intervened.

A More Perfect Union: The Creation of the US Constitution

May 25, 1787, freshly spread dirt covered the cobblestone street in front of the Pennsylvania State House, protecting the men inside from the sound of passing carriages and carts. Guards stood at the entrances to ensure that the curious were kept at a distance. Robert Morris of Pennsylvania, the "financier" of the Revolution, opened the proceedings with a nomination—Gen. George Washington for the presidency of the Constitutional Convention. The vote was unanimous. With characteristic ceremonial modesty, the general expressed his embarrassment at his lack of qualifications to preside over such an august body and apologized for any errors into which he might fall in the course of its deliberations.

To many of those assembled, especially to the small, boyish-looking, 36-year-old delegate from Virginia, James Madison, the general's mere presence boded well for the convention, for the illustrious Washington gave to the gathering an air of importance and legitimacy. But his decision to attend the convention had been an agonizing one. The Father of the Country had almost remained at home.

Suffering from rheumatism, despondent over the loss of a brother, absorbed in the management of Mount Vernon, and doubting that the convention would accomplish very much or that many men of stature would attend, Washington delayed accepting the invitation to attend for several months. Torn between the hazards of lending his reputation to a gathering perhaps doomed to failure and the chance that the public would view his reluctance to attend with a critical eye, the general finally agreed to make the trip. James Madison was pleased.

The Articles of Confederation
The determined Madison had for several years insatiably studied history and political theory, searching for a solution to the political and economic dilemmas he saw plaguing America. The Virginian's labors convinced him of the futility and weakness of confederacies of independent states. America's own government under the Articles of Confederation, Madison was convinced, had to be replaced. In force since 1781, established as a "league of friendship" and a constitution for the 13 sovereign and independent states after the Revolution, the articles seemed to Madison woefully inadequate. With the states retaining considerable power, the central

Based on the Introduction by Roger A. Bruns to A More Perfect Union : The Creation of the United States Constitution. Washington, DC : Published for the National Archives and Records Administration by the National Archives Trust Fund Board, 1986. Used with permission.

government, he believed, had insufficient power to regulate commerce. It could not tax and was generally impotent in setting commercial policy. It could not effectively support a war effort. It had little power to settle quarrels between states. Saddled with this weak government, the states were on the brink of economic disaster. The evidence was overwhelming. Congress was attempting to function with a depleted treasury; paper money was flooding the country, creating extraordinary inflation—a pound of tea in some areas could be purchased for a tidy $100; and the depressed condition of business was taking its toll on many small farmers. Some of them were being thrown in jail for debt, and numerous farms were being confiscated and sold for taxes.

In 1786 some of the farmers had fought back. Led by Daniel Shays, a former captain in the Continental army, a group of armed men, sporting evergreen twigs in their hats, prevented the circuit court from sitting at Northampton, Mass., and threatened to seize muskets stored in the arsenal at Springfield. Although the insurrection was put down by state troops, the incident confirmed the fears of many wealthy men that anarchy was just around the corner. Embellished day after day in the press, the uprising made upper-class Americans shudder as they imagined hordes of vicious outlaws descending upon innocent citizens. From his idyllic Mount Vernon setting, Washington wrote to Madison: "Wisdom and good examples are necessary at this time to rescue the political machine from the impending storm."

Madison thought he had the answer. He wanted a strong central government to provide order and stability. "Let it be tried then," he wrote, "whether any middle ground can be taken which will at once support a due supremacy of the national authority," while maintaining state power only when "subordinately useful." The resolute Virginian looked to the Constitutional Convention to forge a new government in this mold.

The convention had its specific origins in a proposal

A More Perfect Union: The Creation of the US Constitution

offered by Madison and John Tyler in the Virginia assembly that the Continental Congress be given power to regulate commerce throughout the Confederation. Through their efforts in the assembly a plan was devised inviting the several states to attend a convention at Annapolis, Md., in September 1786 to discuss commercial problems. Madison and a young lawyer from New York named Alexander Hamilton issued a report on the meeting in Annapolis, calling upon Congress to summon delegates of all of the states to meet for the purpose of revising the Articles of Confederation. Although the report was widely viewed as a usurpation of congressional authority, the Congress did issue a formal call to the states for a convention. To Madison it represented the supreme chance to reverse the country's trend. And as the delegations gathered in Philadelphia, its importance was not lost to others. The squire of Gunston Hall, George Mason, wrote to his son, "The Eyes of the United States are turned upon this Assembly and their Expectations raised to a very anxious Degree. May God Grant that we may be able to gratify them, by establishing a wise and just Government."

The Delegates

Seventy-four delegates were appointed to the convention, of which 55 actually attended sessions. Rhode Island was the only state that refused to send delegates. Dominated by men wedded to paper currency, low taxes, and popular government, Rhode Island's leaders refused to participate in what they saw as a conspiracy to overthrow the established government. Other Americans also had their suspicions. Patrick Henry, of the flowing red Glasgow cloak and the magnetic oratory, refused to attend, declaring he "smelt a rat." He suspected, correctly, that Madison had in mind the creation of a powerful central government and the subversion of the authority of the state legislatures. Henry along with many other political leaders, believed that the state governments offered the chief protection for personal liberties. He was determined not to lend a hand to any proceeding that seemed to pose a threat to that protection.

With Henry absent, with such towering figures as Jefferson and Adams abroad on foreign missions, and with John Jay in New York at the Foreign Office, the convention was without some of the country's major political leaders. It was, nevertheless, an

Constitutional Convention Delegates

The original states, except Rhode Island, collectively appointed 70 individuals to the Constitutional Convention. A number of these individuals did not accept or could not attend, including Richard Henry Lee, Patrick Henry, Thomas Jefferson, John Adams, Samuel Adams, and John Hancock. In all, 55 delegates attended the Constitutional Convention sessions, but only 39 actually signed the Constitution. The delegates ranged in age from Jonathan Dayton, 26, to Benjamin Franklin, 81, who was so infirm he had to be carried to sessions in a sedan chair.

Connecticut
Oliver Ellsworth*
William. Samuel Johnson
Roger Sherman

Delaware
Richard Bassett
Gunning Bedford, Jr.
Jacob Broom
John Dickinson
George Read

Georgia
Abraham Baldwin
William Few
William Houston*
William L. Pierce*

Maryland
Daniel Carroll
Daniel of St. Thomas Jenifer
Luther Martin*
James McHenry
John F. Mercer*

Massachusetts
Elbridge Gerry*
Nathaniel Gorham
Rufus King
Caleb Strong*

New Hampshire
Nicholas Gilman
John Langdon

New Jersey
David Brearly
Jonathan Dayton
William C. Houston*
William Livingston
William Paterson

New York
Alexander Hamilton
John Lansing, Jr.*
Robert Yates*

North Carolina
William. Blount
William R. Davie*
Alexander Martin*
Richard. Dobbs Spaight
Hugh Williamson

Pennsylvania
George Clymer
Thomas Fitzsimons
Benjamin Franklin
Jared Ingersoll
Thomas Mifflin
Gouverneur Morris
Robert Morris
James Wilson

Rhode Island
Did not send delegates.

South Carolina
Pierce Butler
Charles Pinckney
Charles Cotesworth Pinckney
John Rutledge

Virginia
John Blair
James Madison Jr.
George Mason*
James McClurg*
Edmund J. Randolph*
George Washington
George Wythe*

*Did not sign Constitution.

A More Perfect Union: The Creation of the US Constitution

impressive assemblage. In addition to Madison and Washington, there were Benjamin Franklin of Pennsylvania — crippled by gout, the 81-year-old Franklin was a man of many dimensions: printer, storekeeper, publisher, scientist, public official, philosopher, diplomat, and ladies' man; James Wilson of Pennsylvania — a distinguished lawyer with a penchant for ill-advised land-jobbing schemes, which would force him late in life to flee from state to state avoiding prosecution for debt, the Scotsman brought a profound mind steeped in constitutional theory and law; Hamilton of New York — a brilliant, ambitious former aide-de-camp and secretary to Washington during the Revolution who had, after his marriage into the Schuyler family of New York, become a powerful political figure; Mason of Virginia — the author of the Virginia Bill of Rights whom Jefferson later called "the Cato of his country without the avarice of the Roman"; John Dickinson of Delaware — the quiet, reserved author of the "Farmers' Letters" and chairman of the congressional committee that framed the articles; and Gouverneur Morris of Pennsylvania-- well versed in French literature and language, with a flair and bravado to match his keen intellect, who had helped draft the New York State Constitution and had worked with Robert Morris in the Finance Office.

There were others who played major roles — Oliver Ellsworth of Connecticut; Edmund Randolph of Virginia; William Paterson of New Jersey; John Rutledge of South Carolina; Elbridge Gerry of Massachusetts; Roger Sherman of Connecticut; Luther Martin of Maryland; and the Pinckneys, Charles and Charles Cotesworth, of South Carolina. Franklin was the oldest member and Jonathan Dayton, the 27-year-old delegate from New Jersey, was the youngest. The average age was 42. Most of the delegates had studied law, had served in colonial or state legislatures, or had been in the Congress. Well versed in philosophical theories of government advanced by such philosophers as James Harrington, John Locke, and Montesquieu, profiting from experience gained in state politics, the delegates composed an exceptional body, one that left a remarkably learned record of debate. Fortunately we have a relatively complete record of the proceedings, thanks to the indefatigable Madison. Day after day, the Virginian sat in front of the presiding officer, compiling notes of the debates, not missing a single day or a single major speech. He later remarked that his self-confinement in the hall, which was often oppressively hot in the Philadelphia summer, almost killed him.

The sessions of the convention were held in secret — no reporters or visitors were permitted. Although many of the naturally loquacious members were prodded in the pubs and on the streets, most remained surprisingly discreet. To those suspicious of the convention, the curtain of secrecy only served to confirm their anxieties. Luther Martin of Maryland later charged that the conspiracy in Philadelphia needed a quiet breeding ground. Jefferson wrote John Adams from Paris, "I am sorry they began their deliberations by so abominable a precedent as that of tying up the tongues of their members."

The Virginia Plan

On Tuesday morning, May 29, Edmund Randolph, the tall, 34-year-old governor of Virginia, opened the debate with a long speech decrying the evils that had befallen the country under the Articles of Confederation and stressing the need for creating a strong national government. Randolph then outlined a broad plan that he and his Virginia compatriots had, through long sessions at the Indian Queen tavern, put together in the days preceding the convention. Madison had such a plan on his mind for years. The proposed government had three branches — legislative, executive, and judicial — each branch structured to check the other. Highly centralized, the government would have veto power over laws enacted by state legislatures. The plan, Randolph confessed, "meant a strong consolidated union in which the idea of states should be nearly annihilated." This was, indeed, the rat so offensive to Patrick Henry.

The introduction of the so-called Virginia Plan at the beginning of the convention was a tactical coup. The Virginians had forced the debate into their own frame of reference and in their own terms.

For 10 days the members of the convention discussed the sweeping and, to many delegates, startling Virginia resolutions. The critical issue, described succinctly by Gouverneur Morris on May 30, was the distinction between a federation and a national government, the "former being a mere compact resting on the good faith of the parties; the latter having a compleat and

A More Perfect Union: The Creation of the US Constitution

compulsive operation." Morris favored the latter, a "supreme power" capable of exercising necessary authority, not merely a shadow government, fragmented and hopelessly ineffective.

The New Jersey Plan

This nationalist position revolted many delegates who cringed at the vision of a central government swallowing state sovereignty. On June 13 delegates from smaller states rallied around proposals offered by New Jersey delegate William Paterson. Railing against efforts to throw the states into "hotchpot," Paterson proposed a "union of the States merely federal." The "New Jersey resolutions" called only for a revision of the articles to enable the Congress more easily to raise revenues and regulate commerce. It also provided that acts of Congress and ratified treaties be "the supreme law of the States."

For three days the convention debated Paterson's plan, finally voting for rejection. With the defeat of the New Jersey resolutions, the convention was moving toward creation of a new government, much to the dismay of many small-state delegates. The nationalists, led by Madison, appeared to have the proceedings in their grip. In addition, they were able to persuade the members that any new constitution should be ratified through conventions of the people and not by the Congress and the state legislatures — another tactical coup. Madison and his allies believed that the constitution they had in mind would likely be scuttled in the legislatures, where many state political leaders stood to lose power. The nationalists wanted to bring the issue before "the people," where ratification was more likely.

Hamilton's Plan

On June 18, Hamilton presented his own ideal plan of government. Erudite and polished, the speech, nevertheless, failed to win a following. It went too far. Calling the British government "the best in the world," Hamilton proposed a model strikingly similar — an executive to serve during good behavior or life with veto power over all laws; a senate with members serving during good behavior; the legislature to have power to pass "all laws whatsoever." Hamilton later wrote to Washington that the people were now willing to accept "something not very remote from that which they have lately quitted." What the people had "lately quitted," of course, was monarchy. Some members of the convention fully expected the country to turn in this direction. Hugh Williamson of North Carolina, a wealthy physician, declared that it was "pretty certain…that we should at some time or other have a king." Newspaper accounts appeared in the summer of 1787 alleging that a plot was under way to invite the second son of George III, Frederick, Duke of York, the secular bishop of Osnaburgh in Prussia, to become "king of the United States."

Strongly militating against any serious attempt to establish monarchy was the enmity so prevalent in the revolutionary period toward royalty and the privileged classes. Some state constitutions had even prohibited titles of nobility. In the same year as the Philadelphia convention, Royall Tyler, a Revolutionary War veteran, in his play *The Contract*, gave his own jaundiced view of the upper classes:

> *Exult each patriot heart! this night is shewn*
> *A piece, which we may fairly call our own;*
> *Where the proud titles of "My Lord!" "Your Grace!"*
> *To humble Mr. and plain Sir give place.*

Most delegates were well aware that there were too many Royall Tylers in the country, with too many memories of British rule and too many ties to a recent bloody war, to accept a king. As the debate moved into the specifics of the new government, Hamilton and others of his persuasion would have to accept something less.

By the end of June, debate between the large and small states over the issue of representation in the first chamber of the legislature was becoming increasingly acrimonious. Delegates from Virginia and other large states demanded that voting in Congress be according to population; representatives of smaller states insisted upon the equality they had enjoyed under the articles. With the oratory degenerating into threats and accusations, Franklin appealed for daily prayers. Dressed in his customary gray homespun, the aged philosopher pleaded that "the Father of lights… illuminate our understandings." Franklin's appeal for prayers was never fulfilled; the convention, as Hugh Williamson noted, had no funds to pay a preacher.

On June 29 the delegates from the small states lost the first battle. The convention approved a resolution establishing population as the basis for representation in the House of Representatives, thus favoring the

A More Perfect Union: The Creation of the US Constitution

larger states. On a subsequent small-state proposal that the states have equal representation in the Senate, the vote resulted in a tie. With large-state delegates unwilling to compromise on this issue, one member thought that the convention "was on the verge of dissolution, scarce held together by the strength of an hair."

By July 10, Washington was so frustrated over the deadlock that he bemoaned "having had any agency" in the proceedings and called the opponents of a strong central government "narrow minded politicians…under the influence of local views." Martin of Maryland, perhaps one whom Washington saw as "narrow minded," thought otherwise. A tiger in debate, not content merely to parry an opponent's argument but determined to bludgeon it into eternal rest, Martin had become perhaps the small states' most effective, if irascible, orator. The Marylander leaped eagerly into the battle on the representation issue, declaring, "The States have a right to an equality of representation. This is secured to us by our present articles of confederation; we are in possession of this privilege."

The Great Compromise

Also crowding into this complicated and divisive discussion over representation was the North-South division over the method by which slaves were to be counted for purposes of taxation and representation. On July 12, Ellsworth proposed that representation for the lower house be based on the number of free persons and three-fifths of "all other persons," a euphemism for slaves. In the following week the members finally compromised, agreeing that direct taxation be according to representation and that the representation of the lower house be based on the white inhabitants and three-fifths of the "other people." With this compromise and with the growing realization that such compromise was necessary to avoid a complete breakdown of the convention, the members then approved Senate equality. Sherman had remarked that it was the wish of the delegates "that some general government should be established." With the crisis over representation now settled, it began to look again as if this wish might be fulfilled.

For the next few days the air in the City of Brotherly Love, although insufferably muggy and swarming with blue-bottle flies, had the clean scent of conciliation. In this period of welcome calm, the members decided to appoint a Committee of Detail to draw up a draft constitution. The convention would now at last have something on paper. As Nathaniel Gorham of Massachusetts, John Rutledge, Edmund Randolph, James Wilson, and Oliver Ellsworth went to work, the other delegates voted themselves a much-needed 10-day vacation.

During the adjournment, Gouverneur Morris and Washington rode out along a creek that ran through land that had been part of the Valley Forge encampment 10 years earlier. While Morris cast for trout, Washington pensively looked over the now lush ground where his freezing troops had suffered, at a time when it had seemed as if the American Revolution had reached its end. The country had come a long way.

The First Draft

On Mon., Aug. 6, 1787, the convention accepted the first draft of the Constitution. Here was the article-by-article model from which the final document would result some five weeks later. As the members began to consider the various sections, the willingness to compromise of the previous days quickly evaporated. The most serious controversy erupted over the question of regulation of commerce. The southern states, exporters of raw materials, rice, indigo, and tobacco, were fearful that a New England-dominated Congress might, through export taxes, severely damage the South's economic life. C.C. Pinckney declared that if Congress had the power to regulate trade, the southern states would be "nothing more than overseers for the Northern States."

On August 21 the debate over the issue of commerce became very closely linked to another explosive issue—slavery. When Martin of Maryland proposed a tax on slave importation, the convention was thrust into a strident discussion of the institution of slavery and its moral and economic relationship to the new government. Rutledge of South Carolina, asserting that slavery had nothing at all to do with morality, declared, "Interest alone is the governing principle with nations." Sherman of Connecticut was for dropping the tender issue altogether before it jeopardized the convention. Mason of Virginia expressed concern over unlimited importation of slaves but later indicated that he also favored federal protection of slave property already held. This nagging issue of possible federal

A More Perfect Union: The Creation of the US Constitution

intervention in slave traffic, which Sherman and others feared could irrevocably split northern and southern delegates, was settled by, in Mason's words, "a bargain." Mason later wrote that delegates from South Carolina and Georgia, who most feared federal meddling in the slave trade, made a deal with delegates from the New England states. In exchange for the New Englanders' support for continuing slave importation for 20 years, the southerners accepted a clause that required only a simple majority vote on navigation laws, a crippling blow to southern economic interests.

The bargain was also a crippling blow to those working to abolish slavery. Congregationalist minister and abolitionist Samuel Hopkins of Connecticut charged that the convention had sold out: "How does it appear…that these States, who have been fighting for liberty and consider themselves as the highest and most noble example of zeal for it, cannot agree in any political Constitution, unless it indulge and authorize them to enslave their fellow men…Ah! these unclean spirits, like frogs, they, like the Furies of the poets are spreading discord, and exciting men to contention and war." Hopkins considered the Constitution a document fit for the flames.

On August 31, a weary George Mason, who had three months earlier written so expectantly to his son about the "great Business now before us," bitterly exclaimed that he "would sooner chop off his right hand than put it to the Constitution as it now stands." Mason despaired that the convention was rushing to saddle the country with an ill-advised, potentially ruinous central authority. He was concerned that a "bill of rights," ensuring individual liberties, had not been made part of the Constitution. Mason called for a new convention to reconsider the whole question of the formation of a new government. Although Mason's motion was overwhelmingly voted down, opponents of the Constitution did not abandon the idea of a new convention. It was futilely suggested again and again for more than two years.

One of the last major unresolved problems was the method of electing the executive. A number of proposals, including direct election by the people, by state legislatures, by state governors, and by the national legislature, were considered. The result was the electoral college, a master stroke of compromise, quaint and curious but politically expedient. The large states got proportional strength in the number of delegates, the state legislatures got the right of selecting delegates, and the House the right to choose the president in the event no candidate received a majority of electoral votes. Mason later predicted that the House would probably choose the president 19 times out of 20.

In the early days of September, with the exhausted delegates anxious to return home, compromise came easily. On September 8 the convention was ready to turn the Constitution over to a Committee of Style and Arrangement. Gouverneur Morris was the chief architect. Years later he wrote to Timothy Pickering: "That Instrument was written by the Fingers which wrote this letter." The Constitution was presented to the convention on September 12, and the delegates methodically began to consider each section. Although close votes followed on several articles, it was clear that the grueling work of the convention in the historic summer of 1787 was reaching its end.

Before the final vote on the Constitution on September 15, Randolph proposed that amendments be made by the state conventions and then turned over to another general convention for consideration. He was joined by Mason and Gerry. The three lonely allies were soundly rebuffed. Late in the afternoon the roll of the states was called on the Constitution, and from every delegation the word was "Aye."

On September 17 the members met for the last time, and the venerable Franklin had written a speech that was delivered by his colleague Wilson. Appealing for unity behind the Constitution, Franklin declared, "I think it will astonish our enemies, who are waiting with confidence to hear that our councils are confounded like those of the builders of Babel; and that our States are on the point of separation, only to meet hereafter for the purpose of cutting one another's throats." With Mason, Gerry, and Randolph withstanding appeals to attach their signatures, the other delegates in the hall formally signed the Constitution, and the convention adjourned at 4 o'clock in the afternoon.

Weary from weeks of intense pressure but generally satisfied with their work, the delegates shared a farewell dinner at City Tavern. Two blocks away on Market Street, printers John Dunlap and David Claypoole worked into the night on the final imprint

A More Perfect Union: The Creation of the US Constitution

of the six-page Constitution, copies of which would leave Philadelphia on the morning stage. The debate over the nation's form of government was now set for the larger arena.

As the members of the convention returned home in the following days, Hamilton privately assessed the chances of the Constitution for ratification. In its favor were the support of Washington, commercial interests, men of property, creditors, and the belief among many Americans that the Articles of Confederation were inadequate. Against it were the opposition of a few influential men in the convention and state politicians fearful of losing power, the general revulsion against taxation, the suspicion that a centralized government would be insensitive to local interests, and the fear among debtors that a new government would "restrain the means of cheating Creditors."

The Federalists and the Anti-Federalists

Because of its size, wealth, and influence and because it was the first state to call a ratifying convention, Pennsylvania was the focus of national attention. The positions of the Federalists, those who supported the Constitution, and the anti-Federalists, those who opposed it, were printed and reprinted by scores of newspapers across the country. And passions in the state were most warm. When the Federalist-dominated Pennsylvania assembly lacked a quorum on September 29 to call a state ratifying convention, a Philadelphia mob, in order to provide the necessary numbers, dragged two anti-Federalist members from their lodgings through the streets to the State House where the bedraggled representatives were forced to stay while the assembly voted. It was a curious example of participatory democracy.

On October 5 anti-Federalist Samuel Bryan published the first of his "Centinel" essays in Philadelphia's *Independent Gazetteer*. Republished in newspapers in various states, the essays assailed the sweeping power of the central government, the usurpation of state sovereignty, and the absence of a bill of rights guaranteeing individual liberties such as freedom of speech and freedom of religion. "The United States are to be melted down," Bryan declared, into a despotic empire dominated by "well-born" aristocrats. Bryan was echoing the fear of many anti-Federalists that the new government would become one controlled by the wealthy established families and the culturally refined. The common working people, Bryan believed, were in danger of being subjugated to the will of an all-powerful authority remote and inaccessible to the people. It was this kind of authority, he believed, that Americans had fought a war against only a few years earlier.

The next day Wilson, delivering a stirring defense of the Constitution to a large crowd gathered in the yard of the State House, praised the new government as the best "which has ever been offered to the world." The Scotsman's view prevailed. Led by Wilson, Federalists dominated in the Pennsylvania convention, carrying the vote on December 12 by a healthy 46 to 23.

The vote for ratification in Pennsylvania did not end the rancor and bitterness. Franklin declared that scurrilous articles in the press were giving the impression that Pennsylvania was "peopled by a set of the most unprincipled, wicked, rascally and quarrelsome scoundrels upon the face of the globe." And in Carlisle, on December 26, anti-Federalist rioters broke up a Federalist celebration and hung Wilson and the Federalist chief justice of Pennsylvania, Thomas McKean, in effigy; put the torch to a copy of the Constitution; and busted a few Federalist heads.

In New York the Constitution was under siege in the press by a series of essays signed "Cato." Mounting a counterattack, Hamilton and Jay enlisted help from Madison and, in late 1787, they published the first of a series of essays now known as the Federalist Papers. The 85 essays, most of which were penned by Hamilton himself, probed the weaknesses of the Articles of Confederation and the need for an energetic national government. Thomas Jefferson later called the Federalist Papers the "best commentary on the principles of government ever written."

Against this kind of Federalist leadership and determination, the opposition in most states was disorganized and generally inert. The leading spokesmen were largely state-centered men with regional and local interests and loyalties. Madison wrote of the Massachusetts anti-Federalists, "There was not a single character capable of uniting their wills or directing their measures.... They had no plan whatever." The anti-Federalists attacked wildly on several fronts — the lack of a bill of rights, discrimination against southern states in navigation legislation,

A More Perfect Union: The Creation of the US Constitution

direct taxation, the loss of state sovereignty. Many charged that the Constitution represented the work of aristocratic politicians bent on protecting their own class interests. At the Massachusetts convention one delegate declared, "These lawyers, and men of learning and moneyed men, that…make us poor illiterate people swallow down the pill they will swallow up all us little folks like the great Leviathan; yes, just as the whale swallowed up Jonah!" Some newspaper articles, presumably written by anti-Federalists, resorted to fanciful predictions of the horrors that might emerge. Under the new Constitution pagans and deists could control the government; the use of Inquisition-like torture could be instituted as punishment for federal crimes; even the pope could be elected president.

One anti-Federalist argument gave opponents some genuine difficulty—the claim that the territory of the 13 states was too extensive for a representative government. In a republic embracing a large area, anti-Federalists argued, government would be impersonal, unrepresentative, dominated by men of wealth, and oppressive of the poor and working classes. Had not the illustrious Montesquieu himself ridiculed the notion that an extensive territory composed of varying climates and people, could be a single republican state? Madison, always ready with the Federalist volley, turned the argument completely around and insisted that the vastness of the country would itself be a strong argument in favor of a republic. Claiming that a large republic would counterbalance various political interest groups vying for power, Madison wrote, "The smaller the society, the fewer probably will be the distinct parties and interests composing it; the fewer the distinct parties and interests, the more frequently will a majority be found of the same party and the more easily will they concert and execute their plans of oppression." Extend the size of the republic, Madison argued, and the country would be less vulnerable to separate factions within it.

Ratification

By Jan. 9, 1788, five states of the nine necessary for ratification had approved the Constitution—Delaware, Pennsylvania, New Jersey, Georgia, and Connecticut. But the eventual outcome remained uncertain in pivotal states such as Massachusetts, New York, and Virginia. On February 6, with Federalists agreeing to recommend a list of amendments amounting to a bill of rights, Massachusetts ratified by a vote of 187 to 168. The revolutionary leader, John Hancock, elected to preside over the Massachusetts ratifying convention but unable to make up his mind on the Constitution, took to his bed with a convenient case of gout. Later seduced by the Federalists with visions of the vice presidency and possibly the presidency, Hancock, whom Madison noted as "an idolater of popularity," suddenly experienced a miraculous cure and delivered a critical block of votes. Although Massachusetts was now safely in the Federalist column, the recommendation of a bill of rights was a significant victory for the anti-Federalists. Six of the remaining states later appended similar recommendations.

When the New Hampshire convention was adjourned by Federalists who sensed imminent defeat and when Rhode Island on March 24 turned down the Constitution in a popular referendum by an overwhelming vote of 10 to 1, Federalist leaders were apprehensive. Looking ahead to the Maryland convention, Madison wrote to Washington, "The difference between even a postponement and adoption in Maryland may…possibly give a fatal advantage to that which opposes the constitution." Madison had little reason to worry. The final vote on April 28—63 for, 11 against. In Baltimore, a huge parade celebrating the Federalist victory rolled through the downtown streets, highlighted by a 15-foot float called "Ship Federalist." The symbolically seaworthy craft was later launched in the waters off Baltimore and sailed down the Potomac to Mount Vernon.

On July 2, 1788, the Confederation Congress, meeting in New York, received word that a reconvened New Hampshire ratifying convention had approved the Constitution. With South Carolina's acceptance of the Constitution in May, New Hampshire thus became the ninth state to ratify. The Congress appointed a committee "for putting the said Constitution into operation."

In the next two months, thanks largely to the efforts of Madison and Hamilton in their own states, Virginia and New York both ratified while adding their own amendments. The margin for the Federalists in both states, however, was extremely close. Hamilton figured that the majority of the people in New York actually opposed the Constitution, and it is probable that a majority of people in the entire country opposed

A More Perfect Union: The Creation of the US Constitution

it. Only the promise of amendments had ensured a Federalist victory.

The Bill of Rights

The call for a bill of rights had been the anti-Federalists' most powerful weapon. Attacking the proposed Constitution for its vagueness and lack of specific protection against tyranny, Henry asked the Virginia convention, "What can avail your specious, imaginary balances, your rope-dancing, chain-rattling, ridiculous ideal checks and contrivances." The anti-Federalists, demanding a more concise, unequivocal Constitution, one that laid out for all to see the right of the people and limitations of the power of government, claimed that the brevity of the document only revealed its inferior nature. Richard Henry Lee despaired at the lack of provisions to protect "those essential rights of mankind without which liberty cannot exist." Trading the old government for the new without such a bill of rights, Lee argued, would be trading Scylla for Charybdis.

A bill of rights had been barely mentioned in the Philadelphia convention, most delegates holding that the fundamental rights of individuals had been secured in the state constitutions. Wilson maintained that a bill of rights was superfluous because all power not expressly delegated to the new government was reserved to the people. It was clear, however, that in this argument the anti-Federalists held the upper hand. Even Jefferson, generally in favor of the new government, wrote to Madison that a bill of rights was "what the people are entitled to against every government on earth."

By the fall of 1788 Madison had been convinced that not only was a bill of rights necessary to ensure acceptance of the Constitution but that it would have positive effects. He wrote, on October 17, that such "fundamental maxims of free Government" would be "a good ground for an appeal to the sense of community" against potential oppression and would "counteract the impulses of interest and passion."

Madison's support of the bill of rights was of critical significance. One of the new representatives from Virginia to the First Federal Congress, as established by the new Constitution, he worked tirelessly to persuade the House to enact amendments. Defusing the anti-Federalists' objections to the Constitution, Madison was able to shepherd through 17 amendments in the early months of the Congress, a list that was later trimmed to 12 in the Senate. On Oct. 2, 1789, President Washington sent to each of the states a copy of the 12 amendments adopted by the Congress in September. By Dec. 15, 1791, three-fourths of the states had ratified the 10 amendments now so familiar to Americans as the "Bill of Rights."

Franklin told a French correspondent in 1788 that the formation of the new government had been like a game of dice, with many players of diverse prejudices and interests unable to make any uncontested moves. Madison wrote to Jefferson that the welding of these clashing interests was "a task more difficult than can be well conceived by those who were not concerned in the execution of it." When the delegates left Philadelphia after the convention, few, if any, were convinced that the Constitution they had approved outlined the ideal form of government for the country. But late in his life Madison scrawled out another letter, one never addressed. In it he declared that no government can be perfect, and "that which is the least imperfect is therefore the best government."

The Document Enshrined

The fate of the United States Constitution after its signing on Sept. 17, 1787, can be contrasted sharply to the travels and physical abuse of America's other great parchment, the Declaration of Independence. As the Continental Congress, during the years of the revolutionary war, scurried from town to town, the rolled-up Declaration was carried along. After the formation of the new government under the Constitution, the one-page Declaration, eminently suited for display purposes, graced the walls of various government buildings in Washington, exposing it to prolonged damaging sunlight. It was also subjected to the work of early calligraphers responding to a demand for reproductions of the revered document. As any visitor to the National Archives can readily observe, the early treatment of the now barely legible Declaration took a disastrous toll. The Constitution, in excellent physical condition after more than 200 years, has enjoyed a more serene existence. By 1796 the Constitution was in the custody of the Department of State along with the Declaration and traveled with the federal government from New York to Philadelphia to Washington. Both documents were secretly moved

A More Perfect Union: The Creation of the US Constitution

to Leesburg, Va., before the imminent attack by the British on Washington in 1814. Following the war, the Constitution remained in the State Department while the Declaration continued its travels—to the Patent Office Building from 1841 to 1876, to Independence Hall in Philadelphia during the Centennial celebration, and back to Washington in 1877. On Sept. 29, 1921, President Warren Harding issued an Executive order transferring the Constitution and the Declaration to the Library of Congress for preservation and exhibition. The next day Librarian of Congress Herbert Putnam, acting on authority of Secretary of State Charles Evans Hughes, carried the Constitution and the Declaration in a Model-T Ford truck to the library and placed them in his office safe until an appropriate exhibit area could be constructed. The documents were officially put on display at a ceremony in the library on Feb. 28, 1924. On Feb. 20, 1933, at the laying of the cornerstone of the future National Archives Building, President Herbert Hoover remarked, "There will be aggregated here the most sacred documents of our history—the originals of the Declaration of Independence and of the Constitution of the United States." The two documents however, were not immediately transferred to the Archives. During World War II both were moved from the library to Fort Knox for protection and returned to the library in 1944. It was not until successful negotiations were completed between Librarian of Congress Luther Evans and Archivist of the United States Wayne Grover that the transfer to the National Archives was finally accomplished by special direction of the Joint Congressional Committee on the Library.

On Dec. 13, 1952, the Constitution and the Declaration were placed in helium-filled cases, enclosed in wooden crates, laid on mattresses in an armored Marine Corps personnel carrier, and escorted by ceremonial troops, two tanks, and four servicemen carrying submachine guns down Pennsylvania and Constitution avenues to the National Archives. Two days later, President Harry Truman declared at a formal ceremony in the Archives Exhibition Hall:

"We are engaged here today in a symbolic act. We are enshrining these documents for future ages. This magnificent hall has been constructed to exhibit them, and the vault beneath, that we have built to protect them, is as safe from destruction as anything that the wit of modern man can devise. All this is an honorable effort, based upon reverence for the great past, and our generation can take just pride in it."

Our Founding Fathers

Our Founding Fathers were the patriots who called for independence from Great Britain and framed the constitution of government for our new nation. Many served in the Continental Congress or as officers in the Continental Army or as delegates to the Constitutional Congress, and as the first elected officials of our government, or any combination of the above. Biographies of a few of our Founding Fathers.

John Adams, Massachusetts

John Adams (1735-1826) was a statesman, attorney, diplomat, and writer, who served as the second President of the United States, from 1797 to 1801. Before his presidency, he was a leader of the American Revolution, and he served as the first Vice President of the United States. Adams was a dedicated diarist and regularly corresponded with many important figures in early American history, including his wife and adviser Abigail Adams, and Thomas Jefferson.

A lawyer and political activist prior to the revolution, Adams was devoted to the right to counsel and presumption of innocence. He successfully defended British soldiers against murder charges arising from the Boston Massacre. Adams was a Massachusetts delegate to the Continental Congress and became a principal leader of the Revolution. He assisted in drafting the Declaration of Independence in 1776 and was its foremost advocate in Congress. As a diplomat in Europe, he helped negotiate the peace treaty with Great Britain and secured vital governmental loans. Adams was the primary author of the Massachusetts Constitution in 1780, which influenced the United States' own constitution, as did his earlier *Thoughts on Government.*

Adams was elected to two terms as Vice President under President George Washington and was elected as the second President in 1796. He was the only President elected under the banner of the Federalist Party. During his single term, Adams occupied the newly built Executive Residence in Washington, where he encountered criticism from the Jeffersonian Republicans and from some in his own Federalist Party, led by his rival Alexander Hamilton. Adams signed the controversial Alien and Sedition Acts and built up the Army and Navy in the undeclared "Quasi-War" with France. The main accomplishment of his presidency was a peaceful resolution of the conflict despite public opinion and Hamilton's opposition.

Source: US National Archives. Used with permission.

In his unsuccessful bid for re-election, opposition from Federalists and accusations of despotism from Republicans led to Adams' loss to his former friend Thomas Jefferson. He retired to Massachusetts. He eventually resumed his friendship with Jefferson by initiating a correspondence that lasted 14 years. He and his wife generated a family of politicians, diplomats, and historians now referred to as the Adams political family, which includes their son John Quincy Adams, the sixth President of the United States. John Adams died on July 4, 1826 — the 50th anniversary of the adoption of the Declaration of Independence — hours after Jefferson's death.

Thomas Jefferson, Virginia

Thomas Jefferson (1743-1826) was an American statesman, diplomat, lawyer, architect, philosopher, and Virginia planter who served as the third President from 1801 to 1809. He had previously served as the second Vice President of the U.S. between 1797 and 1801. The principal author of the Declaration of Independence, Jefferson was a proponent of democracy, republicanism, and individual rights, motivating American colonists to break from Great Britain and form a new nation; he produced formative documents and decisions at the state and national levels.

During the American Revolution, Jefferson represented Virginia in the Continental Congress that adopted the Declaration, drafted the law for religious freedom as a Virginia legislator, and served as the second Governor of Virginia from 1779 to 1781, during the war. In May 1785, Jefferson was appointed the U.S. Minister to France, and subsequently, the nation's first secretary of state under President Washington from 1790 to 1793. Jefferson and James Madison organized the Democratic-Republican Party to oppose the Federalist Party during the formation of the First Party System. With Madison, he anonymously wrote the Kentucky and Virginia Resolutions in 1798 and 1799, which sought to strengthen states' rights by nullifying the federal Alien and Sedition Acts.

As President, Jefferson pursued the nation's shipping and trade interests against Barbary pirates and aggressive British trade policies. Starting in 1803,

Our Founding Fathers

Jefferson promoted a western expansionist policy, organizing the Louisiana Purchase, doubling the nation's land area. To make room for settlement, Jefferson began a controversial process of Indian tribal removal from the newly acquired territory. Jefferson was re-elected in 1804. His second term was beset with difficulties at home, including the trial of former Vice President Aaron Burr. In 1807, American foreign trade was diminished when Jefferson implemented the Embargo Act in response to British threats to U.S. shipping. The same year, Jefferson signed the Act Prohibiting Importation of Slaves.

Jefferson's keen interest in religion and philosophy led to his presidency of the American Philosophical Society. A philologist, Jefferson knew several languages. He was a prolific letter writer and corresponded with many prominent people. After retiring from public office, Jefferson founded the University of Virginia. Jefferson died on Independence Day, July 4, 1826, the same day as John Adams.

John Hancock, Massachusetts

John Hancock (1737-1793) was an American merchant, statesman, and prominent proponent of the American Revolution. He served as president of the Second Continental Congress and was the first and third Governor of the Commonwealth of Massachusetts. His signature on the Declaration of Independence was so large (he claimed he wanted to be sure King George III saw it) that "John Hancock" came to be known as a common phrase for "signature."

Before the Revolution, Hancock was one of the wealthiest men in the colonies, having inherited a profitable mercantile business from his uncle. He began his political career in Boston as a follower of Samuel Adams, an influential local politician, though the two men later became foes. Hancock used his wealth to support the colonial cause. He became very popular in Massachusetts, especially after British officials seized his sloop *Liberty* in 1768 and charged him with smuggling. Those charges were eventually dropped.

Hancock was one of Boston's leaders during the Revolutionary crisis. He served more than two years in the Continental Congress in Philadelphia, and he was the first to sign the Declaration of Independence in his position as president of Congress. He returned to Massachusetts and was elected governor of the Commonwealth, serving in that role for most of his remaining years. He used his influence to ensure that Massachusetts ratified the U.S. Constitution in 1788.

John Jay, New York

John Jay (1745-1829) was an American statesman, patriot, diplomat, abolitionist, negotiator and signatory of the Treaty of Paris of 1783, second Governor of New York, and the first Chief Justice of the United States Supreme Court (1789-95). He directed U.S. foreign policy for much of the 1780s and was an important leader of the Federalist Party after the ratification of the U.S. Constitution in 1788.

Jay was born into a wealthy family of merchants and New York City government officials of French and Dutch descent. He became a lawyer and joined the New York Committee of Correspondence, organizing opposition to British policies. Jay was elected to the Second Continental Congress, and served as President of the Congress. From 1779-82, Jay served as the ambassador to Spain, and persuaded Spain to provide financial aid to the fledgling United States. He also served as a negotiator of the Treaty of Paris, in which Britain recognized American independence. Following the end of the war, Jay served as Secretary of Foreign Affairs, directing U.S. foreign policy under the Articles of Confederation government. He also served as the first Secretary of State on an interim basis.

A proponent of strong, centralized government, Jay worked to ratify the Constitution in New York in 1788. He was a co-author of *The Federalist Papers,* along with Hamilton and Madison. After the establishment of the new federal government, Jay was appointed by President George Washington the first Chief Justice of the United States, serving from 1789-95. The court had a light workload, deciding just four cases over six years. In 1794, while serving as Chief Justice, Jay negotiated the highly controversial Jay Treaty with Britain. Jay received a handful of electoral votes in three of the first four presidential elections.

Jay served as the Governor of New York from 1795 to 1801. In the waning days of President John Adams' administration, Jay was confirmed by the Senate for another term as Chief Justice, but he declined the position and retired to his farm in Westchester County, New York.

Our Founding Fathers

Samuel Adams, Massachusetts

Samuel Adams (1722-1803) was an American statesman, political philosopher, and second cousin to his fellow Founding Father, President John Adams. Sam Adams was born in Boston, and brought up in a religious and politically active family. A graduate of Harvard College, he was an unsuccessful businessman and tax collector before entering politics. He was an influential official of the Massachusetts House of Representatives and the Boston Town Meeting in the 1760s, and he became a part of a movement opposed to the British Parliament's efforts to tax the British American colonies without their consent. His 1768 Massachusetts Circular Letter calling for colonial non-cooperation prompted the occupation of Boston by British soldiers, eventually resulting in the Boston Massacre of 1770. Adams and his colleagues devised a committee of correspondence system in 1772 to help coordinate resistance to Great Britain's policies. Continued resistance to British policy resulted in the 1773 Boston Tea Party and the coming of the American Revolution.

Parliament passed the Coercive Acts in 1774, at which time Adams attended the Continental Congress in Philadelphia, which was convened to determine the colonies' response. Adams helped guide Congress towards issuing the Continental Association in 1774 and the Declaration of Independence in 1776, and he helped draft the Articles of Confederation and the Massachusetts Constitution. Adams returned to Massachusetts after the war, where he served in the state senate and was eventually elected governor.

Roger Sherman, Connecticut

Roger Sherman (1721-1793) moved with his family from Massachusetts to Connecticut at a young age. Without benefit of a formal legal education, he was admitted to the bar in 1754 and embarked upon a distinguished judicial and political career. In the period 1755-61, except for a brief interval, he served as a representative in the colonial legislature and held the offices of justice of the peace and county judge. He rose to an associate judge of the Connecticut Superior Court and to representative in both houses of the colonial assembly. Although opposed to extremism, he promptly joined the fight against Britain. Sherman was a longtime and influential member of the Continental Congress (1774-81 and 1783-84). He won membership on the committees that drafted the Declaration of Independence and the Articles of Confederation, as well as those concerned with Indian affairs, national finances, and military matters. To solve economic problems, at both national and state levels, he advocated high taxes rather than excessive borrowing or the issuance of paper currency.

While in Congress, Sherman remained active in state and local politics, continuing to hold the office of judge of the Connecticut Superior Court, as well as membership on the council of safety (1777-79). He was elected mayor of New Haven (1784-86).

Although on the edge of insolvency, mainly because of wartime losses, Sherman could not resist the lure of national service. In 1787 he represented his state at the Constitutional Convention, and attended practically every session. Not only did he sit on the Committee on Postponed Matters, but he also probably helped draft the New Jersey Plan and was a prime mover behind the Connecticut, or Great, Compromise, which broke the deadlock between the large and small states over representation. He was instrumental in Connecticut's ratification of the Constitution. Sherman concluded his career by serving in the U.S. House of Representatives (1789-91) and Senate (1791-93).

John Dickinson, Delaware

John Dickinson (1732-1808), "Penman of the Revolution," studied law with John Moland in Philadelphia. In 1753, Dickinson went to England to continue his studies at London's Middle Temple. Four years later, he returned to Philadelphia and became a prominent lawyer there. By 1770, Dickinson's superior education and talents had propelled him into politics. In 1760, he had served in the assembly of the Three Lower Counties (Delaware), where he held the speakership. Combining his Pennsylvania and Delaware careers in 1762, he won a seat as a Philadelphia member in the Pennsylvania assembly where he remained through 1765. He became the leader of the conservative side in the colony's political battles. His defense of the Quaker charter against the faction led by Benjamin Franklin earned him respect for his integrity, and Franklin lost his seat in the assembly.

In 1771, Dickinson returned to the Pennsylvania legislature and drafted a petition to the king that was unanimously approved. In 1774 he chaired the

Our Founding Fathers

Philadelphia committee of correspondence and briefly sat in the First Continental Congress as a representative from Pennsylvania.

In the Second Continental Congress (1775-76), still a representative of Pennsylvania, he drew up the Olive Branch Petition and the "Declaration of the Causes of Taking Up Arms." In the Pennsylvania assembly in November 1775, he drafted instructions to the delegates to Congress directing them to seek redress of grievances, but ordered them to oppose separation of the colonies from Britain. In June 1776, he wrote new instructions allowing them to vote for independence, but not expressly instructing them to do so.

In Congress, he abstained from the vote on the Declaration of Independence (1776) and refused to sign it. Nevertheless, he then became one of only two contemporary congressional members (with Thomas McKean) who entered the military. During the summer, while on the New Jersey front, he was voted out of the Pennsylvania assembly. When much of his unit deserted, he resigned his colonelcy and accepted re-election to the Pennsylvania assembly in the fall of 1776. When the revolutionary government would not consider amending the new constitution to protect dissenters' rights, he resigned his seat. He then enlisted as a private in the Delaware militia and may have taken part in the Battle of Brandywine.

Dickinson took a seat in the Continental Congress (1779), where he signed the Articles of Confederation, although a much different version from the one he had drafted. In 1781, he became president of Delaware's Supreme Executive Council. In 1786, representing Delaware, he attended and chaired the Annapolis Convention and authored the letter to Congress calling for the Constitutional Convention.

The next year, Delaware sent Dickinson to the Constitutional Convention. He engineered the solution for representation known as the Connecticut Compromise and argued for the end of the slave trade. Because of his premature departure from the convention, he did not actually sign the Constitution but authorized his friend and fellow-delegate George Read to do so for him. In 1792 he served as president of the Delaware Constitutional Convention; in 1795 he led citizen opposition to the Jay Treaty.

Elbridge Gerry, Massachusetts

Elbridge Gerry (1744-1814) was a Harvard graduate and merchant who entered the colonial legislature (1772-74), where he came under the influence of Samuel Adams, and took part in the Marblehead and Massachusetts committees of correspondence. Between 1774 and 1776 Gerry attended the first and second provincial congresses. He served with Samuel Adams and John Hancock on the council of safety and, as chairman of the committee of supply.

In 1776, Gerry entered the Continental Congress, where his congressional specialities were military and financial matters. In Congress and throughout his career his actions often appeared contradictory. He earned the nickname "soldiers' friend" for his advocacy of better pay and equipment, yet he vacillated on the issue of pensions. Despite his disapproval of standing armies, he recommended long-term enlistments.

Gerry was one of the most vocal delegates at the Constitutional Convention of 1787. He presided as chairman of the committee that produced the Great Compromise but disliked the compromise itself. He antagonized nearly everyone by his inconsistency and, according to a colleague, "objected to everything he did not propose." At first an advocate of a strong central government, Gerry ultimately rejected and refused to sign the Constitution because it lacked a bill of rights and because he deemed it a threat to republicanism. He led the drive against ratification in Massachusetts and denounced the document as "full of vices." In 1789, after he announced his intention to support the Constitution, he was elected to the First Congress where, to the chagrin of the Antifederalists, he championed Federalist policies.

Gerry left Congress for the last time in 1793 and retired for four years. In 1800-1803 Gerry, never very popular among the Massachusetts electorate because of his aristocratic haughtiness, met defeat in four bids for the Massachusetts governorship but finally triumphed in 1810. Near the end of his two terms, scarred by partisan controversy, the Democratic-Republicans passed a redistricting measure to ensure their domination of the state senate. In response, the Federalists heaped ridicule on Gerry and coined the pun "gerrymander" to describe the salamander-like shape of one of the redistricted areas.

Our Founding Fathers

Despite his advanced age, frail health, and the threat of poverty brought on by neglect of personal affairs, Gerry served as James Madison's Vice President in 1813 but died of ill health the next year.

Alexander Hamilton, New York

Alexander Hamilton (1757-1804) was born in the British West Indies, the illegitimate son of a common-law marriage between a poor itinerant Scottish merchant of aristocratic descent and an English-French Huguenot mother who was a planter's daughter. In 1772, bearing letters of introduction, Hamilton traveled to New York City. Patrons he met there arranged for him to attend Barber's Academy at Elizabethtown, NJ. During this time, he met and stayed for a while at the home of William Livingston, who would one day be a fellow signer of the Constitution.

Although not yet 20 years of age, in 1774-75 Hamilton wrote several widely read pro-Whig pamphlets. Right after the war broke out, he accepted an artillery captaincy and fought in the principal campaigns of 1776-77. In the latter year, winning the rank of lieutenant colonel, he joined the staff of General Washington as secretary and aide-de-camp and soon became his close confidant as well. In 1781, after some disagreements with Washington, he took a command position under Lafayette in the Yorktown campaign (1781). He resigned his commission that November.

Hamilton then read law at Albany and quickly entered practice, but public service soon attracted him. He was elected to the Continental Congress in 1782-83. Because of his interest in strengthening the central government, he represented his state at the Annapolis Convention in 1786, where he urged the calling of the Constitutional Convention.

In 1787 Hamilton served in the legislature, which appointed him as a delegate to the convention. He sat on the Committee of Style, and he was the only one of the three delegates from his state who signed the finished document. Hamilton's part in New York's ratification the next year was substantial, though he felt the Constitution was deficient in many respects. He collaborated with John Jay and James Madison in writing *The Federalist*. In 1787 Hamilton was again elected to the Continental Congress.

When the new government got under way in 1789, Hamilton won the position of Secretary of the Treasury. He began at once to place the nation's disorganized finances on a sound footing. He proposed establishment of a national bank, funding of the national debt, assumption of state war debts, and the encouragement of manufacturing. Hamilton's policies soon brought him into conflict with Jefferson and Madison. Their disputes with him over his pro-business economic program, sympathies for Great Britain, disdain for the common man, and opposition to the principles and excesses of the French revolution contributed to the formation of the first U.S. party system. It pitted Hamilton and the Federalists against Jefferson and Madison and the Democratic-Republicans.

During most of the Washington administration, Hamilton's views usually prevailed with the President, especially after 1793 when Jefferson left the government. In 1795 family and financial needs forced Hamilton to resign from the Treasury Department and resume his law practice in New York City. Except for a stint as inspector-general of the Army (1798-1800) during the undeclared war with France, he never again held public office.

Meanwhile, when Jefferson and Aaron Burr tied in Presidential electoral votes in 1800, Hamilton threw valuable support to Jefferson. In 1804, when Burr sought the governorship of New York, Hamilton again managed to defeat him. That same year, Burr, taking offense at remarks he believed to have originated with Hamilton, challenged him to a duel, which took place at present Weehawken, NJ, on July 11. Mortally wounded, Hamilton died the next day.

Benjamin Franklin, Pennsylvania

Benjamin Franklin (1706-1790) was born in Boston and later went to work for his half-brother James, a printer, who in 1721 founded the *New England Courant*, the fourth newspaper in the colonies. Benjamin secretly contributed 14 essays to it, his first published writings.

In 1723, Franklin moved to Philadelphia, where he obtained employment as a printer. He spent only a year there and then sailed to London for two more years. Back in Philadelphia, he rose rapidly in the printing industry. He published *The Pennsylvania Gazette* (1730-48), which had been founded by another man in 1728, but his most successful literary venture was the annual *Poor Richard's Almanac* (1733-58). By 1748

Our Founding Fathers

he had achieved financial independence and gained recognition for his philanthropy and the stimulus he provided to such civic causes as libraries, educational institutions, and hospitals. Energetic and tireless, he also found time to pursue his interest in science, as well as to enter politics.

Franklin served as clerk and member of the colonial legislature and as deputy postmaster of Philadelphia and deputy postmaster general of the colonies.

During the years 1757-62 and 1764-75, Franklin resided in England, originally in the capacity of agent for Pennsylvania and later for Georgia, New Jersey, and Massachusetts. During the latter period, which coincided with the growth of colonial unrest, he underwent a political metamorphosis. Until then a contented Englishman in outlook, primarily concerned with Pennsylvania provincial politics, he distrusted popular movements and saw little purpose to be served in carrying principle to extremes. Until the issue of parliamentary taxation undermined the old alliances, he led the Quaker party attack on the Anglican proprietary party and its Presbyterian frontier allies. His purpose throughout the years at London in fact had been displacement of the Penn family administration by royal authority—the conversion of the province from a proprietary to a royal colony.

It was during the Stamp Act crisis that Franklin evolved from leader of a shattered provincial party's faction to celebrated spokesman at London for American rights. Although as agent for Pennsylvania he opposed by every conceivable means the enactment of the bill in 1765, he did not at first realize the depth of colonial hostility. He regarded passage as unavoidable and preferred to submit to it while actually working for its repeal.

Franklin's nomination of a friend and political ally as stamp distributor for Pennsylvania, coupled with his apparent acceptance of the legislation, armed his proprietary opponents with explosive issues. Their energetic exploitation of them endangered his reputation at home until reliable information was published demonstrating his unabated opposition to the act. Subsequently, Franklin's defense of the American position in the House of Commons during the debates over the Stamp Act's repeal restored his prestige at home.

Franklin returned to Philadelphia in May 1775 and immediately became a distinguished member of the Continental Congress. Thirteen months later, he served on the committee that drafted the Declaration of Independence.

But, within less than a year and a half after his return, the aged statesman set sail once again for Europe, beginning a career as diplomat that would occupy him for most of the rest of his life. In the years 1776-79, as one of three commissioners, he directed the negotiations that led to treaties of commerce and alliance with France, where the people adulated him, but he and the other commissioners squabbled constantly. While he was sole commissioner to France (1779-85), he and John Jay and John Adams negotiated the Treaty of Paris (1783), which ended the War for Independence.

Back in the United States, in 1785 Franklin became president of the Supreme Executive Council of Pennsylvania. At the Constitutional Convention, though he did not approve of many aspects of the finished document and was hampered by his age and ill-health, he missed few if any sessions, lent his prestige, soothed passions, and compromised disputes.

Gouverneur Morris, Pennsylvania

Gouverneur Morris (1752-1816) was born into a wealthy family in Westchester (present Bronx) County, N.Y. He was educated by private tutors and at a Huguenot school in New Rochelle. In early life, he lost a leg in a carriage accident. He attended King's College (later Columbia College and University) in New York City, graduating in 1768 at the age of 16. Three years later, after reading law in the city, he gained admission to the bar. In 1775, representing Westchester County, he took a seat in New York's Revolutionary provincial congress (1775-77). In 1776, when he also served in the militia, along with John Jay and Robert R. Livingston he drafted the first constitution of the state. Subsequently he joined its council of safety (1777).

In 1777-78, Morris sat in the legislature and in 1778-79 in the Continental Congress, where he numbered among the youngest and most brilliant members. During this period, he signed the Articles of Confederation and drafted instructions for Benjamin Franklin, in Paris, as well as those that provided a partial basis for the

Our Founding Fathers

treaty ending the War for Independence.

Morris emerged as one of the leading figures at the Constitutional Convention. His speeches, more frequent than those by anyone else, numbered 173. A strong advocate of nationalism and aristocratic rule, he served on many committees, including those on postponed matters and style. Above all, it was apparently he who actually drafted the Constitution. Morris subsequently left public life for a time to devote his attention to business. Having purchased the family home from his half-brother, Lewis, he moved back to New York. Afterward, in 1789, Gouverneur joined in a business venture with Robert Morris (no relation), and traveled to France, where he witnessed the beginnings of the French Revolution.

Morris was to remain in Europe for about a decade. In 1790-91 he undertook a diplomatic mission to London to try to negotiate some of the outstanding problems between the United States and Great Britain. The mission failed, but in 1792 Washington appointed him as Minister to France, to replace Thomas Jefferson. Morris was recalled two years later. Morris returned to the U.S. in 1799. The next year, he was elected to finish an unexpired term in the U.S. Senate. An ardent Federalist, he was defeated in his bid for re-election in 1802 and left office the following year.

Morris retired to a glittering life at Morrisania, where he had built a new residence. During his last years, he continued to speak out against the Democratic-Republicans and strongly opposed the War of 1812.

Robert Morris, Pennsylvania

Robert Morris (1734-1806) was born at Liverpool, England. When he reached 13, he emigrated to Maryland to join his father, a tobacco exporter at Oxford, Md. After brief schooling at Philadelphia, the youth obtained employment with Thomas and Charles Willing's well-known shipping-banking firm. In 1754 he became a partner and for almost four decades was one of the company's directors as well as an influential Philadelphia citizen.

During the Stamp Act turmoil in 1765, Morris joined other merchants in protest, but not until the outbreak of hostilities a decade later did he fully commit himself to the Revolution. In 1775 the Continental Congress contracted with his firm to import arms and ammunition, and he was elected to the Pennsylvania council of safety (1775-76), the committee of correspondence, the provincial assembly, the legislature, and the Continental Congress. In the last body, on July 1, 1776, he voted against independence, which he personally considered premature, but the next day he purposely absented himself to facilitate an affirmative ballot by his delegation.

Morris, a key congressman, specialized in financial affairs and military procurement. Although he and his firm profited handsomely, had it not been for his assiduous labors the Continental Army would probably have been forced to demobilize. He worked closely with General Washington, wheedled money and supplies from the states, borrowed money in the face of overwhelming difficulties, and on occasion even obtained personal loans to further the war cause.

Immediately following his congressional service, Morris sat for two more terms in the Pennsylvania legislature (1778-81). He embarked on the most dramatic phase of his career by accepting the office of Superintendent of Finance (1781-84) under the Articles of Confederation. Congress, recognizing the perilous state of the nation's finances and its impotence to provide remedies, granted him dictatorial powers and acquiesced to his condition that he be allowed to continue his private commercial enterprises. He slashed all governmental and military expenditures, personally purchased army and navy supplies, tightened accounting procedures, prodded the states to fulfill quotas of money and supplies, and when necessary strained his personal credit by issuing notes over his own signature or borrowing from friends.

To finance Washington's Yorktown campaign in 1781, Morris obtained a sizable loan from France. He used part of it, along with some of his own fortune, to organize the Bank of North America, chartered that December. The first government-incorporated bank in the United States, it aided war financing.

Although Morris was re-elected to the Pennsylvania legislature for 1785-86, his private ventures consumed most of his time. In the latter year, he attended the Annapolis Convention, and the following year the Constitutional Convention, where he sympathized with the Federalists. In 1789, declining Washington's offer of appointment as the first Secretary of the Treasury, he took instead a U.S. Senate seat (1789-95).

Our Founding Fathers

In 1794, in financial trouble, Morris attempted to escape creditors by retreating to The Hills, the country estate along the Schuylkill River on the edge of Philadelphia that he had acquired in 1770.

Arrested at the behest of creditors in 1798 and forced to abandon completion of the mansion, Morris was thrown into the Philadelphia debtor's prison, where he was nevertheless well treated. By the time he was released in 1801, under a federal bankruptcy law, however, his property and fortune had vanished, his health had deteriorated, and his spirit had been broken. He lingered on in poverty and obscurity, living in a simple Philadelphia home on an annuity obtained for his wife by fellow-signer Gouverneur Morris (unrelated).

James Wilson, Pennsylvania

James Wilson (1741-1798) was born near St. Andrews, Scotland, and educated at the universities of St. Andrews, Glasgow, and Edinburgh. He then emigrated to America, arriving in the midst of the Stamp Act agitations in 1765. In 1768, the year after his admission to the Philadelphia bar, Wilson set up practice at Reading, Pa. Two years later, he moved westward to the Scotch-Irish settlement of Carlisle.

Wilson became involved in Revolutionary politics. In 1774 he took over chairmanship of the Carlisle committee of correspondence, attended the first provincial assembly, and completed preparation of a political tract that was circulated widely in England and America and established him as a Whig leader.

The next year, Wilson was elected to both the provincial assembly and the Continental Congress, where he sat mainly on military and Indian affairs committees. In 1776, he voted in the affirmative and signed the Declaration of Independence on August 2.

Wilson's strenuous opposition to the republican Pennsylvania constitution of 1776, besides indicating a switch to conservatism on his part, led to his removal from Congress the following year. To avoid the clamor among his frontier constituents, he repaired to Annapolis during the winter of 1777-78 and then took up residence in Philadelphia.

In the fall of 1779, during a period of inflation and food shortages, a mob which included many militiamen and was led by radical constitutionalists, set out to attack the republican leadership. Wilson was a prime target. He and some 35 of his colleagues barricaded themselves in his home at Third and Walnut Streets, thereafter known as "Fort Wilson." During a brief skirmish, several people on both sides were killed or wounded.

During 1781 Congress appointed Wilson as one of the directors of the Bank of North America.

Wilson reached the apex of his career in the Constitutional Convention (1787), where his influence was probably second only to that of Madison. Rarely missing a session, he sat on the Committee of Detail and in many other ways applied his excellent knowledge of political theory to convention problems. Only Gouverneur Morris delivered more speeches.

That same year, overcoming powerful opposition, Wilson led the drive for ratification in Pennsylvania, the second state to endorse the instrument. The new commonwealth constitution, drafted in 1789-90 along the lines of the U.S. Constitution, was primarily Wilson's work and represented the climax of his 14-year fight against the constitution of 1776.

For his services President Washington named him as an associate justice in 1789. He was also chosen as the first law professor at the College of Philadelphia.

Wilson, who wrote only a few opinions, did not achieve the success on the Supreme Court that his capabilities and experience promised. Indeed, during those years he was the object of much criticism and barely escaped impeachment. He tried to influence the enactment of legislation in Pennsylvania favorable to land speculators. Between 1792 and 1795 he also made unwise land investments in western New York and Pennsylvania, as well as in Georgia. This did not stop him from conceiving a grandiose but ill-fated scheme, involving vast sums of European capital, for the recruitment of European colonists and their settlement in the West.

John Rutledge, South Carolina

John Rutledge (1739-1800), elder brother of Edward Rutledge, signer of the Declaration of Independence, was born near Charleston in 1739. After studying law at London's Middle Temple in 1760, he was admitted to English practice. But, almost at once, he sailed back to Charleston to begin a legal career and to amass a fortune in plantations and slaves. In 1761 Rutledge became politically active when he was

Our Founding Fathers

elected to the provincial assembly where he held his seat until the War for Independence. For 10 months in 1764 he temporarily held the post of provincial attorney general. In 1774 Rutledge was sent to the First Continental Congress, where he pursued a moderate course. After spending the next year in the Second Continental Congress, he returned to South Carolina and helped reorganize its government. In 1776 he served on the committee of safety and took part in the writing of the state constitution. That year, he also became president of the lower house of the legislature, a post he held until 1778.

In 1779, he was elected as governor. It was a difficult time. The British were invading South Carolina, and the military situation was desperate. Early in 1780, by which time the legislature had adjourned, Charleston was besieged. In May it fell, the American army was captured, and the British confiscated Rutledge's property. He ultimately escaped to North Carolina and set about attempting to rally forces to recover South Carolina. In 1781, aided by Gen. Nathanael Greene and a new Continental Army force, he re-established the government. In January 1782 he resigned the governorship and took a seat in the lower house of the legislature.

One of the most influential delegates at the Constitutional Convention, where he maintained a moderate nationalist stance and chaired the Committee of Detail, he attended all the sessions, spoke often and effectively, and served on five committees. Like his fellow South Carolina delegates, he vigorously advocated southern interests.

The new government under the Constitution soon lured Rutledge. He was a Presidential elector in 1789 and Washington then appointed him as Associate Justice of the U.S. Supreme Court, but for some reason he apparently served only a brief time. In 1791 he became chief justice of the South Carolina supreme court. Four years later, Washington again appointed him to the U.S. Supreme Court, this time as Chief Justice to replace John Jay. But Rutledge's outspoken opposition to Jay's Treaty (1794), and the intermittent mental illness he had suffered from since the death of his wife in 1792, caused the Federalist-dominated Senate to reject his appointment and end his public career.

James Madison, Virginia

James Madison (1751-1836) was born at Port Conway, King George County, Va., while his mother was visiting her parents. In a few weeks she journeyed back with her newborn son to Montpelier estate, in Orange County, which became his lifelong home. An excellent scholar though frail and sickly in his youth, in 1771 he graduated from the College of New Jersey (later Princeton). Back at Montpelier, still undecided on a profession, Madison soon embraced the patriot cause, and state and local politics absorbed much of his time. In 1775 he served on the Orange County committee of safety; the next year at the Virginia convention, which, besides advocating various Revolutionary steps, framed the Virginia constitution; in 1776-77 in the House of Delegates; and in 1778-80 in the Council of State.

In 1780 Madison was chosen to represent Virginia in the Continental Congress. Although originally the youngest delegate, he played a major role in the deliberations of that body. Meantime, in the years 1784-86, he had again sat in the Virginia House of Delegates. He was a guiding force behind the Mount Vernon Conference (1785), attended the Annapolis Convention (1786), and was otherwise highly instrumental in the convening of the Constitutional Convention in 1787.

Madison was clearly the preeminent figure at the convention. Some of the delegates favored an authoritarian central government; others, retention of state sovereignty; and most occupied positions in the middle of the two extremes. Madison, who was rarely absent and whose Virginia Plan was in large part the basis of the Constitution, tirelessly advocated a strong government, though many of his proposals were rejected. Despite his poor speaking capabilities, he took the floor more than 150 times. Madison was also a member of numerous committees, the most important of which were those on postponed matters and style. His journal of the convention is the best single record of the event.

Playing a lead in the ratification process in Virginia, too, Madison defended the document against such powerful opponents as Patrick Henry, George Mason, and Richard Henry Lee. In New York, where Madison was serving in the Continental Congress,

Our Founding Fathers

he collaborated with Alexander Hamilton and John Jay in a series of essays that in 1787-88 appeared in the newspapers and were soon published in book form as *The Federalist* (1788). This set of essays is a classic of political theory and a lucid exposition of the republican principles that dominated the framing of the Constitution.

In the U.S. House of Representatives (1789-97), Madison helped frame and ensure passage of the Bill of Rights. He also assisted in organizing the executive department and creating a system of federal taxation. As leaders of the opposition to Hamilton's policies, he and Jefferson founded the Democratic-Republican Party.

In 1798 he wrote the Virginia Resolutions, which attacked the Alien and Sedition Acts. While he served as Secretary of State (1801-09), his wife, Dolley, often served as President Jefferson's hostess.

In 1809 Madison succeeded Jefferson. Like the first three Presidents, Madison was enmeshed in the ramifications of European wars. Diplomacy had failed to prevent the seizure of U.S. ships, goods, and men on the high seas, and a depression wracked the country. Madison continued to apply diplomatic techniques and economic sanctions, eventually effective to some degree against France. But continued British interference with shipping, as well as other grievances, led to the War of 1812.

The war, for which the young nation was ill prepared, ended in stalemate in December 1814 when the inconclusive Treaty of Ghent, which nearly restored prewar conditions, was signed. But, thanks mainly to Andrew Jackson's spectacular victory at the Battle of New Orleans (Chalmette) in January 1815, most Americans believed they had won. Twice tested, independence had survived, and an ebullient nationalism marked Madison's last years in office, during which period the Democratic-Republicans held virtually uncontested sway.

George Mason, Virginia

George Mason (1725-1792) established himself as an important figure in his community. As owner of Gunston Hall he was one of the richest planters in Virginia. In 1752 he acquired an interest in the Ohio Company, an organization that speculated in western lands. When the crown revoked the company's rights in 1773, Mason, the company's treasurer, wrote his first major state paper. During these years Mason also pursued his political interests. He was a justice of the Fairfax County court, and between 1754 and 1779 Mason was a trustee of the city of Alexandria. In 1759 he was elected to the Virginia House of Burgesses. When the Stamp Act of 1765 aroused outrage in the colonies, Mason wrote an open letter explaining the colonists' position to a committee of London merchants to enlist their support.

In 1774 Mason assisted in drawing up the Fairfax Resolves, a document that outlined the colonists' constitutional grounds for their objections to the Boston Port Act. Virginia's Declaration of Rights, framed by Mason in 1776, was widely copied in other colonies, served as a model for Jefferson in the first part of the Declaration of Independence, and was the basis for the federal Constitution's Bill of Rights.

Mason supported the disestablishment of the church and was active in the organization of military affairs, especially in the West. The influence of his early work is seen in the 1783 peace treaty with Great Britain, which fixed the Anglo-American boundary at the Great Lakes instead of the Ohio River. After independence, Mason drew up the plan for Virginia's cession of its western lands to the United States.

By the early 1780s, however, Mason grew disgusted with the conduct of public affairs and retired. In 1785 he attended the Mount Vernon meeting that was a prelude to the Annapolis convention of 1786, but, though appointed, he did not go to Annapolis.

At Philadelphia in 1787 Mason was one of the five most frequent speakers at the Constitutional Convention. He exerted great influence, but during the last two weeks of the convention he decided not to sign the document.

Mason's refusal prompted surprise, especially since his name is so closely linked with constitutionalism. He explained his reasons at length, citing the absence of a declaration of rights as his primary concern. He then discussed the provisions of the Constitution point by point, beginning with the House of Representatives. The House he criticized as not truly representative of the nation, the Senate as too powerful. He also claimed that the power of the federal judiciary would destroy the state judiciaries, render justice unattainable, and

Our Founding Fathers

enable the rich to oppress and ruin the poor. These fears led Mason to conclude that the new government was destined to either become a monarchy or fall into the hands of a corrupt, oppressive aristocracy. Two of Mason's greatest concerns were incorporated into the Constitution. The Bill of Rights answered his primary objection, and the 11th amendment addressed his call for strictures on the judiciary.

Edmund Randolph, Virginia

Edmund Randolph (1753-1813) attended the College of William and Mary and continued his education by studying the law under his father's tutelage. When the Revolution broke out, father and son followed different paths. John Randolph, a Loyalist, followed the royal governor, Lord Dunmore, to England, in 1775. Edmund then lived with his uncle. During the war Edmund served as an aide-de-camp to General Washington and also attended the convention that adopted Virginia's first state constitution in 1776. He was the convention's youngest member at age 23.

Randolph became mayor of Williamsburg and Virginia's attorney-general. In 1779 he was elected to the Continental Congress, and in November 1786 Randolph became Governor of Virginia. In 1786 he was a delegate to the Annapolis Convention.

Four days after the opening of the federal convention in Philadelphia, on May 29, 1787, Randolph presented the Virginia Plan for creating a new government. This plan proposed a strong central government composed of three branches—legislative, executive, and judicial—and enabled the legislative to veto state laws and use force against states that failed to fulfill their duties. After many debates and revisions, including striking the section permitting force against a state, the Virginia Plan became in large part the basis of the Constitution.

Randolph fluctuated between the Federalist and Antifederalist points of view. He sat on the Committee of Detail that prepared a draft of the Constitution, but by the time the document was adopted, Randolph declined to sign. He felt it was not sufficiently republican, and he was especially wary of creating a one-man executive. He preferred a three-man council since he regarded "a unity in the Executive" to be the "foetus of monarchy." In a Letter…on the Federal Constitution, dated Oct. 10, 1787, Randolph explained at length his objections to the Constitution. Randolph was a strong advocate of the process of amendment. He feared that if the Constitution were submitted for ratification without leaving the states the opportunity to amend it, the document might be rejected and thus close off any hope of another plan of union. However, he hoped that amendments would be permitted and second convention called to incorporate the changes.

By the time of the Virginia convention for ratification, Randolph supported the Constitution and worked to win his state's approval of it. He stated his reason for his switch: "The accession of eight states reduced our deliberations to the single question of Union or no Union."

Under President Washington, Randolph became Attorney General. After Thomas Jefferson resigned as Secretary of State, Randolph assumed that post for the years 1794-95. During the Jefferson-Hamilton conflict he tried to remain unaligned. After retiring from politics in 1795, Randolph resumed his law practice and was regarded as a leading figure in the legal community. When Aaron Burr went on trial for treason in 1807, Randolph acted as his senior counsel.

George Washington, Virginia

The eldest of six children from his father's second marriage, George Washington was born into the landed gentry in 1732 at Wakefield Plantation, Va. Until reaching 16 years of age, he lived there and at other plantations along the Potomac and Rappahannock Rivers, including the one that later became known as Mount Vernon. His education was rudimentary, probably being obtained from tutors but possibly also from private schools, and he learned surveying. After he lost his father when he was 11 years old, his half-brother Lawrence, who had served in the Royal Navy, acted as his mentor. As a result, the youth acquired an interest in pursuing a naval career, but his mother discouraged him from doing so.

At the age of 16, in 1748, Washington joined a surveying party sent out to the Shenandoah Valley by Lord Fairfax, a land baron. For the next few years, Washington conducted surveys in Virginia and present West Virginia and gained a lifetime interest in the West. In 1751-52 he also accompanied Lawrence on a visit he made to Barbados, West Indies, for health reasons just before his death.

Our Founding Fathers

The next year, Washington began his military career when the royal governor appointed him to an adjutantship in the militia, as a major. That same year, as a gubernatorial emissary, accompanied by a guide, he traveled to Fort Le Boeuf, Pa., in the Ohio River Valley, and delivered to French authorities an ultimatum to cease fortification and settlement in English territory. During the trip, he tried to better British relations with various Indian tribes.

In 1754, winning the rank of lieutenant colonel and then colonel in the militia, Washington led a force that sought to challenge French control of the Ohio River Valley, but met defeat at Fort Necessity, Pa., an event that helped trigger the French and Indian War (1754-63). Late in 1754, irked by the dilution of his rank because of the pending arrival of British regulars, he resigned his commission. That same year, he leased Mount Vernon, which he was to inherit in 1761.

In 1755, Washington re-entered military service with the courtesy title of colonel, as an aide to Gen. Edward Braddock, and barely escaped death when the French defeated the general's forces in the Battle of the Monongahela, Pa. As a reward for his bravery, Washington rewon his command of the Virginia militia forces, charged with defending the colony's frontier. Late in 1758 or early in 1759, disillusioned over governmental neglect of the militia and irritated at not rising in rank, he resigned and headed back to Mount Vernon.

During 1759-74, he managed his plantations and sat in the Virginia House of Burgesses. He supported the initial protests against British policies; took an active part in the nonimportation movement in Virginia; and, in time, particularly because of his military experience, became a Whig leader.

Strongly sympathetic to the Whig position and resentful of British restrictions and commercial exploitation, Washington represented Virginia at the First and Second Continental Congresses. In 1775, after the bloodshed at Lexington and Concord, Congress appointed him as commander in chief of the Continental Army. Overcoming severe obstacles, especially in supply, he eventually fashioned a well-trained and disciplined fighting force.

The strategy Washington evolved consisted of continual harassment of British forces while avoiding general actions. Although his troops yielded much ground and lost a number of battles, they persevered even during the dark winters at Valley Forge and Morristown, N.J. Finally, with the aid of the French fleet and army, he won a climactic victory at the Battle of Yorktown, Va., in 1781.

During the next two years, while still commanding the Continental Army, which was underpaid and poorly supplied, Washington denounced proposals that the military take over the government, including one that planned to appoint him as king, but supported army petitions to the Continental Congress for proper compensation. Once the Treaty of Paris (1783) was signed, he resigned his commission and returned once again to Mount Vernon.

Dissatisfied with national progress under the Articles of Confederation, Washington advocated a stronger central government. He hosted the Mount Vernon Conference (1785) at his estate after its initial meetings in Alexandria, though he apparently did not directly participate in the discussions. Despite his sympathy with the goals of the Annapolis Convention (1786), he did not attend. But, the following year, encouraged by many of his friends, he presided over the Constitutional Convention, whose success was immeasurably influenced by his presence and dignity. Following ratification of the new instrument of government in 1788, the electoral college unanimously chose him as the first President.

The next year, after a triumphal journey from Mount Vernon to New York City, Washington took the oath of office at Federal Hall. During his two precedent-setting terms, he governed with dignity as well as restraint. He also provided the stability and authority the emergent nation so sorely needed, gave substance to the Constitution, and reconciled competing factions and divergent policies within the government and his administration. Although not averse to exercising presidential power, he respected the role of Congress and did not infringe upon its prerogatives. He also tried to maintain harmony between his Secretary of State Thomas Jefferson and Secretary of the Treasury Alexander Hamilton, whose differences typified evolving party divisions which Washington disdained.

Yet, usually leaning upon Hamilton for advice, Washington supported his plan for the assumption of

Our Founding Fathers

state debts, concurred in the constitutionality of the bill establishing the Bank of the United States, and favored enactment of tariffs by Congress to provide federal revenue and protect domestic manufacturers. Washington took various other steps to strengthen governmental authority, including suppression of the Whisky Rebellion (1794). To unify the country, he toured the Northeast in 1789 and the South in 1791. During his tenure, the government moved from New York to Philadelphia in 1790. He superintended planning for relocation to the District of Columbia, and he laid the cornerstone of the Capitol (1793).

In foreign affairs, despite opposition from the Senate, Washington exerted dominance. He fostered United States interests on the North American continent by treaties with Britain and Spain. Yet, until the nation was stronger, he insisted on the maintenance of neutrality. For example, when the French Revolution created war between France and Britain, he ignored the remonstrances of pro-French Jefferson and pro-English Hamilton.

Although many people encouraged Washington to seek a third term, he was weary of politics and refused to do so. In his "Farewell Address" (1796), he urged his countrymen to forswear party spirit and sectional differences and to avoid entanglement in the wars and domestic policies of other nations.

Washington enjoyed only a few years of retirement at Mount Vernon. Even then, demonstrating his continued willingness to make sacrifices for his country in 1798 when the nation was on the verge of war with France he agreed to command the army, though his services were not ultimately required. He died at the age of 67 in 1799. In his will, he emancipated his slaves.

National Anthem

To celebrate a victory over British forces during the War of 1812, U.S. soldiers raised a large American flag at Fort McHenry in Baltimore, Maryland, on Sept. 14, 1814. Inspired by those events, Francis Scott Key wrote a poem called "Defence of Fort M'Henry," which eventually became *The Star Spangled Banner* and the United States national anthem.

The Star-Spangled Banner

O say can you see, by the dawn's early light,

What so proudly we hail'd at the twilight's last gleaming,

Whose broad stripes and bright stars through the perilous fight

O'er the ramparts we watch'd were so gallantly streaming?

And the rocket's red glare, the bombs bursting in air,

Gave proof through the night that our flag was still there,

O say does that star-spangled banner yet wave

O'er the land of the free and the home of the brave?

On the shore dimly seen through the mists of the deep

Where the foe's haughty host in dread silence reposes,

What is that which the breeze, o'er the towering steep,

As it fitfully blows, half conceals, half discloses?

Now it catches the gleam of the morning's first beam,

In full glory reflected now shines in the stream,

'Tis the star-spangled banner - O long may it wave

O'er the land of the free and the home of the brave!

And where is that band who so vauntingly swore,

That the havoc of war and the battle's confusion

A home and a Country should leave us no more?

Their blood has wash'd out their foul footstep's pollution.

No refuge could save the hireling and slave

From the terror of flight or the gloom of the grave,

And the star-spangled banner in triumph doth wave

O'er the land of the free and the home of the brave.

O thus be it ever when freemen shall stand

Between their lov'd home and the war's desolation!

Blest with vict'ry and peace may the heav'n rescued land

Praise the power that hath made and preserv'd us a nation!

Then conquer we must, when our cause it is just,

And this be our motto - "In God is our trust,"

And the star-spangled banner in triumph shall wave

O'er the land of the free and the home of the brave.

Gettysburg Address

Four score and seven years ago our fathers brought forth on this continent, a new nation, conceived in Liberty, and dedicated to the proposition that all men are created equal.

Now we are engaged in a great civil war, testing whether that nation, or any nation so conceived and so dedicated, can long endure. We are met on a great battle-field of that war. We have come to dedicate a portion of that field, as a final resting place for those who here gave their lives that that nation might live. It is altogether fitting and proper that we should do this.

But, in a larger sense, we can not dedicate — we can not consecrate — we can not hallow — this ground. The brave men, living and dead, who struggled here, have consecrated it, far above our poor power to add or detract. The world will little note, nor long remember what we say here, but it can never forget what they did here. It is for us the living, rather, to be dedicated here to the unfinished work which they who fought here have thus far so nobly advanced. It is rather for us to be here dedicated to the great task remaining before us — that from these honored dead we take increased devotion to that cause for which they gave the last full measure of devotion — that we here highly resolve that these dead shall not have died in vain — that this nation, under God, shall have a new birth of freedom — and that government of the people, by the people, for the people, shall not perish from the earth.

Abraham Lincoln
November 19, 1863

Oath of Allegiance

I hereby declare, on oath, that I absolutely and entirely renounce and abjure all allegiance and fidelity to any foreign prince, potentate, state, or sovereignty of whom or which I have heretofore been a subject or citizen; that I will support and defend the Constitution and laws of the United States of America against all enemies, foreign and domestic; that I will bear true faith and allegiance to the same; that I will bear arms on behalf of the United States when required by the law; that I will perform noncombatant service in the Armed Forces of the United States when required by the law; that I will perform work of national importance under civilian direction when required by the law; and that I take this obligation freely without any mental reservation or purpose of evasion; so help me God.

Oath of Office-US President

"I, (name), do solemnly swear (or affirm) that I will faithfully execute the Office of President of the United States, and will to the best of my Ability, preserve, protect and defend the Constitution of the United States.

Oath of Office-Congress

I, (name), do solemnly swear (or affirm) that I will support and defend the Constitution of the United States against all enemies, foreign and domestic; that I will bear true faith and allegiance to the same; that I take this obligation freely, without any mental reservation or purpose of evasion; and that I will well and faithfully discharge the duties of the office on which I am about to enter. [So help me God.]

Oath of Office-Judiciary

I, (name), do solemnly swear (or affirm) that I will administer justice without respect to persons, and do equal right to the poor and to the rich, and that I will faithfully and impartially discharge and perform all the duties incumbent upon me as (office) under the Constitution and laws of the United States. [So help me God.]

US Citizenship

The United States of America is a sovereign nation bound not by race or religion but by the shared values of freedom, liberty, and equality under the law.

Throughout our history, the United States has welcomed newcomers from all over the world. Immigrants have helped shape and define the country we know today. Their contributions help preserve our legacy as a land of freedom and opportunity. More than 200 years after our founding, naturalized citizens are still an important part of our republic.

Citizenship offers many benefits but also equally important responsibilities. Some of these responsibilities are legally required of every citizen, but all are important to ensuring that America remains a free and prosperous nation.

Rights:

- Freedom to express yourself.
- Right to assemble and protest grievances.
- Right to criticize the government without reprisal.
- Freedom to worship as you wish.
- Right to a prompt, fair trial by jury.
- Right to vote in elections for public officials.
- Right to apply for federal employment requiring U.S. citizenship.
- Right to run for elected office.
- Right to "life, liberty, and the pursuit of happiness."
- Right to travel freely among the States, and overseas.
- Right to bear arms.
- Enforcement of legal contracts.

Responsibilities:

- Support and defend the Constitution.
- Stay informed of the issues affecting your community.
- Participate in the democratic process.
- Respect and obey federal, state, and local laws.
- Respect the rights, beliefs, and opinions of others.
- Participate in your local community.
- Pay income and other taxes honestly, and on time, to federal, state, and local authorities.
- Serve on a jury when called upon.
- Serve in the armed forces and defend the country if necessary.

Pledge of Allegiance

I pledge allegiance to the Flag of the United States of America, and to the Republic for which it stands, one Nation under God, indivisible, with liberty and justice for all.

National Holidays

New Year's Day

Birthday of Martin Luther King, Jr. — 3rd Monday of January (Born on Jan. 15, 1929)

Washington's Birthday (Presidents Day)—3rd Monday in February (Washington was born on Feb. 22, 1732 and Lincoln was born on Feb. 12, 1809)

Memorial Day—Last Monday in May

Independence Day—July 4th

Labor Day—1st Monday in September

Columbus Day—2nd Monday in October

Veterans Day—November 11 (date of WWI armistice in 1918)

Thanksgiving Day—4th Thursday in November

Christmas Day—December 25th

On Memorial Day, America honors those who died while serving in the military.

On Veterans Day, the country celebrates everyone who has served in the military.

Some holidays honor specific groups and events, such as Valentine's Day (Feb. 14), St. Patrick's Day (March 17), Easter (March 22-April 25; Sunday; date varies), Mother's Day (May 8-14; Sunday; date varies), Father's Day (June 15-21; Sunday; date varies), Flag Day (June 14), Halloween (October 31), and New Year's Eve (December 31). These are not federal holidays. Some holidays and observances receive presidential proclamations.

US Flag and Flag Code

On June 14, 1777, the Continental Congress declared the uniform design for the US flag; before then the flag had various designs — Betsy Ross flag, Grand Union flag, Sons of Liberty flag, New England flag, and others. Stars were added on an irregular basis as new states were added to the Union. In 1942, President Franklin D. Roosevelt signed the Federal Flag Code, which regulates how the US flag is to be handled, displayed, and destroyed. On Feb. 23, 1945, US Marines planted the US Flag atop Mount Suribachi on Iwo Jima. On July 20, 1969, astronaut Neil Armstrong placed the US flag on the Moon.

The U.S. flag stands for our nation and the shared history, pride, principles, and commitment of its people. When we properly display this powerful symbol, we signal our respect for everything it represents.

- The flag shouldn't be flown in inclement weather unless it's an all-weather flag.
- Flags displayed at night should be properly illuminated.
- In a time of national mourning, hang the flag at half-mast.

The flag can be flown every day, but it is often flown to show patriotism on these observances:

- New Year's Day
- Inauguration Day
- Martin Luther King Jr.'s Birthday
- Lincoln's Birthday
- Washington's Birthday (Presidents Day)
- National Vietnam War Veterans Day
- Easter Sunday
- Armed Forces Day
- Memorial Day
- Flag Day
- Independence Day
- National Korean War Veterans Armistice Day
- Labor Day
- Constitution Day
- Columbus Day
- Navy Day
- Veterans Day
- Thanksgiving Day
- Christmas Day

When displaying the flag...

- From your porch, place the union (blue section) at the peak of the staff.
- Against a wall or on a window, place the union (blue section) at the top left corner.
- On your vehicle, clamp the staff to the right front fender.
- With another flag, place the U.S. flag to your left when crossed.

Keep your flag completely dry and folded properly — into a triangle, with the union (blue section) visible — before storing it in a well-ventilated area. If the flag is damaged or worn out, it should be disposed of with dignity.

The flag should not touch anything below it or rest on the ground.

The flag should never be worn as an article of clothing, e.g., as a cape or scarf.

[Consult Federal Flag Code for complete guidelines.]

US Flag Myths (American Legion)

A flag that has been used to cover a casket cannot be used for any other proper display purpose.
A flag that has been used to cover a casket can be used for any proper display purpose to include displaying this flag from a staff or flagpole.

The Flag Code prohibits the display of a United States flag of less than 50 stars.
According to the U.S. Army Institute of Heraldry, the United States flag never becomes obsolete. Any officially approved American flag, irrespective of the number or arrangement of the stars and/or stripes may continue to be used and displayed until no longer serviceable.

The Flag Code does provide for penalties for violations of any of its provisions.
The Flag Code is simply a guideline for proper flag etiquette. The law does not provide penalties for violation of any of its provisions.

You must destroy the flag when it touches the ground.
As long as the flag remains suitable for display, the flag may continue to be displayed as a symbol of our great country.

The Flag Code prohibits the washing or dry-cleaning of the flag.
There are no provisions of the Flag Code which prohibit the washing or dry-cleaning of the flag. The decision to wash or dry-clean would, of course, depend upon the type of material.

The Flag Code no longer requires the flag to be properly illuminated during the hours of darkness.
There has been NO CHANGE to Flag Code section 6(a), which states: "It is the universal custom to display the flag only from sunrise to sunset on buildings and on stationary flag staffs in the open. However, when a patriotic effect is desired, the flag may be displayed 24 hours a day if properly illuminated during the hours of darkness."

The mayor, a town official, or the Post Commander can order the flag to be displayed at half-staff.
The gesture of placing the flag at half-staff means that the Nation or the state mourns the death of a highly regarded National or state figure, hence only the President of the United States or the Governor of the state may order the Flag to be half-staffed in accordance with Flag Code section 7(m). Those individuals and agencies that usurp authority and display the flag at half-staff on inappropriate occasions are quickly eroding the honor and reverence accorded this solemn act.

The Flag Code states that when the flag is no longer a fitting emblem for display it is to be disposed of by burning in private.
The Flag Code as revised and adopted by the Congress of the United States in 1942 has never included the word(s) "private" or "in privacy." Section 8(k) of the Flag Code states: "The flag, when it is in such a condition that it is no longer a fitting emblem for display, should be destroyed in a dignified way, preferably by burning." Since 1937, The American Legion has promoted the use of a public flag disposal ceremony. This ceremony is a fitting tribute and an overt expression of patriotism, which enhances the public's understanding of honor and respect due the American flag.

The Flag Code prohibits the "fringing" of the flag.
Fringing of the flag is neither approved of nor prohibited by the Flag Code. The American Legion considers that fringe is used as an honorable enrichment to the Flag. Additionally the courts have deemed without merit and frivolous, lawsuits that contend that the gold fringe adorning the flag conferred Admiralty/Maritime jurisdiction.

The Flag Code is The American Legion Flag Code.
On Flag Day, June 14, 1923, The American Legion and representatives of 68 other patriotic, fraternal, civic and military organizations met in Washington, D.C. for the purpose of drafting a code of flag etiquette. The 77th Congress adopted this codification of rules as public law on June 22, 1942. It is Title 4, United States Code Chapter 1.

USA *third largest country in the world*

The United States of America is the world's third-largest country by size (after Russia and Canada) and by population (after China and India). The nation covers 3,796,742 square miles, including 264,836 sq. mi. of water. It is about half the size of Russia; about three-tenths the size of Africa; about half the size of South America (or slightly larger than Brazil); slightly larger than China; more than twice the size of the European Union. It is estimated that 27 percent of the total land area is owned by the federal government.

The USA has 7,486 miles of border, including 1,539 miles on the Canadian-Alaska border and 1,960 miles on the border with Mexico.

The US Naval Base at Guantanamo Bay, Cuba is leased by the US and is part of Cuba.

The Mississippi River is the second-longest river in North America, flowing 2,350 miles from its source at Lake Itasca to the Gulf of Mexico. The Missouri River, a tributary of the Mississippi River, is about 100 miles longer. The Mississippi River is the third longest river system in the world, if the length of Missouri and Ohio Rivers are added to the Mississippi's main stem. The Mississippi River drains an area of about 1.2 million square miles, including all or parts of 32 states (about 40 percent of the continental US). The Mississippi River watershed is the fourth largest in the world.

The lowest point in North America is Death Valley at 282 feet below sea level. The highest point in North America is Denali (Mount McKinley) at 20,308 feet above sea level. Eleven of the 20 highest peaks in the USA are in Alaska; 14 of the highest 30 are in Colorado.

The peak of Mauna Kea (13,802 feet above sea level) on the island of Hawaii rises about 33,465 feet above the Pacific Ocean floor. By this measurement, it is the world's tallest mountain, higher than Mount Everest (29,035 feet).

The USA has significant deposits of coal, copper, lead, molybdenum, phosphates, rare earth elements, uranium, bauxite, gold, iron, mercury, nickel, potash, silver, tungsten, zinc, petroleum, natural gas, timber, and arable land. The USA has the world's largest coal reserves, with 491 billion short tons, accounting for 27 percent of the world's total.

The western coast of the United States and southern coast of Alaska lie along the Ring of Fire, a belt of active volcanoes and earthquake epicenters bordering the Pacific Ocean; up to 90 percent of the world's earthquakes and some 75 percent of the world's volcanoes occur within the Ring of Fire. The Aleutian Islands are a chain of volcanic islands that divide the Bering Sea (north) from the main Pacific Ocean (south); they extend about 1,118 mi. westward from the Alaskan Peninsula; the archipelago consists of 14 larger islands, 55 smaller islands, and hundreds of islets; there are 41 active volcanoes on the islands, which together form a large northern section of the Ring of Fire.

Mammoth Cave, in west-central Kentucky, is the world's longest known cave system with more than 405 miles of surveyed passageways, which is nearly twice as long as the second-longest cave system, the Sac Actun underwater cave in Mexico, the world's longest underwater cave system.

Kazumura Cave on the island of Hawaii is the world's longest and deepest lava tube cave; it has been surveyed at 41 mi. long and 3,614 ft. deep.

Bracken Cave outside of San Antonio, Texas is the world's largest bat cave, the summer home to the largest colony of bats in the world. An estimated 20 million Mexican free-tailed bats roost in the cave from March to October, making it the world's largest known concentration of mammals.

US Territories-Location	Date of Acquisition	Pop. (2018)
American Samoa (South Pacific)	1900	50,826
Guam in Micronesia (North Pacific)	1899	167,772
Northern Mariana Islands in Micronesia	1986	51,994
Puerto Rico in Caribbean	1899	3,294,626
US Virgin Islands in Caribbean	1917	106,977

Currency, Federal Reserve, Time Zones

Currency is produced by the US Department of Treasury, Bureau of Engraving (Washington, D.C. and Fort Worth, Texas) and Printing, and US Mints. The BEP prints billions of dollars—referred to as Federal Reserve notes—each year for delivery to the Federal Reserve System. U.S. currency is used as a medium of exchange and store of value around the world. According to the Federal Reserve, there is more than $1 trillion worth of Federal Reserve notes in circulation. There are currently four active coin-producing mints: Philadelphia, Denver, San Francisco, and West Point. The US Mint produces many commemorative and bullion coins.

US Paper Currency (Federal Reserve Notes)

$1	George Washington
$2	Thomas Jefferson
$5	Abraham Lincoln
$10	Alexander Hamilton
$20	Andrew Jackson
$50	US Grant
$100	Benjamin Franklin

Coins

1 cent	Abraham Lincoln
5 cents	Thomas Jefferson
10 cents	Franklin D. Roosevelt
25 cents	George Washington
50 cents	John F. Kennedy

Federal Reserve System
The Federal Reserve Act was passed by the 63rd Congress and signed into law by President Woodrow Wilson on Dec. 23, 1913. The law created the Federal Reserve System, the central banking system of the US. The Federal Reserve Bank is a regional bank of the Federal Reserve System, the central banking system of the United States. There are 12, one for each of the 12 Federal Reserve Districts: Boston, New York, Philadelphia, Cleveland, Richmond, Atlanta, Chicago, St. Louis, Minneapolis, Kansas City, Dallas, and San Francisco. The banks are jointly responsible for implementing the monetary policy set forth by the Federal Open Market Committee. The whole system is headquartered at the Eccles Building in D.C.

Fort Knox

The US Bullion Depository in Kentucky, commonly known as Fort Knox for the nearby US Army post, holds 147.34 million troy ounces (4,583 metric tons) of gold reserves with a market value of $285 billion, representing 56.35 percent of the gold reserves of the United States. The depository was built by the Treasury in 1936 on land transferred to it from Fort Knox. It has also safeguarded other precious items, such as the Constitution of the United States and the Declaration of Independence.

Time Zones

The continental U.S. (including Alaska) spans five time zones. American Samoa, Hawaii, Guam, the Northern Mariana Islands, Puerto Rico, and the U.S. Virgin Islands are located in additional time zones. The continental time zones are Pacific, Mountain, Central, and Eastern.

Daylight Saving Time is a widely used system that adjusts the official local time forward one hour during spring and summer months. Clocks are moved ahead one hour on the second Sunday in March at 2:00 am (local time). Clocks are moved back one hour on the first Sunday in November at 2:00 am (local time). "Spring forward, fall back."

Daylight Saving Time is not observed in Hawaii, American Samoa, Guam, Puerto Rico, the U.S. Virgin Islands, and most of Arizona.

Constitutional Republic Form of Government

The USA is a constitutional republic and representative democracy, regulated by a system of checks and balances defined by the US Constitution, which serves as the country's supreme legal document. In the USA, citizens are subject to three levels of government — federal, state, and local. The original text of the Constitution establishes the structure and responsibilities of the federal government and its relationship with the individual states. The Constitution has been amended 27 times, including the first 10 amendments, the Bill of Rights, which guarantees the inalienable rights of citizens as expressed in the declaration.

The Constitution divides the federal government into three branches to ensure a central government in which no individual or group gains too much control:

Legislative — Makes laws. The legislative branch enacts legislation, confirms or rejects presidential appointments, and has the authority to declare war. This branch comprises Congress (the Senate and House of Representatives) and several agencies that provide support services to Congress.

Executive — Carries out laws. The executive branch carries out and enforces laws. It includes the president, vice president, the Cabinet, executive departments, independent agencies, and other boards, commissions, and committees.

Judicial — Evaluates laws. The judicial branch interprets the meaning of laws, applies laws to individual cases, and decides if laws violate the Constitution. The judicial branch comprises the Supreme Court and other federal courts.

Each branch of government can change acts of the other branches as follows:

- The president can veto legislative bills passed by Congress before they become law (subject to Congressional override).
- Congress confirms or rejects the president's appointments and can remove the president from office in exceptional circumstances.
- The justices of the Supreme Court, who can overturn unconstitutional laws, are appointed by the president and confirmed by the Senate.

The legislative branch consists of 100 Senators and 435 Representatives, plus:

Architect of the Capitol
US Botanic Garden
Government Accounability Office
Government Printing Office
Library of Congress
Congressional Budget Office
US Capitol Police.

The executive branch consists of the President, Vice President, Executive Office of the President, and 15 Cabinet Members:

State
Justice
Defense
Treasury
Homeland Security

Congressional Salaries

1789–1815	$6.00 per diem
1815–1817	$1,500 per annum
1817–1855	$8.00 per diem
1855–1865	$3,000 per annum
1865–1871	$5,000
1871–1873	$7,500
1873–1907	$5,000
1907–1925	$7,500
1925–1932	$10,000
1932–1933	$9,000
1933–1935	$8,500
1935–1947	$10,000
1947–1955	$12,500
1955–1965	$22,500
1965–1969	$30,000
1969–1975	$42,500
1975–1977	$44,600
1977–1978	$57,500
1979–1983	$60,662.50
1983	$69,800
1984	$72,600
1985–1986	$75,100
Feb 4, 1987	$89,500
Feb 1, 1990	$98,400
Aug 15, 1991	$125,100
1991	$101,900
1992	$129,500
1993	$133,600
1998	$136,700
1999	$136,700
2000	$141,300
2001	$145,100
2002	$150,000
2003	$154,700
2004	$158,100
2005	$162,100
2006	$165,200
2007	$165,200
2008	$169,300
2009	$174,000
2010	$174,000
2015	$174,000
2020	$174,000

Constitutional Republic Form of Government

Interior
Agriculture
Education
Commerce
Energy
Health and Human Services
Housing and Urban Development
Labor
Transportation
Veterans Affairs

The executive branch also consists of:

White House Office
Office of the Vice President
Council of Economic Advisers
Council on Environmental Quality
National Security Council
Office of Administration
Office of Management and Budget
Office of National Drug Control Policy
Office of Policy Development
Office of Science and Technology Policy
Office of US Trade Representative

The judicial branch consists of the Supreme Court of the United States, a Chief Justice and eight Associate Justices, plus:

US Court of Appeals
US District Courts
Territorial Courts
US Court of International Trade
US Court of Federal Claims
Administrative Office of the US Courts
Federal Judicial Center
US Sentencing Commission

Other significant federal reporting entities:

Environmental Protection Agency
General Services Administration
National Aeronautics and Space Administration
National Science Foundation
Office of Personnel Management
Small Business Administration
Social Security Administration
US Agency for International Development
US Nuclear Regulatory Commission
Defense Security Cooperation Agency
Export-Import Bank of the US
Farm Credit System Insurance Corporation
Federal Communications Commission
Federal Deposit Insurance Corporation
General Fund of the US Government
Milennium Challenge Corporation
National Credit Union Administration
Overseas Private Investment Corporation
Pension Benefit Guaranty Corporation
Railroad Retirement Board
Securities and Exchange Commission
Smithsonian Institution
Tennessee Valley Authority
US Postal Service

American Indian tribal government structure

The federal government recognizes 573 Indian tribes in the contiguous 48 states and Alaska. The USA observes tribal sovereignty of the American Indian nations to a limited degree, as it does with the states' sovereignty. American Indians are US citizens and tribal lands are subject to the jurisdiction of the US Congress and the federal courts. Like the states, the tribal governments have a great deal of autonomy with respect to their members, including the power to tax, govern, and try them in court, but also like the states, tribes are not allowed to make war, engage in their own foreign relations, or print and issue currency.

State Governments

Legislative

All 50 states have legislatures made up of elected representatives, who consider matters brought forth by the governor or introduced by its members to create legislation that becomes law. The legislature also approves a state's budget and initiates tax legislation and articles of impeachment. The latter is part of a system of checks and balances among the three branches of government that mirrors the federal system and prevents any branch from abusing its power.

Every state except one has a bicameral legislature made up of two chambers: a smaller upper house and a larger lower house. Together the two chambers make state laws and fulfill other governing responsibilities. The smaller upper chamber is always called the Senate, and its members generally serve

Constitutional Republic Form of Government

longer terms, usually four years. The larger lower chamber is most often called the House of Representatives, but some states call it the Assembly or the House of Delegates. Its members usually serve shorter terms, often two years. Nebraska is the lone state that has just one chamber in its legislature.

Executive

In every state, the executive branch is headed by a governor who is directly elected by the people. In most states, other leaders in the executive branch are also directly elected, including the lieutenant governor, the attorney general, the secretary of state, and auditors and commissioners. States reserve the right to organize in any way, so they often vary greatly with regard to executive structure. No two state executive organizations are identical.

Judicial

Most states have a supreme court that hears appeals from lower-level state courts. Court structures and judicial appointments/elections are determined either by legislation or by the state constitution. The state supreme court usually focuses on correcting errors made in lower courts and therefore holds no trials. Rulings made in state supreme courts are normally binding; however, when questions are raised regarding consistency with the US Constitution, matters may be appealed directly to the US Supreme Court.

Local Governments

There are 90,075 local government units consisting of 38,779 general purpose governments (3,031 county, 19,495 municipalities, 16,253 townships) and 51,296 special district governments, including 12,754 independent school districts and 38,542 other districts, which include:

- air transportation
- cemeteries
- corrections
- electric power
- fire protection
- gas supply
- health
- highways
- hospitals
- housing and community development
- industrial development
- libraries
- mortgage credit
- natural resources
- parking facilities
- parks and recreation
- sea and inland port facilities
- sewerage
- solid waste management
- transit
- water supply

Much of the information for this section taken from reports by USAFacts Institute, a Delaware nonprofit, nonstock corporation.

— Land of the Free, Home of the Brave —

Concise History of the United States of America

Colonial Period

In search of religious freedom and trade, English colonize East Coast of US while French explore interior in search of furs, pelts. Spanish establish Catholic missions in Southwest. Spanish conquistador Hernando de Soto explores Southeast in search of gold and treasure in early 1500s.

English establish footholds at Jamestown (1607), Plymouth (1620), and unsuccessful attempt at Roanoke Colony (1585). Four great waves of English settlement–Puritans to Massachusetts (1629-41), Cavaliers and indentured servants to Virginia (1642-75); Quakers to Delaware Valley (1675-1725), and Borderlands (Scots-Irish) to BackCountry (1717-75). Germans (Germantown-1683) and Dutch (New Amsterdam-1613) also settle in Pennsylvania and Hudson Valley respectively.

Relations between European explorers, hunters, and settlers and indigenous tribes are contentious and often lead to warfare. Diseases carried by Europeans to vulnerable Indians in New World prove devastating and deadly. Colonists trade for slave labor brought from Africa, to be exploited on plantations.

During French and Indian War (1754-63), American colonists and British army defeat French and Indian allies for right to settle America. Although English subjects, American colonists govern themselves to large extent and grow to resent English intrusion into their affairs. Conflict with Great Britain and King George III eventually leads to American independence.

Birth of a Nation

Population of 13 colonies in 1770 is 2,205,000.

April 19, 1775–Massachusetts "minutemen" fire upon British troops at Lexington and Concord.

June 17, 1775–Battle of Bunker Hill in Boston. British victory but with heavy losses.

1775-76–Patriots unsuccessfully attempt to invade Quebec, Canada. Newly created Continental Army under Gen. George Washington forces British military out of Boston in March 1776. British capture New York City and its strategic harbor that summer, which they hold for duration of war. Not all Americans are Patriots; some remain loyal to King George III.

July 4, 1776–Declaration of Independence, written by Thomas Jefferson, adopted by 2nd Continental Congress at Independence Hall in Philadelphia. Declaration of independence from rule by Great Britain resulted from several prior events, such as French and Indian War (1754-63), Stamp Act of 1765, Townsend Acts of 1767, Boston Massacre of 1770, Boston Tea Party of 1773, Intolerable Acts of 1774, and battles of Lexington and Concord on April 19, 1775.

Aug. 27, 1776–Battle of Long Island. Largest battle of war. Washington loses but evacuates to Manhattan Island.

Sept. 22, 1776–Before being executed by British for spying, Capt. Nathan Hale declares, "I only regret that I have but one life to lose for my country."

Nov. 16, 1776–British capture Hudson River fort and 3,000 prisoners, and nearby Fort Lee four days later.

Dec. 26, 1776–Battle of Trenton, NJ. Washington crosses Delaware to surprise-attack and defeat Hessians.

Jan. 3, 1777–Battle of Princeton. British defeated and evacuate New Jersey.

June 14, 1777–Continental Congress authorizes flag with 13 red/white stripes and 13 white stars on field of blue.

July 2, 1777–Vermont becomes first political entity in world to abolish slavery.

Concise History of the United States of America

Sept. 11, 1777–British defeat Washington at Battle of Brandywine, Pa.

Oct. 17, 1777–British under Gen. Burgoyne surrender to Patriot forces under Gen. Gates and Bendict Arnold at Saratoga, NY. Victory leads to assistance from French under King Louis XVI.

1777-78–Continental Army winters, trains at Valley Forge, Pa.

June 28, 1778–Battle of Monmouth. British harassed in New Jersey on retreat to New York.

Dec. 29, 1778–Savannah, Ga. captured by British as Southern campaign begins.

Feb. 25, 1779–Patriots under George Rogers Clark successfully lay siege to Fort Vincennes on Wabash River in what is now Indiana.

May 12, 1780–British recapture Charleston, SC after 6-week seige.

Aug. 16, 1780–Battle of Camden, SC is British victory.

Oct. 7, 1780–Overmountain men defeat Loyalist forces under Major Patrick Ferguson at Kings Mountain, SC.

Jan. 17, 1781–Battle of Cowpens, SC. Infantry and cavalry under Gen. Daniel Morgan defeat British cavalry of Col. Banastre Tarleton.

March 1, 1781–Original 13 states (Massachusetts, New Hampshire, Connecticut, Rhode Island, New York, Pennsylvania, New Jersey, Maryland, Delaware, Virginia, North Carolina, South Carolina, and Georgia) adopt Articles of Confederation, which creates weak Congress and leads to creation of US Constitution.

Sept. 5, 1781–Battle of Chesapeake. French ships defeat British in naval battle.

Oct. 19, 1781–Yorktown, Va. British forces under Cornwallis surrender to Patriots led by Washington, aided by French forces under Comte de Rochambeau, following 3-week siege.

Sept. 3, 1783–Treaty of Paris ends Revolutionary War, grants territory to US west to Mississippi River (except Spanish Florida). Ratified in US on Jan. 14, 1784. One hundred thousand Loyalists flee US, mainly to Nova Scotia.

Affirmation and Growth

Jan. 25, 1787–Shays Rebellion. Massachusetts farmers, faced with high taxes, eviction, and imprisonment for debt, attack Springfield arsenal.

May 14, 1787– Constitutional Convention convenes at Independence Hall. Delegates from the states hammer out new plan. Federals in favor of Constitution, namely Alexander Hamilton, James Madison, and John Jay, publish Federalist Papers.

July 13, 1787–Northwest Ordinance establishes system of government and prohibits slavery in territory (now Midwest states).

Feb. 4, 1789–Electoral College selects George Washington as first President. New York City is the capital.

May 29, 1790–Final state, Rhode Island, ratifies US Constitution as supreme law of land.

Nov. 4, 1791 — Massacre at the Wabash, as nine Indian tribes unite to defeat Gen. St. Clair's army. Largest Indian victory over US Army ever.

Land of the Free, Home of the Brave

Concise History of the United States of America

Dec. 15, 1791–First ten amendments to Constitution ratified as Bill of Rights.

Dec. 21, 1791–Samuel Slater opens first cotton mill in Pawtucket, R.I.

Oct. 28, 1793–Eli Whitney patents cotton gin (engine).

July-November, 1794–President Washington shuts down Whiskey Rebellion, tax revolt by farmers in Pennsylvania.

May 31, 1797–XYZ Affair. France demands $10 million loan and bribes to negotiate treaty with US, which refuses.

1798–Alien and Sedition Acts give President Adams power to imprison or deport foreigners believed to be dangerous to US, make it crime to attack government with "false, scandalous, or malicious" statements.

Jan. 20, 1801–John Marshall appointed Chief Justice of US Supreme Court.

April 30, 1801–President Jefferson purchases Louisiana Territory from Napoleon–800,000 square miles for $15 million.

Feb. 24, 1803–Supreme Court establishes principle of judicial review in case of *Marbury v. Madison* — court rules federal law unconstitutional.

May 14, 1804–Lewis and Clark Expedition explores 8,000 miles along Missouri and Columbia Rivers as far as Pacific, returning in 1806.

July 11, 1804–Federalist party leader Alexander Hamilton killed in duel with Vice President Aaron Burr. Burr later charged with treason, acquitted.

Sept. 4, 1807–Robert Fulton sails steamship *Clermont* on Hudson River, inaugurating steam-powered transportation.

Jan. 1, 1808–African slave trade prohibited. Hundreds of thousands of slaves illegally imported during next 50 years.

Nov. 7, 1811–Future President William Henry Harrison and 800 soldiers defeat Tenskwatawa, Shawnee prophet, and destroy Prophetstown. On Oct. 5, 1814, Indian leader Tecumseh (his brother) killed at Thames in Canada.

June 18, 1812–US declares war against Great Britain over interference with American shipping and impressments of American seamen.

1814–First U.S. factory opens able to convert raw cotton into cloth using power machinery.

May 27, 1814–Gen. Andrew Jackson defeats Creeks at Horseshoe Bend, opening Deep South to settlement.

Aug. 24, 1814–British avenge American raid on York, Ontario (now Toronto), capital of Upper Canada, by setting fire to White House and Capitol.

Sept. 10, 1814–Lt. Oliver Hazzard Perry wins naval victory at Battle of Lake Erie, declares "We have met the enemy and they are ours."

Sept. 14, 1814–Lawyer Francis Scott Key, detained on British warship, writes *Star-Spangled Banner* about Fort McHenry. Song later becomes national anthem.

Dec. 15, 1814-January 1815–Hartford Convention. Federalists in New England call for changes to Constitution, threatening secession from Union. Their demands are not met; they do not secede.

Dec. 24, 1814–Peace treaty ending War of 1812 signed at Ghent, Belgium.

———————— Land of the Free, Home of the Brave ————————

Concise History of the United States of America

Jan. 8, 1815–General Jackson and ragtag army defeat British forces at New Orleans.

July 4, 1817–Construction of Erie Canal begins, connecting Great Lakes to Eastern Seaboard. Opens in 1825.

1819–First major economic depression strikes. At this point, US population is 9,638,453.

March 3, 1820–Missouri Compromise prohibits slavery in North. Missouri admitted as slave state, and Maine admitted as free state.

Dec. 2, 1823–President Monroe declares Western Hemisphere closed to European colonization (Monroe Doctrine).

May 24, 1824–Samuel Morse sends first message by telegraph "What hath God wrought," from Washington to Baltimore.

Jan. 3, 1825–Englishman Robert Owen creates secular utopian village of New Harmony, Indiana.

Age of Jackson

May 28, 1830–President Jackson signs Indian Removal Acts. In 1838, Cherokees forcibly marched to Oklahoma on "Trail of Tears," with 4,000 dying along way.

April 6, 1832–Black Hawk War begins when Sauk Indians cross back over from Iowa to Illinois. Capt. Abraham Lincoln takes part in conflict. Sauk surrender in August.

January 1835–For only time in American history, US free from debt, with surplus of $400,000 in Treasury.

July 8, 1835–Liberty Bell cracks as it tolls death of Chief Justice Marshall.

Feb. 25, 1836–Samuel Colt granted patent for six-shooter, first handgun with revolving cylinder.

March 2, 1836– Texas declares independence from Mexico. Four days later, Mexican troops storm Alamo, killing 182 Texans, including David Crockett and James Bowie. On March 27, Mexican leader Santa Anna orders 330 Texas prisoners executed at Goliad. On April 21, Gen. Sam Houston's troops defeat Mexican Army and capture Santa Anna, forcing him to recognize Texas independence.

April 4, 1841 — William H. Harrison first President to die in office; succeeded by VP John Tyler amid controversy.

May 13, 1846–Congress declares war on Mexico after President Polk contends Mexico has "invaded our territory and shed American blood on American soil."

Sept. 14, 1847–Gen. Winfield Scott captures Mexico City.

Jan. 24, 1848–James Marshall discovers gold at Sutter's sawmill near Sacramento. By next year, 80,000 people, mostly men, migrate to California.

Feb. 2, 1848–Treaty of Guadalupe Hidalgo ends Mexican War. US acquires vast territory (California, Nevada, Utah, New Mexico, and parts of Arizona, Colorado, Kansas and Wyoming) for $15 million.

March 29, 1848–John Jacob Astor dies richest man in US, his fortune deriving from fur trade and real estate.

August 1850–Compromise of 1850 admits California as free state, but does not forbid slavery in territories acquired from Mexico. Includes strict law requiring return of runaway slaves to their masters.

March 20, 1852–Harriet Beecher Stowe publishes *Uncle Tom's Cabin,* which sells million copies in 16 months.

Concise History of the United States of America

Dec. 30, 1853–Gadsden Purchase. Mexico sells 29,640 square miles of territory (southern Arizona and New Mexico) for $10 million.

May 21, 1856–Pro-slavery forces in Kansas burn buildings in Lawrence. Four days later, John Brown and six others murder five pro-slavery men at Pottawatomie Creek, leading to other killings in "Bleeding Kansas."

March 6, 1857–In case of Dred Scott, Supreme Court rules US Constitution does not apply to blacks, and Missouri Compromise unconstitutional.

March 23, 1857–Elisha Otis installs first passenger elevator in New York department store.

Aug. 21 to Oct. 15, 1858– Abraham Lincoln and Stephen Douglas, candidates for US Senate from Illinois, hold seven debates. Douglas elected to Senate; Lincoln gains notoriety.

Oct. 16, 1859–John Brown leads unsuccessful raid on federal arsenal at Harpers Ferry, Va. He is later hanged, becomes abolitionist martyr.

War Between the States

Nov. 6, 1860–Lincoln elected President of US, 2nd Republican to run (John Fremont lost in 1856).

Dec. 20, 1860–South Carolina secedes from US, followed by Mississippi, Florida, Alabama, Georgia, Louisiana, and Texas. Following Lincoln's call for volunteer troops to quash rebellion, Virginia, Arkansas, North Carolina, and Tennessee also secede. Missouri, Kentucky, and Maryland, slave states, are known as "border states." On Feb. 8, 1861, provisional constitution for Confederate States of America adopted. On May 29, 1861, CSA capital moves from Montgomery, Ala. to Richmond, Va. Jefferson Davis serves as president; Alexander Stephens as vice-president.

April 12, 1861–Civil War begins as Confederates fire on Fort Sumter in Charleston harbor.

July 21, 1861–Battle of First Bull Run (Manassas), Va. Federal soldiers flee back to Washington, DC.

Feb. 6, 1862–US naval forces (ironclad gunboats) capture Fort Henry on Tennessee River.

Feb. 16, 1862–Land forces under US Grant capture Fort Donelson on Cumberland River, 13,000 rebels surrender.

Feb. 26, 1862–US forces capture Nashville, capital of Tennessee. New Orleans falls in May, Memphis in June.

March 8-9, 1862–First clash of ironclad gunboats, at Hampton Roads, Va. They battle to a draw.

April 6-7, 1862–Battle of Shiloh (Pittsburg Landing) in Tennessee, first battle with mass casualties.

Aug. 14-Oct. 10, 1862–Kentucky Campaign fails to bring state into Confederacy.

Sept. 17, 1862–Battle of Antietam (Sharpsburg), Gen. Robert E. Lee's invasion of Maryland fails.

Jan, 1, 1863–Lincoln issues Emancipation Proclamation, declaring free all persons held in bondage in Confederate states.

May 10, 1863–Gen. Stonewall Jackson dies, accidentally shot by own troops following victory at Chancellorsville, Va.

July 1-3, 1863–Battle of Gettysburg, Pa. Meade's Federals outlast Lee's Confederates in 3 days of desperate fighting, culminating in futile Pickett's Charge.

July 4, 1863–Vicksburg, Miss. garrison of 30,000 surrenders to US Grant after six-week siege.

Concise History of the United States of America

Sept. 18-20, 1863–Battle of Chickamauga. Confederate victory in Georgia.

Nov. 19, 1863–Lincoln's famed Gettysburg Address.

Nov. 24-25, 1863–Battles of Lookout Mountain and Missionary Ridge drive Confederates out of Chattanooga.

May-June 1864– Wilderness campaign in Virginia, in which Grant sustains heavy casualties but continues to turn Lee's flank, resulting in ten-month siege of Richmond and Petersburg.

Sept. 1, 1864–Sherman enters Atlanta as Hood's army evacuates, following campaign beginning in May 1864.

Dec. 15-16, 1864–Battle of Nashville. Massive Union victory ends major fighting in Western Theater.

Dec. 21, 1864–Sherman enters Savannah, Ga., following March to Sea, continues destruction north into South Carolina.

April 9, 1865–US Grant accepts surrender of Robert E. Lee, commander of Army of Northern Virginia, at farmhouse in Appomattox, Va.

April 14, 1865–Lincoln assassinated at Ford's Theater in Washington, DC by actor John Wilkes Booth, who is killed by Union troops April 26. Vice-President Andrew Johnson sworn in as 17th President.

April 26, 1865–Joseph Johnston surrenders Confederate army to Sherman at Bennett Place, Durham, NC.

US Population

Year	Population	% Change
1770	2,205,000	--
1780	2,781,000	26.1
1790	3,929,625	41.3
1800	5,236,631	33.3
1810	7,239,881	38.3
1820	9,638,453	33.1
1830	12,866,020	33.5
1840	17,069,453	32.7
1850	23,191,876	35.9
1860	31,443,321	35.6
1870	39,818,449	22.6
1880	50,155,783	28.0
1890	62,947,714	27.6
1900	75,994,575	21.0
1910	91,972,266	21.0
1920	105,710,620	15.0
1930	123,203,000	16.2
1940	132,165,000	7.3
1950	150,697,361	14.5
1960	179,323,175	18.5
1970	203,211,926	13.3
1980	227,225,000	11.5
1990	249,623,000	9.8
2000	282,172,000	13.2
2010	309,330,000	9.7
2020	330,000,000	6.7

Reconstruction

Dec. 6, 1865–13th Amendment abolishes slavery.

July 24, 1866–Tennessee first Confederate state readmitted into Union.

March 2, 1867–Congress passes first of three Reconstruction Acts, imposing martial law in South, splitting South into five military districts, and requiring states to ratify 14th, 15th Amendments to be readmitted.

Feb. 24, 1868–House votes to impeach President Johnson. Following trial, Senate falls one vote short of convicting.

May 10, 1869–Transcontinental railroad completed at Promontory Point, Utah.

1871–PT Barnum opens "Greatest Show on Earth" circus.

Oct. 8-10, 1871–Great Chicago Fire kills 300 people, consumes 3.3 square miles of city.

Feb. 14, 1876–Alexander Graham Bell patents telephone.

May 10, 1876–Nation's Centennial opens with International Exhibition in Philadelphia.

June 25, 1876–Gen. George Custer and soldiers killed by Sioux Indians led by Sitting Bull and Crazy Horse at Little Big Horn in Montana.

— Land of the Free, Home of the Brave —

Concise History of the United States of America

March 2, 1877–Compromise of 1877, following disputed 1876 election, provides for troop withdrawal in South, end of Reconstruction, and election of President Rutherford B. Hayes.

Industry and the Gilded Age

Dec. 6, 1877–Thomas Edison invents phonograph. Two years later, he invents electric light bulb.

July 2, 1881–President Garfield shot by Charles Guiteau, disgruntled office-seeker. Garfield dies on Sept. 19. Vice-President Chester Arthur becomes President.

May 24, 1883–Brooklyn Bridge opens in New York City.

Nov. 18, 1883–Railroads in US and Canada adopt system of standard time.

May 1, 1884–Construction begins in Chicago on first skyscraper.

May 1, 1886–Workers demonstrate for eight-hour workday. Three days later, Haymarket Square bombing in Chicago kills seven police officers and wounds 60. On May 10, Supreme Court holds that corporations entitled to due process.

Oct. 28, 1886–President Grover Cleveland unveils Statue of Liberty.

May 31, 1889–Johnstown, Pa. flooded after reservoir failure, killing 2,295 people.

1890 –US population is 62,947,714. Census Bureau declares western frontier closed.

July 2, 1890–Congress passes Sherman Anti-Trust Act.

Dec. 29, 1890–Wounded Knee Massacre. US Army kills 250 Lakota men, women, children.

December 1891– James Naismith invents basketball in Springfield, Mass.

Jan. 1, 1892–Ellis Island in NY opens to screen immigrants. Twenty million pass through before closing in 1954.

Oct. 12, 1892–World's Columbian Exhibition opens in Chicago to commemorate 300th anniversary of Columbus' discovery of New World, and features first Ferris wheel.

May 18, 1896–*Plessy v. Ferguson* holds that segregation of blacks and whites permitted as long as both races provided equal facilities.

Feb. 15, 1898–Battleship *USS Maine* explodes in Havana, Cuba harbor. Spanish-American War rages April 25 to August 12. On May 1, Commodore Dewey's flotilla defeats Spanish fleet at Manila Bay in Philippines. US acquires Puerto Rico, Guam, and Philippine Islands.

Feb. 4, 1899-July 2, 1902–Philippine Insurrection pits US army against revolutionary forces under Emilio Aguinaldo.

Jan. 10, 1901–Oil (petroleum) discovered at Spindletop near Beaumont, Texas.

March 3, 1901–U.S. Steel organized, country's first billion-dollar corporation.

Sept. 6, 1901–President McKinley shot in Buffalo, NY by anarchist Leon Czolgosz. President dies on Sept. 14, succeeded by VP Theodore Roosevelt.

Concise History of the United States of America

The Progressive Era

Dec. 17, 1903–Wright brothers Orville and Wilbur fly powered aircraft for 12 seconds at Kitty Hawk, NC.

April 18, 1906–San Francisco earthquake and fires kill 3,000 and destroy 80 percent of city.

Oct. 1, 1908–Henry Ford introduces Model T automobile. In 1913 he introduces assembly line, institutes $5 work day.

June 1, 1909–National Association for Advancement of Colored People (NAACP) organized.

Feb. 25, 1913–16th Amendment permits federal income tax.

April 8, 1913–17th Amendment provides for popular election of US Senators rather than appointment by state legislatures.

Dec. 23, 1913–Federal Reserve System established, providing central control over nation's currency and credit.

July 6, 1915–Erich Muenter commits suicide after bombing US Senate and shooting financier J.P. Morgan.

March 9, 1916–Mexican revolutionary Pancho Villa crosses US border to attack Columbus, NM. President Wilson orders Gen. John Pershing to capture Villa.

World War I

April 6, 1917– US declares war on Central Powers (Germany, Austria-Hungary, Ottoman Empire, Bulgaria) which have been waging war against Allies (Great Britain, France, Russia, Italy) since 1914.

July 3, 1917– First wave of American Expeditionary Force lands in France commanded by Gen. Pershing.

Jan. 8, 1918–President Wilson issues 14 Point Plan for lasting peace.

October 1918–Deadly influenza epidemic begins, killing nearly 675,000 Americans.

Nov. 11, 1918–World War I ends as Germany and Allies sign Armistice.

Roaring Twenties and Great Depression

Jan. 29, 1919–18th Amendment bans manufacture, sale, or transportation of liquor.

March 19, 1920–Senate votes 49-35 to join League of Nations, seven votes short of ratification.

Aug. 18, 1920–Woman's Suffrage Amendment to U.S. Constitution ratified.

July 1925–Monkey Trial in Dayton, Tenn. debates theory of evolution.

May 21, 1927–Charles Lindbergh lands in Paris after flying solo over Atlantic Ocean from Long Island, NY.

Feb. 14, 1929–St. Valentine's Day Massacre in Chicago. Seven mobsters gunned down by rival gang.

Oct. 29, 1929–Black Tuesday on NY Stock Exchange as stocks lose $26 billion in value over next three months.

March 1, 1932–Lindbergh's infant son kidnapped, murdered. Bruno Hauptman convicted of crime, executed.

March 4, 1933–President Franklin Roosevelt launches New Deal of federal programs, many job-related, designed to combat national financial Depression.

Concise History of the United States of America

Sept. 18, 1933–Tennessee Valley Authority (TVA) created to provide regional flood control, navigation, and rural electrification.

Dec. 5, 1933–Prohibition of liquor repealed.

Aug. 1-16, 1936–Jesse Owens wins four gold medals at Olympics in Berlin, Nazi Germany.

1941–Mount Rushmore completed. Begun in 1927, monument features likenesses of Presidents Washington, Jefferson, T. Roosevelt, and Lincoln. Crazy Horse Memorial built nearby.

World War II

March 11, 1941–Lend-Lease Act provides supplies to Great Britain, at war with Nazi Germany since invasion of Poland in September 1939.

Dec. 7, 1941–Japanese naval warplanes surprise-attack US ships in Pearl Harbor, Hawaii. Congress declares war on Japan next day. Germany declares war on US on Dec. 11.

April 10, 1942–Bataan Death March begins as Corregidor falls to Japanese. Gen. Douglas MacArthur ordered to flee Philippines to Australia.

April 18, 1942–Morale-boosting air raid on Tokyo as Gen. Jimmy Doolittle leads carrier-based bombers.

June 3-6, 1942–Battle of Midway. US aircraft repel Japanese assault in Central Pacific, sinking 17 ships and shooting down 250 airplanes.

Nov. 8, 1942–Operation Torch landings in North Africa begin, leading to victory in Tunisia in May 1943.

June 4, 1944–US army captures Rome following invasion of Sicily (July 10, 1943), subsequent fighting in southern Italy.

June 6, 1944–Allies storm beaches of Normandy France, beginning invasion of Nazi-occupied Europe. Americans suffer heavy losses at Omaha Beach. By August 25, Paris is liberated.

Oct. 22-27, 1944– Battle of Leyte Gulf, largest naval battle in history, resounding US victory over Japan.

Dec. 16, 1944–Battle of Bulge begins in Ardennes, with German forces eventually repulsed.

May 7, 1945–V-E Day. German forces surrender to Allies.

Aug. 6, 1945–US drops atomic bomb over Hiroshima, Japan, followed 3 days later by another bomb over Nagasaki.

Sept. 2, 1945–Japan formally surrenders in ceremonies aboard *USS Missouri* in Tokyo Bay.

Cold War Begins

1946-47–Cold War begins between US, Allies and communist Soviet Union.

Oct. 14, 1947–Air Force Capt. Chuck Yeager first pilot to exceed speed of sound.

March 8, 1948–Congress authorizes Marshall Plan to rescue economies of war-ravaged Western Europe.

June 25, 1950–Korean War begins when North Korean forces invade South. President Truman wins UN mandate to drive out communist forces.

Sept. 15, 1950–UN forces under Gen. MacArthur land behind enemy lines at Inchon in Korea.

Concise History of the United States of America

April 11, 1951–President Truman fires Gen. MacArthur; replaced by Gen. Matthew Ridgway.

July 27, 1953–Armistice ends Korean War.

March 1, 1954–Five members of Congress shot in House by Puerto Rican nationalists.

May 17, 1954–In *Brown v. Board of Education,* Supreme Court rules segregated schools are unconstitutional.

Turbulent Times

1960–US scientists patent laser, first retirement community opens in Sun City, Ariz., FDA approves birth control pill.

May 5, 1960–U2 spy plane piloted by Francis Gary Powers shot down over USSR.

April 17, 1961–US-backed invasion of Cuba at Bay of Pigs fails.

May 5, 1961–Alan Shepard first American in space. For US space program events, see separate article.

October-November 1962–Cuban Missile Crisis. US confronts USSR, which backs down after it places missiles in Cuba, controlled by communist Fidel Castro.

August 1963–March on Washington and "I Have A Dream" speech by civil rights leader Rev. Dr. Martin Luther King.

Aug. 5, 1963–US, Soviet Union, Britain sign treaty banning nuclear tests in atmosphere, outer space, and underwater.

Nov. 22, 1963–President Kennedy assassinated during trip to Dallas, Texas. Vice-President Lyndon Johnson becomes President. Two days later, alleged assassin, Lee Harvey Oswald, shot to death at Dallas jail by Jack Ruby.

Feb. 7, 1964–Beatles land in US, perform 32 concerts in 24 cities in 33 days.

July 2, 1964–President Johnson signs Civil Rights Act of 1964.

Aug. 2, 1964–Gulf of Tonkin Incident. Congress authorizes President to take military action, in effect start of Vietnam War.

Feb. 21, 1965–Followers of Black Muslim leader Elijah Muhammad shoot and kill black nationalist leader Malcolm X.

March 8, 1965–US Marines, first US ground troops, land at South Vietnam beach.

Aug. 11-16, 1965–Arson and looting erupt in Watts district of Los Angeles.

April 28, 1967–Heavyweight boxing champion Muhammad Ali arrested for refusing military induction. Boxing officials strip him of his title.

July 1967–Riots rock Newark, NJ and Detroit, Mich.

Jan. 14, 1968–Green Bay Packers world champions three years in a row after winning Super Bowl II.

Jan. 30, 1968–US forces staggered by surprise Tet Offensive in South Vietnam but emerge victorious.

April 4, 1968–Rev. King assassinated in Memphis, Tenn., touching off riots in many US cities.

June 5, 1968–Presidential candidate Robert F. Kennedy assassinated in Los Angeles after California primary.

Aug. 25-29, 1968–Demonstrators battle police at Democratic National Convention in Chicago.

Concise History of the United States of America

Aug. 16, 1969–Gigantic rock concert at Woodstock, NY.

May 4, 1970–National Guard kills four students at Kent State University in Ohio during protests against Cambodia invasion.

June 13, 1971–Pentagon Papers published by *New York Times*.

Sept. 13, 1971–Attica Prison in New York stormed; 31 prisoners and nine guards being held hostage die.

May 15, 1972–Presidential candidate George Wallace shot in Laurel, Md.

June 17, 1972–Five burglars caught at Democratic headquarters in Watergate office complex in Washington, DC.

Jan. 28, 1973–Paris Peace Accords signed by US and North Vietnam ending war, following massive US bombing of Hanoi and Haiphong.

July 16, 1973–Former aide reveals to Senate Watergate investigators that President Nixon maintained secret tape-recording system in White House.

July 27, 1974–House Judiciary Committee recommends impeachment of President Nixon.

Aug. 8, 1974–Nixon first president to resign office. Gerald Ford becomes 38th President, and on Sept. 8 pardons Nixon.

Bicentennial Year of 1976

January 18 – Super Bowl X. Pittsburgh Steelers defeat Dallas Cowboys, 21-17, in Miami. Throughout the year, Philadelphia served as host for the 1976 NBA All-Star Game, the 1976 National Hockey League All-Star Game, the 1976 NCAA Final Four, and the 1976 Major League Baseball All-Star Game at which President Ford threw out the first pitch.

March 9-11 – Two coal mine explosions claim 26 lives in Letcher County, Ky.

April 1 – Apple Computer formed by Steve Jobs and Steve Wozniak.

April 13 – US Treasury reintroduces $2 bill on Thomas Jefferson's 233rd birthday.

May 30 – Indianapolis 500. Johnny Rutherford wins shortest race (254 miles, shortened due to rain).

June 4 – Boston Celtics defeat Phoenix Suns, 128-126, in triple overtime in Game 5 of NBA Finals at Boston Garden.

July 1 – Smithsonian opens new home of National Air and Space Museum.

July 4 – Large international fleet of tall-masted sailing ships gather first in New York City on Independence Day and then in Boston one week later.

November 2 – Democrat Jimmy Carter defeats incumbent President Gerald Ford in presidential election.

Land of the Free, Home of the Brave

Presidents of the United States

1

George Washington
1789-1797
Federalist
VP: John Adams

Born 02-22-1732 in Pope's Creek, Westmoreland, VA
Died 12-14-1799; Buried at Mount Vernon, VA
First Lady: Martha Dandridge Custis (1731-1802)

Virginia planter; General of Continental Army during Revolutionary War; president of Constitutional Convention; inaugurated 04-30-1789 at Federal Hall, NYC. Set standard for all subsequent Presidents. "First in war, first in peace, first in the hearts of his countrymen." Shut down Whiskey Rebellion (1794). Gave up power, retired peacefully to private life.

2

John Adams
1797-1801
Federalist
VP: Thomas Jefferson

Born 10-30-1735 in Braintree (Quincy), MA
Died 07-04-1826; Buried at 1st Unitarian Church, Quincy, MA
First Lady: Abigail Smith (1744-1818)

New England Yankee, lawyer, defended British soldiers after Boston Massacre; a leader of Continental Congress; supported Alien and Sedition Acts; first to occupy White House; died on 4th of July, 50th anniversary of Declaration; more remarkable as political philosopher than as politician. Wife Abagail was major adviser.

3

Thomas Jefferson
1801-1809
Democratic-Republican
VPs: Aaron Burr, George Clinton

Born 04-13-1743 in Goochland (Albemarle County), VA
Died 07-04-1826; Buried at Monticello, Charlottesville, VA
Wife: Martha W. Skelton (1748-1782)

Virginia planter, lawyer, statesman, intellectual, served in Continental Congress, minister to France, governor of VA (Statute of Religious Freedom-1786), author of Declaration of Independence; negotiated Louisiana Purchase; Embargo Act; no vetoes of Congress; died same day as Adams. Foe of Chief Justice John Marshall.

4

James Madison
1809-1817
Democratic-Republican
VP: George Clinton

Born 03-16-1751 in Port Conway, VA
Died 06-28-1836; Buried at Montpelier, VA
First Lady: Dorothea "Dolley" Payne Todd (1768-1849)

Diminutive Virginia planter, member of Continental Congress and Constitutional Convention; main author of the US Constitution, co-author of Federalist Papers; wartime President during War of 1812 with Great Britain; British burned down White House, other govt buildings; First Lady avid social hostess.

5

James Monroe
1817-1825
Democratic-Republican
VP: Daniel Tompkins

Born 04-28-1758 in Westmoreland County, VA
Died 07-04-1831; Buried at Hollywood Cemetery, Richmond, VA
First Lady: Elizabeth Kortright (1768-1830)

Virginia planter, officer in Revolutionary War, US Senator, minister to France, term as President known as Era of Good Feelings; advocated Monroe Doctrine, forbidding foreign intervention in Western Hemisphere; Missouri Compromise dealt with new states as slave-holding or free; supported internal (infrastructure) improvements.

6

John Quincy Adams
1825-1829
Democratic-Republican
VP: John C. Calhoun

Born 07-11-1767 in Braintree (Quincy), MA
Died 02-23-1848; Buried at First Unitarian Church, Quincy, MA
First Lady: Louisa Catherine Johnson (1774-1852)

Son of the 2nd President, Harvard graduate, world-traveling diplomat. US Senator. As Secretary of State, Oregon and Florida obtained from England and Spain respectively. Single term was tumultuous. Distinguished anti-slavery Congressman in later years. Beneficiary of "Corrupt Bargain."

Land of the Free, Home of the Brave

Presidents of the United States

7

Andrew Jackson
1829-1837
Democrat
VPs: John C. Calhoun, Martin Van Buren

Born 03-15-1767 in The Waxhaws, SC
Died 06-08-1845; Buried at The Hermitage, Nashville, TN
Wife: Rachel Donelson Robards (1767-1828)
Died after election but before inauguration.

Strong-willed, lawyer, duelist, known as Old Hickory, frontier lawyer, general of militia, Indian fighter, hero of Horseshoe Bend and 1815 Battle of New Orleans, military governor of Florida, rowdy campaigner, 1st Westerner elected as Pres., defeated 2nd National Bank, stood down Calhoun and nullification, supported spoils system, Kitchen Cabinet, signed Indian Removal Act.

8

Martin Van Buren
1837-1841
Democrat
VP: Richard M. Johnson

Born 12-05-1782 in Kinderhook, NY
Died 07-24-1862; Buried at Kinderhook (NY) Cemetery
Wife: Hannah Hoes (1783-1819)

Lawyer, astute politician, founder of Democrat Party, Jackson Vice President and supporter, governor of NY, US senator, secretary of state, elder statesman, abolitionist who led Free Soil Party in 1848. Only President to speak English as 2nd language (Dutch was 1st). Portrayed as patrician elitist. One-termer.

9

William Henry Harrison
1841
Whig
VP: John Tyler

Born 02-09-1773 in Charles City County, VA
Died 04-04-1841; Buried at Wm Henry Harrison State Park, North Bend, OH
First Lady: Anna Tuthill Symmes (1775-1864)

Served only one month, dying at age 68 of pneumonia caught during lengthy inauguration speech outdoors in damp cold. Born into wealth, he campaigned as being born in log cabin "Tippecanoe and Tyler Too." General instrumental in victories at Fallen Timbers, Tippecanoe, and Thames, and opening Northwest Territory to settlement. Governor of Indiana Territory. Congressman, Senator from Ohio.

10

John Tyler
1841-1845
Whig
VP: None

Born 03-29-1790 in Charles City County, VA
Died 01-18-1862; Buried at Hollywood Cemetery, Richmond, VA
First Ladies: Leitia Christian (1790-1842); Julia Gardiner (1820-89)

First President born in USA (Virginia). First VP to assume Presidency upon death of President. Known as His Accidency. Strict Constitutional constructionist. Supported Texas annexation as slave state. Battled with own Whig party. Vetoed bills, Cabinet resigned. Supporter of states' rights, Manifest Destiny. Father of 15 children (most of any President).

11

James K. Polk
1845-1849
Democrat
VP: George M. Dallas

Born 11-02-1795 in Mecklenburg County, NC
Died 06-15-1849; Buried at Tennessee State Capitol, Nashville
First Lady: Sarah Childress (1803-1891)

Lawyer, known as Young Hickory. Wife was astute political adviser. First "dark horse" to be elected Pres. Kept promise to serve only one term. Accomplished all 4 goals: Won war with Mexico and US acquired most of Southwest; acquired Oregon from Great Britain; reduced tariffs; independent Treasury. Washington Monument, US Naval Academy and Smithsonian begun.

12

Zachary Taylor
1849-1850
Whig
VP: Millard Fillmore

Born 11-24-1784 in Orange County, VA
Died 07-09-1850; Buried at Zachery Taylor National Cemetery, Louisville, KY
First Lady: Margaret M. Smith (1788-1852)

Son of prominent Virginia planters, Indian fighter. Major general and hero of Mexican War (battles of Monterrey and Buena Vista). First President with no prior political office. Reluctant candidate. Set groundwork for Compromise of 1850 over slavery. Died 16 mos. into term of natural causes.

Presidents of the United States

13

Millard Fillmore
1850-1853
Whig
VP: None

Born 01-07-1800 in Cayuga County, NY
Died 03-08-1874; Buried at Forest Lawn Cemetery, Buffalo, NY

First Lady: Abigail Powers (1798-1853);
2nd Wife: Caroline C. McIntosh (1813-81)

Lawyer who rose from poverty. Congressman from NY, Vice President. Anti-slavery but argued federal govt had no role. Compromise of 1850. Fugitive Slave Act passed. Last Whig President. Ran in 1856 as Know-Nothing Party candidate. Helped found University of Buffalo.

14

Franklin Pierce
1853-1857
Democrat
VP: William R. King

Born 11-23-1804 in Hillsboro, NH
Died 10-08-1869; Buried at Old North Cemetery, Concord, NH

First Lady: Jane M. Appleton (1806-1863)

Lawyer. US Senator. Northern Democrat who saw abolition of slavery as threat to Union. Signed Kansas-Nebraska Act and Gadsden Purchase. Tried to acquire Cuba from Spain. Vocal critic of Pres. Lincoln during war. Heavy drinker. Wife suffered from depression; all their children died young. Son died in ghastly train accident shortly before inauguration.

15

James Buchanan
1857-1861
Democrat
VP: John C. Breckinridge

Born 04-23-1791 in Cove Gap, PA
Died 06-01-1868; Buried at Woodward Hill Cemetery, Lancaster, PA

First Lady: None

Pennsylvania lawyer, Congressman, minister to Russia, secretary of state, minister to Britain. Only bachelor President. States' rights advocate. Supported Dred Scott case. Bank Panic of 1857. Utah War against Mormons. Violence in Kansas over slavery. Pledged to serve only one term. Did not react to secessionists.

16

Abraham Lincoln
1861-1865
Republican
VPs: Hannibal Hamlin, Andrew Johnson

Born 02-12-1809 in Hardin County, KY
Died 04-15-1865; Buried at Oak Ridge Cemetery, Springfield, IL

First Lady: Mary Todd (1818-1882)

Frontier lawyer, US Congressman, first Republican elected President. Debated Stephen Douglas. Successfully prosecuted War of the Rebellion (Civil War) while contending with War Democrats, Radical Republicans, and hesitant generals. Issued Emancipation Proclamation. Promoted 13th Amendment. Gettysburg Address. Assasssinated April 14, 1865 at Ford's Theater in DC.

17

Andrew Johnson
1865-1869
Democrat
VP: None

Born 12-29-1808 in Raleigh, NC
Died 07-31-1875; Buried at Andrew Johnson National Cemetery, Greeneville, TN

First Lady: Eliza McCardle (1810-1876)

Self-educated. Tailor by trade. Southern Democrat. Emerged from poverty to hold numerous political offices at all levels. Governor and military governor of Tenn. Lincoln's VP. Staunch Constitutionalist. 1st President to be impeached; avoided conviction by one vote. Opposed ex-slave citizenship. Opposed Radical Reconstruction. US Senator following term.

18

Ulysses S. Grant
1869-1877
Republican
VPs: Schuyler Colfax, Henry Wilson

Born 04-27-1822 in Point Pleasant, OH
Died 07-23-1885; Buried at Grant's Tomb, New York City, NY

First Lady: Julia B. Dent (1826-1902)

West Point graduate. Mexican War hero. Commanding Gen. of Army and hero of Civil War. Accepted Lee's surrender at Appomattox. Created Justice Dept., fought Ku Klux Klan. Panic of 1873 severe economic depression. Created Civil Service Commission. Suffered from corruption of official appointees. Toured world after term. Wrote celebrated memoirs.

Land of the Free, Home of the Brave

Presidents of the United States

19

Rutherford B. Hayes
1877-1881
Republican
VP: William Wheeler

Born 10-04-1822 in Delaware, OH
Died 01-17-1893; Buried at Spiegel Grove State Park, Fremont, OH
First Lady: Lucy Webb (1831-1889)

Lawyer, abolitionist, Harvard Law School, Congressman, Ohio governor. General in Civil War. Elected via Compromise of 1877 that ended Reconstruction. Withdrew troops from South. Supported gold standard and meritocratic government. Banished liquor from WH. Civil service reform. Kept pledge not to run for re-election.

20

James Garfield
1881
Republican
VP: Chester Arthur

Born 11-19-1831 in Orange, OH
Died 09-19-1881; Buried at Lakeview Cemetery, Cleveland, OH
First Lady: Lucretia Rudolph (1832-1918)

Born in poverty, self-educated. General in Civil War. Ohio Congressman. Skilled orator. Supported civil rights, gold standard. Compromise candidate, conducted "front porch" campaign. Only sitting House member elected President. Served only 6 mos. Shot in 1881 by a delusional office seeker. He died months later from infections caused by his doctors.

21

Chester Arthur
1881-1885
Republican
VP: None

Born 10-05-1829 in Fairfield, VT
Died 11-17-1886; Buried at Rural Cemetery, Albany, NY
Wife: Ellen L. Herndon (1837-1880)

Son of Baptist preacher, lawyer, quartermaster in Civil War, NY Port Customs Collector. VP under Garfield. Champion of civil service reform. Member of boss Conkling's Stalwarts. DC's most eligible bachelor. Revitalized US Navy. Dignified, tall, handsome. Solid performer despite failing health (fatal kidney disease).

22

Grover Cleveland
1885-1889
Democrat
VP: Thomas Hendricks

Born 03-18-1837 in Caldwell, NJ
Died 06-24-1908; Buried at Princeton, NJ
First Lady: Frances Fulsom (1864-1947)

Son of Presbyterian minister, lawyer, county sheriff, Buffalo mayor, NY governor, pro-business and fiscal conservative. First Democrat President since Civil War. Reformer, fought corruption and patronage. Opposed imperialism and government subsidies. Supported gold standard. Interstate Commerce Act. Denied special interests. Known for his good character.

23

Benjamin Harrison
1889-1893
Republican
VP: Levi P. Morton

Born 08-20-1833 in North Bend, OH
Died 03-13-1901; Buried at Crown Hill Cemetery, Indianapolis, IN
First Lady: Caroline L. Scott (1832-92),
2nd Wife: Mary S.L. Dimmick (1858-1948)

Grandson of President Wm H. Harrison. Indiana lawyer. General in Civil War. US Senator. Imposed protective tariffs and Sherman Antitrust Act. Created national forest reserves. Six states admitted to Union (most of any President). Modernized US Navy. Federal spending reached $1 billion for first time. Failed to secure voting rights enforcement for blacks.

24

Grover Cleveland
1893-1897
Democrat
VP: Adlai Stevenson Sr.

Born 03-18-1837 in Caldwell, NJ
Died 06-24-1908; Buried at Princeton, NJ
First Lady: Frances Fulsom (1864-1947)

Only President to serve non-consecutive terms. Panic of 1893 caused economic depression. Intervened in railroad strike. Wed in White House. Wife youngest First Lady at age 21. Unpopular President by end of 2nd term. Fathered 2 illegitimate children as young man.

Land of the Free, Home of the Brave

Presidents of the United States

25

William McKinley
1897-1901
Republican
VP: Theodore Roosevelt

Born 01-29-1843 in Niles, OH

Died 09-14-1901; Buried at Canton, OH

First Lady: Ida Saxton (1847-1907)

Lawyer, last President to have served in Civil War. Ohio governor, US Congressman, expert on tariffs, led US to victory in Spanish-American War, supported high tariffs and hard-money gold standard. Rapid economic growth. Start of Progressive Era. US acquired Hawaii. Assassinated in 1901 by anarchist and died 8 days later, shortly after re-election.

26

Theodore Roosevelt
1901-1909
Republican
VP: Charles W. Fairbanks

Born 10-27-1858 in New York City, NY

Died 01-06-1919; Buried at Young's Memorial Cemetery, Oyster Bay, NY

First Lady: Edith K. Carow (1861-1948);
1st Wife: Alice H. Lee (1861-84)

Sickly as child, exurberant personality, Teddy or TR, NYC Police Commissioner, Rough Rider on San Juan Hill, NY Governor, VP under McKinley, youngest President at 42, Progressive Republican, "bully pulpit," battled big business trusts, established national parks, supervised building of Panana Canal, expanded US Navy. Founded Bull Moose Party. Explored Amazon. Son killed in WWI, another served as General in WWII.

27

William Howard Taft
1909-1913
Republican
VP: James S. Sherman

Born 09-15-1857 in Cincinnati, OH

Died 03-08-1930; Buried at Arlington National Cemetery, VA

First Lady: Helen "Nellie" Herron (1861-1943)

Father was US Attorney General. Yale grad, judge in his 20s, solicitor general, governor of Philippines. Supported by TR, then fell out of grace. Reduced trade tariffs, suffered from conflict within party. Named in 1921 as Chief Justice of Supreme Court, only Pres. to hold that position. Weighed over 300 lbs.

28

Woodrow Wilson
1913-1921
Democrat
VP: Thomas Marshall

Born 12-28-1856 in Staunton, VA

Died 02-03-1924; Buried at National Cathedral, Washington, DC

First Ladies: Ellen L. Axson (1860-1914),
Edith B. Galt (1872-1961)

Southerner. President of Princeton University, NJ governor. Reformer. Progressive policies. Led US into World War I. Established first modern propaganda office, Espionage and Sedition Acts. Architect of League of Nations. Federal income tax, estate tax, Federal Reserve System created. Disabled at end of term. Awarded 1919 Nobel Peace Prize.

29

Warren G. Harding
1921-1923
Republican
VP: Calvin Coolidge

Born 11-02-1865 in Blooming Grove, OH

Died 08-02-1923; Buried at Hillside Cemetery, Marion, OH

First Lady: Florence K. De Wolfe (1860-1924)

Newspaper owner, US Senator from Ohio. Theme was "return to normalcy." Conducted "front porch" campaign. 1st sitting Senator elected President. Distinguished Cabinet. Pro-business. Naval Conference tackled disarmament. Died in office in San Francisco of heart attack while on tour. Scandals, inc. Teapot Dome and extramarital affairs, tarnished reputation.

30

Calvin Coolidge
1923-1929
Republican
VP: Charles G. Dawes

Born 07-04-1872 in Plymouth Notch, VT

Died 01-05-1933; Buried at Plymouth Cemetery, Plymouth, VT

First Lady: Grace A. Goodhue (1879-1957)

New England lawyer, Massachusetts governor who broke Boston Police Strike. VP under Harding. Small government conservative and man of few words. Frugal with dry sense of humor. Vivacious wife. Signed law restricting immigration. Kellogg-Briand Act tried to outlaw war. Used press and radio to his advantage. Declined to run for re-election.

Land of the Free, Home of the Brave

Presidents of the United States

31

Herbert Hoover
1929-1933
Republican
VP: Charles Curtis

Born 08-10-1874 in West Branch, IA
Died 10-20-1964; Buried at Hoover Presidential Library, West Branch, IA
First Lady: Lou Henry (1875-1944)

Stanford grad, wealthy mining engineer, businessman, commerce secretary, led starvation relief for Belgium after WWI. Led response to Flood of 1927. Bolstered radio and air travel. Stock market crash led to Great Depression. Blamed for not using federal govt to counteract financial crisis. Conservative statesman during lengthy retirement.

32

Franklin D. Roosevelt
1933-1945
Democrat
VPs: John Garner, Henry Wallace, Harry S. Truman

Born 01-30-1882 in Hyde Park, NY
Died 04-12-1945; Buried at Hyde Park, NY
First Lady: Anna Eleanor Roosevelt (1884-1962)

Born into wealth, FDR battled paralysis of legs at age 33, NY governor. Only Pres. elected to 4 terms. Died in office at beginning of 4th term. Led nation through Great Depression with controversial New Deal programs and as commander-in-chief during World War II against Germany, Italy, and Japan. Court-packing plan. Wife Eleanor was activist. Fireside chats with citizens via radio.

33

Harry S Truman
1945-1953
Democrat
VP: Alben Barkley

Born 05-08-1884 in Lamar, MO
Died 12-26-1972; Buried at Independence, MO
First Lady: Elizabeth "Bess" Wallace (1885-1982)

Missouri farmer and businessman, artillery captain in WWI, county judge, US Senator. Investigated WWII govt. contracts. VP under FDR. Authorized use of atomic weapons against Japan. Oversaw Berlin Airlift, Marshall Plan, and UN military response to Communist aggression in Korea. Racially integrated US military. Fired Gen. MacArthur. Plain spoken, poker player.

34

Dwight D. Eisenhower
1953-1961
Republican
VP: Richard Nixon

Born 10-14-1890 in Denison, TX
Died 03-28-1969; Buried at Eisenhower Museum, Abilene, KS
First Lady: Marie "Mamie" Doud (1896-1979)

Kansas farmboy. West Point graduate. Served as Supreme Commander of Allied Forces in Europe in WWII. Army Chief of Staff, NATO Commander, president of Columbia University. Conservative. Anti-isolationist. Ike supervised Interstate Highway System, warned against military-industrial complex. Eisenhower Doctrine against Communist aggression. Avid golfer.

35

John F. Kennedy
1961-1963
Democrat
VP: Lyndon B. Johnson

Born 05-29-1917 in Brookline, MA
Died 11-22-1963; Buried at Arlington National Cemetery, VA
First Lady: Jacqueline "Jackie" Bouvier (1929-1994)

Son of wealthy New England dynasty. Harvard graduate. Served in Navy in WWII. US Senator. Won close race in 1960 as youthful sophisticate. JFK's Camelot. Bay of Pigs and Cuban Missile Crisis. Beginnings of Vietnam involvement. Vowed to reach Moon by end of decade. Assassinated in Dallas, Texas during political trip. One of 2 Presidents buried at Arlington Cemetery.

36

Lyndon B. Johnson
1963-1969
Democrat
VP: Hubert Humphrey

Born 08-27-1908 in Stonewall, TX
Died 01-22-1973; Buried at LBJ Ranch, Stonewall, TX
First Lady: Claudia "Lady Bird" Taylor (1912-2007)

Known as LBJ. Texan. Gregarious and domineering. Longtime Congressional leader. Senate Majority Leader. VP under Kennedy. Activist President. Great Society social programs and War on Poverty. Civil Rights Act of 1964. Sidetracked by escalation of Vietnam War, protests, and civil unrest. Declined to run for 2nd full term. Addressed citizens on TV as "my fellow Americans."

Land of the Free, Home of the Brave

Presidents of the United States

37

Richard M. Nixon
1969-1974
Republican
VPs: Spiro Agnew, Gerald Ford

Born 01-09-1913 in Yorba Linda, CA
Died 04-22-1994; Buried at Nixon Library, Yorba Linda, CA
First Lady: Thelma C. "Pat" Ryan (1912-1993)

Californian, lawyer, Congressman, VP under Eisenhower, Checkers Speech; lost close race in 1960; opened relations to Communist China; negotiated Vietnam War Peace Accords; created EPA; campaigned on law and order; won re-election handily; only President to resign office, under threat of impeachment due to Watergate scandal. VP Agnew resigned due to a scandal.

38

Gerald R. Ford Jr.
1974-1977
Republican
VP: Nelson Rockefeller

Born 07-14-1913 in Omaha, NE
Died 12-26-2006; Buried at Gerald Ford Presidential Museum, Grand Rapids, MI
First Lady: Elizabeth "Betty" Ann Warren (1918-2011)

Born Leslie L. King Jr. Natural athlete. Served in Navy in WWII. House Minority Leader. VP under Nixon. Only VP and Pres. not to be elected to either office. Moderate. Vetoed many Congressional bills. Pardoned Nixon of crimes. Helsinki Accords. Stagnant economy. Fall of Vietnam. Shortest term of any Pres. who didn't die in office. Lost 1976 re-election bid.

39

James Earl Carter Jr.
1977-1981
Democrat
VP: Walter Mondale

Born 10-01-1924 in Plains, GA
First Lady: Rosalynn Smith (1927-)

Georgia peanut farmer and Governor. Served in Navy in WWII. Pardoned draft resistors. Camp David Accords, SALT II, returned Panama Canal, energy crisis, Iran hostage crisis and failed rescue attempt, boycotted Olympics over Soviets in Afghanistan. Sluggish economy. Lost re-election in 1980. 2002 Nobel Peace Prize winner for Carter Center work.

40

Ronald W. Reagan
1981-1989
Republican
VP: George H.W. Bush

Born 02-06-1911 in Tampico, IL
Died 06-05-2004; Buried at Reagan Presidential Library and Museum, Simi Valley, CA
First Lady: Nancy Davis (1921-2016);
1st Wife: Jane Wyman (1914-2007)

Illinois native. Lifeguard. California rancher, governor. Longtime Hollywood actor, union leader. Modern conservative. Iran hostage release. Survived assassination attempt in 1981. Grenada invasion, bombing of Libya. Escalated arms race and engineered collapse of Soviet Union. Lopsided re-election. Iran-Contra affair. Tough on unions, violent protesters. Affable personality.

41

George H.W. Bush
1989-1993
Republican
VP: Dan Quayle

Born 06-12-1924 in Milton, MA
Died 11-30-2018; Buried at George H.W. Bush Presidential Library and Museum, College Station, TX
First Lady: Barbara Pierce (1925-2018)

Wealthy family. Moved to Texas, became oilman. Served in Navy in WWII. Yale graduate. Congressman. Ambassador to UN. Director of CIA. VP under Reagan. Saw end of Cold War. Invasion of Panama. Commander of successful US-led Gulf War to liberate Kuwait. Supported NAFTA. Economic recession. Raised taxes after pledging not to. Lost re-election in 1992.

42

William J. Clinton
1993-2001
Democrat
VP: Al Gore Jr.

Born 08-19-1946 in Hope, AR
First Lady: Hilary Rodham (1947-)

Rhodes Scholar. Arkansas governor. Centrist "third-way" politician. Whitewater scandal. Welfare reform. Bosnia and Kosovo Wars. Oklahoma City bombing. Impeached for perjury over relations with White House intern; acquitted by Senate. Wife later served as Sec. of State, US Senator, and VP under Obama. Known as 1st Boomer President. Handily won re-election.

Land of the Free, Home of the Brave

Presidents of the United States

43

George W. Bush
2001-2009
Republican
VP: Dick Cheney

Born 07-06-1946 in New Haven, CT

First Lady: Laura Welch (1946-)

Son of 41st President. Businessman. Yale graduate. Governor of Texas. Won contested election in 2000. Presided over wars in Afghanistan and Iraq following 9/11 terrorist attacks in US. Patriot Act. Hurricane Katrina. Recession and 2008 financial crisis. No Child Left Behind Act. Campaigned on "compassionate conservatism." Advocate of veterans' affairs.

44

Barack H. Obama
2009-2017
Democrat
VP: Joe Biden

Born 08-04-1961 in Honolulu, HI

First Lady: Michelle L. Robinson (1964-)

First African-American elected President. Lawyer, community organizer, US Senator. Affordable Care health act, Consumer Protection Act, economic stimulist act and other "progressive" activism. Ended military involvement in Iraq, ordered operations in Libya. Ambassador assassinated in Benghazi. Ordered killing of Osama bin Laden. Brokered nuclear deal with Iran.

45

Donald J. Trump
2017 - 2021
Republican
VP: Michael Pence

Born 06-14-1946 in New York, NY

First Lady: Melania Knauss (1970-);
2nd Wife: Marla Maples (1963-);
1st Wife: Ivana Zelnickova (1949-)

NY businessman, real estate developer. Surprise populist candidate; oldest 1st-term President. Proponent of tax cuts, border enforcement, and foreign "America-first" policy. Covid-19 virus health crisis. Civil rights unrest; anarchist riots. Accused of complicity with Russians in 2016 election. Impeached, acquitted in Senate. Feuds with mainstream media over "fake news."

Presidential Factoids

Four Presidents died in office of natural causes: WH Harrison, Taylor, Harding, FD Roosevelt

Four Presidents were assassinated: Lincoln, Garfield, McKinley, Kennedy

Three Presidents were impeached: A Johnson, Clinton, Trump

One President resigned: Nixon, facing impeachment

Five Presidents elected but did not win popular vote: Trump, GW Bush, B. Harrison, Hayes, JQ Adams

Five Presidents never elected President: Tyler, Fillmore, A Johnson, Arthur, Ford

Twelve Presidents ran for re-election and failed: GHW Bush, Carter, Ford, Hoover, T Roosevelt, Taft, B Harrison, Cleveland, Fillmore, Van Buren, JQ Adams, J Adams

President serving the longest: FD Roosevelt (4,422 days)

President serving the shortest: WH Harrison (31 days)

Oldest President upon taking office: Trump (70)

Youngest President upon taking office: T. Roosevelt (42)

President with longest retirement: Carter (also longest-lived President)

President with shortest retirement: Polk (103 days)

One President later served as Chief Justice of the US Supreme Court: Taft

One President later served in the House of Representatives: JQ Adams

One President later served in the US Senate: A Johnson

Six Presidents lived into their 90s: GHW Bush, Ford, Carter, Reagan, Hoover, J Adams

Father and son Presidents: John Adams and John Quincy Adams; George HW Bush and George W Bush

Grandfather and grandson Presidents: William H Harrison and Benjamin Harrison

Three Presidents within six weeks: Van Buren, Harrison, Tyler

Two Presidents in 20 years: FD Roosevelt, Truman

Only bachelor President: Buchanan

Only President married three times: Trump

First divorcee elected President: Reagan

First President born in the USA: Tyler

Two Presidents buried at Arlington National Cemetery: Taft, Kennedy

Two Presidents buried at Hollywood Cemetery, Richmond: Monroe, Tyler

Four Presidents awarded Nobel Peace Prize: T. Roosevelt, Wilson, Carter, Obama

Number of women who have run for President: 28

Most vetoes by a President: 635 by FD Roosevelt (9 overridden)

Presidents who have served as Vice President: 14

Presidents who have served as Governors: 20

Presidents who have served as US Senators: 15

Presidents who have served as US Representatives: 18

Presidential Elections

2016	Electoral	Popular
Donald Trump (R)	304	62,979,636
Hilary Clinton (D)	227	65,844,610

2012	Electoral	Popular
Barack Obama (D)	332	65,915,795
Mitt Romney (R)	206	60,933,504

2008	Electoral	Popular
Barack Obama (D)	365	69,498,516
John McCain (R)	173	59,948,323

2004	Electoral	Popular
George W Bush (R)	286	62,040,610
John Kerry (D)	251	59,028,444

2000	Electoral	Popular
George W Bush (R)	271	50,456,002
Al Gore (D)	266	50,999,897

1996	Electoral	Popular
Bill Clinton (D)	379	47,401,054
Robert Dole (R)	159	39,197,350
Ross Perot (Reform)	0	8,085,285

1992	Electoral	Popular
Bill Clinton (D)	370	44,909,326
George HW Bush (R)	168	39,103,882
Ross Perot (Reform)	0	19,741,657

1988	Electoral	Popular
George HW Bush (R)	426	48,886,097
Michael Dukakis (D)	112	41,809,074

1984	Electoral	Popular
Ronald Reagan (R)	525	54,455,075
Walter Mondale (D)	13	37,577,185

1980	Electoral	Popular
Ronald Reagan (R)	489	43,904,153
Jimmy Carter (D)	49	35,483,883
John Anderson (I)	0	5,720,060

1976	Electoral	Popular
Jimmy Carter (D)	297	40,830,763
Gerald Ford (R)	240	39,147,793

1972	Electoral	Popular
Richard Nixon (R)	520	47,169,911
George McGovern (D)	17	29,170,383

1968	Electoral	Popular
Richard Nixon (R)	301	31,785,480
Hubert Humphrey (D)	191	31,275,166
George Wallace (I)	46	9,906,473

1964	Electoral	Popular
Lyndon B. Johnson (D)	486	43,129,566
Barry Goldwater (R)	52	27,178,188

1960	Electoral	Popular
John F. Kennedy (D)	303	34,226,731
Richard Nixon (R)	219	34,108,157
Harry Bird (Southern-D)	15	324,050

1956	Electoral	Popular
Dwight Eisenhower (R)	457	35,590,472
Adlai Stevenson (D)	73	26,022,752

1952	Electoral	Popular
Dwight Eisenhower (R)	442	33,936,234
Adlai Stevenson (D)	89	27,314,992

1948	Electoral	Popular
Harry S Truman (D)	303	24,179,345
Thomas Dewey (R)	189	21,991,291
Strom Thurman*	39	1,176,125
Henry Wallace**	--	1,157,326

*States Rights **Progressive

1944	Electoral	Popular
Franklin Roosevelt (D)	432	25,612,610
Thomas Dewey (R)	99	22,017,617

1940	Electoral	Popular
Franklin Roosevelt (D)	449	27,313,041
Wendell Willkie (R)	82	22,348,480

1936	Electoral	Popular
Franklin Roosevelt (D)	523	27,757,333
Alfred Landon (R)	8	16,684,231

1932	Electoral	Popular
Franklin Roosevelt (D)	472	22,829,501
Herbert Hoover (R)	59	15,760,684

Presidential Elections

1928	Electoral	Popular
Herbert Hoover (R)	444	21,437,277
Alfred E. Smith (D)	87	15,007,698

1924	Electoral	Popular
Calvin Coolidge (R)	382	15,719,921
John W. Davis (D)	136	8,386,704
Robert La Follette	13	4,832,532

1920	Electoral	Popular
Warren G. Harding (R)	404	16,153,115
James M. Cox (D)	127	9,133,092

1916	Electoral	Popular
Woodrow Wilson (D)	277	9,126,300
Charles E. Hughes (R)	254	8,546,789

1912	Electoral	Popular
Woodrow Wilson (D)	435	6,293,152
Theodore Roosevelt*	88	4,119,207
William H. Taft (R)	8	3,486,333

*Progressive

1908	Electoral	Popular
William H. Taft (R)	321	7,676,258
William Bryan (D)	162	6,406,801

1904	Electoral	Popular
Theodore Roosevelt (R)	336	7,626,593
Alton Parker (D)	140	5,082,898

1900	Electoral	Popular
William McKinley (R)	292	7,218,039
William Bryan (D)	155	6,358,345

1896	Electoral	Popular
William McKinley (R)	271	7,108,480
William Bryan (D)	176	6,511,495

1892	Electoral	Popular
Grover Cleveland (D)	277	5,553,898
Benjamin Harrison (R)	145	5,190,819
James Weaver	22	1,026,595

1888	Electoral	Popular
Benjamin Harrison (R)	233	5,443,892
Grover Cleveland (D)	168	5,534,488

1884	Electoral	Popular
Grover Cleveland (D)	219	4,914,482
James Blaine (R)	182	4,856,903

1880	Electoral	Popular
James Garfield (R)	214	4,446,158
Winfield Hancock (D)	155	4,444,260

1876	Electoral	Popular
Rutherford B. Hayes (R)	185	4,034,311
Samuel Tilden (D)	184	4,288,546

1872	Electoral	Popular
Ulysses S. Grant (R)	286	3,596,235
Horace Greeley*	63	2,834,791

*Liberal Republican

1868	Electoral	Popular
Ulysses S. Grant (R)	214	3,013,650
Horatio Seymour (D)	80	2,708,744

1864	Electoral	Popular
Abraham Lincoln*	212	2,218,388
George McClellan (D)	21	1,812,807

*National Union

1860	Electoral	Popular
Abraham Lincoln (R)	180	1,865,908
Stephen Douglas (D)	12	1,380,202
John C. Breckenridge*	72	848,019
John Bell**	39	590,901

*Southern Democrat
**National Constitutional Union

1856	Electoral	Popular
James Buchanan (D)	174	1,836,072
John Fremont (R)	114	1,342,345
Millard Fillmore*	8	873,053

*Know-Nothing

1852	Electoral	Popular
Franklin Pierce (D)	254	1,607,510
Winfield Scott (Whig)	42	1,386,942

1848	Electoral	Popular
Zachary Taylor (Whig)	163	1,361,393
Lewis Cass (D)	127	1,223,460

Presidential Elections

1844	Electoral	Popular
James K. Polk (D)	170	1,339,494
Henry Clay (Whig)	105	1,300,004

1840	Electoral	Popular
Wm H. Harrison (Whig)	234	1,274,624
Martin Van Buren (D)	60	1,127,781

1836	Electoral	Popular
Martin Van Buren (D)	170	764,176
Wm H. Harrison (Whig)	73	550,816
Hugh White (Whig)	26	146,107
Daniel Webster (Whig)	14	41,201
Willie Mangrum*	11	1,234

*Anti-Jacksonian

1832	Electoral	Popular
Andrew Jackson (D)	219	701,780
Henry Clay (Whig)	49	484,205
John Floyd (Nullifier)	11	100,715
William Wirt*	7	7,273

*Anti-Masonic

1828	Electoral	Popular
Andrew Jackson (D)	178	642,553
John Quincy Adams*	83	500,897

*National Republican

1824	Electoral	Popular
Andrew Jackson (D)	99	153,544
John Quincy Adams*	84	108,740
William Crawford*	41	46,618
Henry Clay*	37	47,136

* Democratic-Republican
No candidate with majority; House elected Adams.

1820	Electoral	Popular
James Monroe*	231	NA
John Quincy Adams**	1	NA

*Democratic-Republican
**Independent-Republican

1816	Electoral	Popular
James Monroe*	183	NA
Rufus King (Federalist)	34	NA

*Democratic-Republican

1812	Electoral	Popular
James Madison*	128	NA
DeWitt Clinton (Fusion)	89	NA

*Democratic-Republican

1808	Electoral	Popular
James Madison*	122	NA
Chas Pinckney (Federalist)	47	NA
George Clinton**	6	NA

*Democratic-Republican
**Independent-Republican

1804	Electoral	Popular
Thomas Jefferson*	162	NA
Chas Pinckney (Federalist)	14	NA

*Democratic-Republican

1800	Electoral	Popular
Thomas Jefferson*	73	NA
Aaron Burr *	73	NA
John Adams (Federalist)	65	NA
Chas Pinckney (Federalist)	64	NA
John Jay (Federalist)	1	NA

*Democratic-Republican
Each elector voted for 2 men (revised by 12th Amend.);
House elected Jefferson

1796	Electoral	Popular
John Adams (Federalist)	71	NA
Thomas Jefferson*	68	NA
Thomas Pinckney**	59	NA
Aaron Burr*	30	NA
Samuel Adams*	15	NA
Oliver Ellsworth**	11	NA
7 others	22	NA

*Democratic-Republican
**Federalist

1792	Electoral	Popular
George Washington	132	NA
John Adams	77	NA
George Clinton	50	NA
Thomas Jefferson	4	NA

1789	Electoral	Popular
George Washington	69	NA
John Adams	34	NA
10 others	35	NA

The White House

Our first president, George Washington, selected the site for the White House in 1791. The cornerstone was laid in 1792 and a competition design submitted by Irish-born architect James Hoban was chosen. After eight years of construction, President John Adams and his wife, Abigail, moved into the unfinished house in 1800. During the War of 1812, the British set fire to the President's House in 1814. Hoban was appointed to rebuild the house, and President James Monroe moved into the building in 1817. During Monroe's administration, the South Portico was constructed in 1824, and Andrew Jackson oversaw the addition of the North Portico in 1829. During the late 19th century, various proposals were made to significantly expand the President's House or to build an entirely new house for the president, but these plans were never realized.

In 1902, President Theodore Roosevelt began a major renovation of the White House, including the relocation of the president's offices from the Second Floor of the Residence to the newly constructed temporary Executive Office Building (now known as the West Wing). The Roosevelt renovation was planned and carried out by the famous New York architectural firm McKim, Mead and White. Roosevelt's successor, President William Howard Taft, had the Oval Office constructed within an enlarged office wing.

Less than fifty years after the Roosevelt renovation, the White House was showing signs of serious structural weakness. President Harry S. Truman began a renovation of the building in which everything but the outer walls were dismantled. The reconstruction was overseen by architect Lorenzo Winslow, and the Truman family moved back into the White House in 1952.

Every president since John Adams has occupied the White House, and the history of this building extends far beyond the construction of its walls. From the Ground Floor Corridor rooms, transformed from their early use as service areas, to the State Floor rooms, where countless leaders and dignitaries have been entertained, the White House is both the home of the President of the United States and his family, and a museum of American history.

There are 132 rooms, 35 bathrooms, and 6 levels in the Residence. There are also 412 doors, 147 windows, 28 fireplaces, 8 staircases, and 3 elevators.

The White House kitchen is able to serve dinner to as many as 140 guests and hors d'oeuvres to more than 1,000.

The White House requires 570 gallons of paint to cover its outside surface.

At various times in history, the White House has been known as the "President's Palace," the "President's House," and the "Executive Mansion."

President Theodore Roosevelt officially gave the White House its current name in 1901.

———————— Land of the Free, Home of the Brave ————————

National Statuary Hall Collection

The National Statuary Hall Collection holds statues donated by each of the states, depicting notable persons in the histories of the respective states. Displayed in the National Statuary Hall and other parts of the United States Capitol in Washington, D.C., the collection includes two statues from each state, plus one from the District of Columbia, plus Rosa Parks, making a total of 102.

By act of Congress, which commissioned the statue in 2005, Rosa Parks was added, though not representing a state. The year was 2013, the centenary of her birth. Hers is the only statue in the Hall not linked with a state. Later that year (on Juneteenth, 2013), by act of Congress, a statue of Frederick Douglass was added as a choice of the District of Columbia.

Alabama
Helen Keller
Joseph Wheeler

Alaska
Edward Lewis "Bob" Bartlett
Ernest Gruening

Arizona
Barry Goldwater
Eusebio Kino

Arkansas
Uriah Milton Rose
James Paul Clarke

California
Ronald Reagan
Junípero Serra

Colorado
Florence R. Sabin
Jack Swigert

Connecticut
Roger Sherman
Jonathan Trumbull

District of Columbia
Frederick Douglass

Delaware
John Middleton Clayton
Caesar Rodney

Florida
John Gorrie
Edmund Kirby Smith

Georgia
Crawford Long
Alexander Hamilton Stephens

Hawaii
Father Damien
Kamehameha I

Idaho
George Laird Shoup
William Borah

Illinois
James Shields
Frances E. Willard

Indiana
Oliver P. Morton
Lew Wallace

Iowa
Samuel Jordan Kirkwood
Norman Borlaug

Kansas
John James Ingalls
Dwight D. Eisenhower

Kentucky
Henry Clay
Ephraim McDowell

Louisiana
Huey Pierce Long
Edward Douglass White

Maine
William King
Hannibal Hamlin

Maryland
Charles Carroll
John Hanson

Massachusetts
Samuel Adams
John Winthrop

Michigan
Lewis Cass
Gerald Ford

Minnesota
Henry Mower Rice
Maria Sanford

Mississippi
Jefferson Davis
James Zachariah George

Missouri
Thomas Hart Benton
Francis Preston Blair Jr.

Montana
Charles Marion Russell
Jeannette Rankin

Nebraska
Standing Bear
J. Sterling Morton

Nevada
Patrick Anthony McCarran
Sarah Winnemucca

New Hampshire
John Stark
Daniel Webster

New Jersey
Philip Kearny
Richard Stockton

New Mexico
Dennis Chávez
Po'pay

New York
George Clinton
Robert R. Livingston

―――――――――――――― Land of the Free, Home of the Brave ――――――――――――――

National Statuary Hall Collection

North Dakota
John Burke
Sakakawea

Ohio
James A. Garfield
Thomas Edison

Oklahoma
Sequoyah
Will Rogers

Oregon
Jason Lee
John McLoughlin

Pennsylvania
Robert Fulton
John Peter Gabriel Muhlenberg

Rhode Island
Nathanael Greene
Roger Williams

South Carolina
John C. Calhoun
Wade Hampton

South Dakota
William Henry Harrison Beadle
Joseph Ward

Tennessee
Andrew Jackson
John Sevier

Texas
Stephen F. Austin
Sam Houston

Utah
Brigham Young
Philo T. Farnsworth

Vermont
Ethan Allen
Jacob Collamer

Virginia
Robert Edward Lee
George Washington

Washington
Marcus Whitman
Mother Joseph

West Virginia
John Edward Kenna
Francis Harrison Pierpont

Wisconsin
Jacques Marquette
Robert M. La Follette Sr.

Wyoming
Esther Hobart Morris
Washakie

Rosa Parks

Replacements:

George Washington Glick, Kansas (removed in favor of Dwight D. Eisenhower in 2003)

Thomas Starr King, California (removed in favor of Ronald Reagan in 2009)

Jabez Lamar Monroe Curry, Alabama (removed in favor of Helen Keller in 2009)

Zachariah Chandler, Michigan (removed in favor of Gerald R. Ford in 2011)

James Harlan, Iowa (removed in favor of Norman Borlaug in 2014)

William Jennings Bryan, Nebraska (removed in favor of Chief Standing Bear in 2019)

John Campbell Greenway, Arizona (removed in favor of Barry M. Goldwater in 2015)

William Allen, Ohio (removed in favor of Thomas A. Edison in 2016)

On February 28, 2018, the governor of North Carolina requested from the Architect of the Capitol replacement of the statue of Charles Brantley Aycock with one of evangelist Billy Graham, pursuant to legislation signed in 2015.

On March 19, 2018, the governor of Florida signed legislation to replace the statue of Confederate General Edmund Kirby Smith with one of the African-American educator and Civil Rights advocate, Mary McLeod Bethune.

On April 23, 2018, the Governor of Nebraska, Pete Ricketts, signed legislation that would replace the statue of U.S. Secretary of Agriculture Julius Sterling Morton with author Willa Cather.

On April 4, 2019, the Governor of Utah, Gary Herbert, signed legislation that would replace inventor Philo T. Farnsworth with Martha Hughes Cannon, who was the nation's first female state senator.

On April 17, 2019, the Governor of Arkansas, Asa Hutchinson, signed legislation that would replace statues of lawyer and Confederate supporter Uriah Milton Rose and former governor and avowed white supremacist James Paul Clarke with musician Johnny Cash and civil rights icon Daisy Lee Gatson Bates.

On July 11, 2019, the Governor of Missouri, Mike Parson, signed legislation that would replace the statue of U.S. Senator Thomas Hart Benton with Harry S. Truman, the 33rd President of the United States.

Lain in State or Honor at US Capitol Rotunda

Congressman John R. Lewis
July 27-28, 2020
Member of the House of Representatives from Georgia, One Hundredth and the sixteen succeeding Congresses, 1987-2020, serving until his death; prominent civil rights leader.

George Herbert Walker Bush
December 3–5, 2018
Member of the House of Representatives from Texas, January 3, 1967, to January 3, 1971; United States Ambassador to the United Nations, 1971–1973; chairman, Republican National Committee, 1973–1974; chief United States liaison officer, People's Republic of China, 1974–1976; director, Central Intelligence Agency, 1976–1977; Vice President of the United States from January 20, 1981, to January 20, 1989; President of the United States from January 20, 1989, to January 20, 1993. Died November 30, 2018, in Houston, Texas.

John S. McCain III
August 31, 2018
Member of the House of Representatives from Arizona, January 3, 1983, to January 3, 1987. U.S. Senator from Arizona, January 3, 1987, to his death. Died August 25, 2018, in Sedona, Arizona.

Billy Graham
February 28 – March 1, 2018; lay in honor
Minister, evangelist and adviser to presidents. Died February 21, 2018, in Montreat, North Carolina.

Daniel K. Inouye
December 20, 2012
Senator Inouye was the first congressman to represent Hawaii when it became a state in 1959. He served in the U.S. Senate from 1963 until his death on December 17, 2012. Inouye was the second-longest serving senator in history and served as president pro tempore of the U.S. Senate. He was a World War II hero, given the Medal of Honor for his service.

Gerald R. Ford Jr.
December 30, 2006 – January 2, 2007
Ford was a member of the House of Representatives from Michigan, January 3, 1949 to December 6, 1973, when he resigned to become Vice President. He was Vice President of the United States from December 6, 1973, to August 9, 1974, when President Richard M. Nixon resigned. Ford served as President of the United States from August 9, 1974 to January 20, 1977. He died December 26, 2006, in Rancho Mirage, California.

Rosa Parks
October 30-31, 2005; lay in honor
Parks is best known as a civil rights pioneer. She died on October 24, 2005, in Detroit, Michigan.

Ronald Wilson Reagan
June 9-11, 2004
Reagan was governor of California from 1967 to 1975 and President of the United States from January 20, 1981 to January 20, 1989. He died June 5, 2004, in Bel Air, California.

Jacob Joseph Chestnut and **John Michael Gibson**
July 28, 1998; lay in honor
Chestnut and Gibson were United States Capitol Police officers killed at the U.S. Capitol in the line of duty on July 24, 1998.

Claude Denson Pepper
June 1-2, 1989
Pepper served as U.S. Senator from Florida November 4, 1936 to January 3, 1951. He was a member of the House of Representatives from Florida from January 3, 1963, until his death on May 30, 1989, in Washington, D.C.

Unknown Soldier of the Vietnam Conflict
May 25-28, 1984
Chosen to honor the unknown Americans who lost their lives while serving in the Armed Forces of the United States in Southeast Asia during 1959-1972.

Hubert H. Humphrey
January 14-15, 1978
Humphrey served as U.S. Senator from Minnesota from January 3, 1949 to December 29, 1964, when he resigned to become Vice President. He was Vice President of the United States from January 20, 1965 to January 20, 1969. Humphrey then returned to the Senate from November 3, 1970, until his death. He died on January 14, 1978, in Waverly, Minnesota.

Lyndon Baines Johnson
January 24-25, 1973
Johnson was a member of the House of Representatives from Texas from April 10, 1937 to January 3, 1949. He was a U.S. Senator from Texas from January 3, 1949 to January 3, 1961, when he resigned, having been elected Vice President of the United States. Johnson served as Vice President from January 20, 1961, to November 22, 1963, when he assumed the Presidency. He served as President until January 20, 1969. Johnson died on January 22, 1973, near Johnson City, Texas.

Lain in State or Honor at US Capitol Rotunda

J. Edgar Hoover
May 3-4, 1972
Hoover was the first Director of the Federal Bureau of Investigation, serving from 1924 until his death. He died on May 2, 1972, in Washington, D.C.

Everett McKinley Dirksen
September 9-10, 1969
Member of the House of Representatives from Illinois, March 4, 1933 to January 3, 1949. U.S. Senator from Illinois, January 3, 1951, until his death. Died September 7, 1969, in Washington, D.C.

Dwight D. Eisenhower
March 30-31, 1969
Eisenhower graduated from the U.S. Military Academy at West Point in 1915, was promoted to General of the Army in 1944, and was named President of Columbia University in 1948. He served as President of the United States from January 20, 1953, to January 20, 1961. Eisenhower died March 28, 1969, in Washington, D.C.

Herbert Clark Hoover
October 23-25, 1964
Hoover served as Secretary of Commerce for Presidents Warren G. Harding and Calvin Coolidge. He was Food Administrator under President Woodrow Wilson. Hoover also served as Chairman of the Commission on the Organization of Executive Branch of Government in 1947-1949 and 1953-1955. He was President of the United States from March 4, 1929, to March 3, 1933. Hoover died October 20, 1964, in New York City.

Douglas MacArthur
April 8-9, 1964
MacArthur was Superintendent of the U.S. Military Academy at West Point from 1919-1922; appointed Chief of Staff of the Army on November 21, 1930; and was appointed General of the Army on December 18, 1944. From July 26, 1941, through April 11, 1951, he served in the Pacific and Far East in various allied commands. MacArthur died April 5, 1964, in Washington, D.C.

John F. Kennedy
November 24-25, 1963
Kennedy was a member of the House of Representatives from Massachusetts, January 3, 1947, to January 3, 1953. U.S. Senator from Massachusetts, January 3, 1953, to December 22, 1960, when he resigned to become President. President of the United States from January 20, 1961, until his death. Assassinated in Dallas, Texas, on November 22, 1963.

Unknown Soldiers of World War II and the Korean War
May 28-30, 1958
Chosen to honor and perpetuate the memory of the heroes who gave their lives while serving overseas in the Armed Forces of the United States during World War II and the Korean War, and whose identities were unknown.

Robert A. Taft
August 2-3, 1953
Taft served as U.S. Senator from Ohio, January 3, 1939, until his death. He died July 31, 1953, in New York City.

John Joseph Pershing
July 18-19, 1948
Pershing was General of the Armies of the United States. He graduated from the U.S. Military Academy at West Point in 1886 and devoted his entire life to military service. He served as Chief of Staff of the Army 1921-24; Commander of American Expeditionary Forces, World War I; distinguished service during the Philippine insurrection and Spanish-American War. Pershing died July 15, 1948, in Washington, D.C.

William Howard Taft
March 11, 1930
Taft served as President of United States from March 4, 1909 to March 4, 1913. He was Chief Justice of the United States from July 11, 1921 to February 3, 1930. Taft died on March 8, 1930, in Washington, D.C.

Warren G. Harding
August 8, 1923
Harding served as U.S. Senator from Ohio, March 4, 1915, to January 13, 1921, when he resigned, having been elected President. He was President of United States March 4, 1921, until his death. Harding died August 2, 1923, in San Francisco, California.

Unknown Soldier of World War I
November 9-11, 1921
Chosen to honor and perpetuate the memory of the heroes who gave their lives in World War I, the body was that of an unknown American who served as a member of the American Expeditionary Forces in Europe.

George Dewey
January 20, 1917
Dewey was admiral of the Navy and was a hero of Manila Bay in the Spanish-American War. He died January 16, 1917, in Washington, D.C.

Lain in State or Honor at US Capitol Rotunda

Pierre Charles L'Enfant
(re-interment) April 28, 1909
L'Enfant was the planner of the city of Washington, D.C. He died June 14, 1825, and was buried on Digges farm in Prince George's County, Maryland. His remains were brought to the U.S. Capitol on April 28, 1909, to be re-interred at Arlington National Cemetery.

William McKinley, Jr.
September 17, 1901
McKinley was a member of House of Representatives from Ohio, March 4, 1877, to May 27, 1884, and again from March 4, 1885, to March 3, 1891. He served as governor of Ohio from 1892 to 1896 and as President of United States, March 4, 1897, until his death. McKinley was assassinated September 6, 1901, in Buffalo, New York, and died there September 14, 1901.

John A. Logan
December 30-31, 1886
Logan was a member of House of Representatives from Illinois, March 4, 1859, to April 2, 1862, when he resigned to enter the Union Army, and again from March 4, 1867, until March 3, 1871. He served as U.S. Senator from Illinois, March 4, 1871, to March 3, 1877, and again from March 4, 1879, to December 26, 1886. Logan died on December 26, 1886, in Washington, D.C.

James A. Garfield
September 21-23, 1881
Garfield was a member of House of Representatives from Ohio, March 4, 1863, to November 8, 1880, when he resigned, having been elected President. He served as President of the United States from March 4, 1881, until his death. Garfield was assassinated July 2, 1881, in Washington, D.C., and died September 19, 1881, in Elberon, New Jersey.

Henry Wilson
November 25-26, 1875
Wilson served as a U.S. Senator from Massachusetts, January 31, 1855, to March 3, 1873, when he resigned to become Vice President of the United States. He was Vice President from March 4, 1873, until his death on November 22, 1875. Wilson died in the Vice President's room in the Capitol Building in Washington, D.C.

Charles Sumner
March 13, 1874
Sumner served as U.S. Senator from Massachusetts, April 24, 1851, until his death, March 11, 1874. He died in Washington, D.C.

Thaddeus Stevens
August 13-14, 1868
Stevens was a member of the House of Representatives from Pennsylvania, March 4, 1849, to March 3, 1853, and again from March 4, 1859, until his death on August 11, 1868. He died in Washington, D.C.

Abraham Lincoln
April 19-21, 1865
Lincoln was a member of the House of Representatives from Illinois, March 4, 1847, to March 3, 1849. He was President of the United States from March 4, 1861, until his death. Lincoln was assassinated April 14, 1865, in Washington, D.C., and died there April 15, 1865 after adjournment of the 38th Congress, 2nd Session. The historic catafalque was constructed to support Lincoln's casket during his lying in state.

Henry Clay
July 1, 1852
Henry Clay was a member of the House of Representatives for five non-consecutive terms (1811-25). He served as Speaker of the House in 1811-14, 1815-20, and 1823-25. He was Secretary of State from 1825 to 1829. Clay also served as U.S. Senator from Kentucky intermittently for 18 years between 1806 and 1852. He died June 29, 1852, in Washington, D.C. during the 32nd Congress, 1st Session, becoming the first person honored by a funeral ceremony in the Capitol Rotunda.

Land of the Free, Home of the Brave

★ ★ ★ ★ ★ ★ THE 50 STATES ★ ★ ★ ★ ★ ★

State	Nickname	Capital and Largest City	Date of Admission (Rank)	Population (Rank)	Sq. Mi. (rank)
Alabama (AL)	Yellowhammer State	Montgomery (123,456) Birmingham (209,403)	Dec. 14, 1819 (22)	4,903,185 (24)	52,420 (30)
Alaska (AK)	Last Frontier	Juneau (31,974) Anchorage (288,000)	Jan. 3, 1959 (49)	731,545 (49)	665,384 (1)
Arizona (AZ)	Grand Canyon State	Phoenix (1,680,992)	Feb. 14, 1912 (48)	7,278,717 (14)	113,990 (6)
Arkansas (AR)	Natural State	Little Rock (197,312)	June 15, 1836 (25)	3,017,804 (34)	53,179 (29)
California (CA)	Golden State	Sacramento (513,624) Los Angeles (3,979,576)	Sept. 9, 1850 (31)	39,512,223 (1)	163,695 (3)
Colorado (CO)	Centennial State	Denver (727,211)	Aug. 1, 1876 (38)	5,758,736 (21)	104,094 (8)
Connecticut (CT)	Constitution State	Hartford (122,105) Bridgeport (144,399)	Jan. 9, 1788 (5)	3,565,278 (29)	5,543 (48)
Delaware (DE)	First State	Dover (38,166) Wilmington (70,166)	Dec. 7, 1787 (1)	973,764 (46)	2,489 (49)
Florida (FL)	Sunshine State	Tallahassee (194,500) Jacksonville (911,507)	March 3, 1845 (27)	21,477,737 (3)	65,758 (22)
Georgia (GA)	Peach State	Atlanta (506,811)	Jan. 2, 1788 (4)	10,617,423 (8)	59,425 (24)
Hawaii (HI)	Aloha State	Honolulu (345,064)	Aug. 21, 1959 (50)	1,415,872 (41)	10,932 (43)
Idaho (ID)	Gem State	Boise (228,959)	July 3, 1890 (43)	1,787,065 (40)	83,569 (14)
Illinois (IL)	Prairie State	Springfield (114,230) Chicago (2,693,976)	Dec. 3, 1818 (21)	12,671,821 (6)	57,914 (25)
Indiana (IN)	Hoosier State	Indianapolis (876,384)	Dec. 11, 1816 (19)	6,732,219 (17)	36,420 (38)
Iowa (IA)	Hawkeye State	Des Moines (214,237)	Dec. 28, 1846 (29)	3,155,070 (32)	56,273 (26)
Kansas (KS)	Sunflower State	Topeka (125,310) Wichita (389,938)	Jan. 29, 1861 (34)	2,913,314 (36)	82,278 (15)
Kentucky (KY)	Bluegrass State	Frankfort (27,755) Louisville (617,638)	June 1, 1792 (15)	4,467,673 (26)	40,408 (37)
Louisiana (LA)	Pelican State	Baton Rouge (220,236) New Orleans (390,144)	April 30, 1812 (18)	4,648,794 (25)	52,378 (31)
Maine (ME)	Pine Tree State	Augusta (18,697) Portland (66,215)	March 15, 1820 (23)	1,344,212 (43)	35,380 (39)
Maryland (MD)	Old Line State	Annapolis (39,223) Baltimore (593,490)	April 28, 1788 (7)	6,045,680 (19)	12,406 (42)
Massachusetts (MA)	Bay State	Boston (692,600)	Feb. 6, 1788 (6)	6,892,503 (15)	10,554 (44)
Michigan (MI)	Great Lakes State	Lansing (118,210) Detroit (670,031)	Jan. 26, 1837 (26)	9,986,857 (10)	96,714 (11)
Minnesota (MN)	North Star State	St. Paul (308,096) Minneapolis (429,606)	May 11, 1858 (32)	5,639,632 (22)	86,936 (12)
Mississippi (MS)	Magnolia State	Jackson (160,628)	Dec. 10, 1817 (20)	2,976,149 (35)	48,432 (32)
Missouri (MO)	Show-Me State	Jefferson City (42,708) Kansas City (495,327)	Aug. 10, 1821 (24)	6,137,428 (18)	69,707 (21)
Montana (MT)	Treasure State	Helena (33,124) Billings (109,577)	Nov. 8, 1889 (41)	1,068,778 (44)	147,040 (4)

Land of the Free, Home of the Brave

★ ★ ★ ★ ★ ★ THE 50 STATES ★ ★ ★ ★ ★ ★

State	Nickname	Capital and Largest City	Date of Admission (Rank)	Population (Rank)	Sq. Mi. (rank)
Nebraska (NE)	Cornhusker State	Lincoln (289,102) Omaha (478,192)	March 1, 1867 (37)	1,934,408 (38)	77,348 (16)
Nevada (NV)	Silver State	Carson City (55,916) Las Vegas (651,319)	Oct. 31, 1864 (36)	3,080,156 (33)	110,572 (7)
New Hampshire (NH)	Granite State	Concord (43,627) Manchester (112,673)	June 21, 1788 (9)	1,359,711 (42)	9,349 (46)
New Jersey (NJ)	Garden State	Trenton (83,203) Newark (282,011)	Dec. 18, 1787 (3)	8,882,190 (11)	8,723 (47)
New Mexico (NM)	Land of Enchantment	Santa Fe (84,683) Albuquerque (560,513)	Jan. 6, 1912 (47)	2,096,829 (37)	121,590 (5)
New York (NY)	Empire State	Albany (96,460) New York (8,336,817)	July 26, 1788 (11)	19,453,561 (4)	54,555 (27)
North Carolina (NC)	Tar Heel State	Raleigh (474,069) Charlotte (885,708)	Nov. 21, 1789 (12)	10,488,084 (9)	53,819 (28)
North Dakota (ND)	Peace Garden State	Bismarck (73,529) Fargo (124,662)	Nov. 2, 1889 (39)	762,062 (48)	70,698 (19)
Ohio (OH)	Buckeye State	Columbus (898,553)	March 1, 1803 (17)	11,689,100 (7)	44,826 (34)
Oklahoma (OK)	Sooner State	Oklahoma City (655,057)	Nov. 16, 1907 (46)	3,956,971 (28)	69,899 (20)
Oregon (OR)	Beaver State	Salem (174,365) Portland (654,741)	Feb. 14, 1859 (33)	4,217,737 (27)	98,379 (9)
Pennsylvania (PA)	Keystone State	Harrisburg (49,271) Philadelphia (1,584,064)	Dec. 12, 1787 (2)	12,801,989 (5)	46,054 (33)
Rhode Island (RI)	Ocean State	Providence (179,883)	May 29, 1790 (13)	1,059,361 (45)	1,545 (50)
South Carolina (SC)	Palmetto State	Columbia (131,674) Charleston (137,566)	May 23, 1788 (8)	5,148,714 (23)	32,020 (40)
South Dakota (SD)	Mt Rushmore State	Pierre (13,867) Sioux Falls (183,793)	Nov. 2, 1889 (40)	884,659 (47)	77,116 (17)
Tennessee (TN)	Volunteer State	Nashville (670,820)	June 1, 1796 (16)	6,829,174 (16)	42,144 (36)
Texas (TX)	Lone Star State	Austin (978,908) Houston (2,320,268)	Dec. 29, 1845 (28)	28,995,881 (2)	268,596 (2)
Utah (UT)	Beehive State	Salt Lake City (200,567)	Jan. 4, 1896 (45)	3,205,958 (30)	84,897 (13)
Vermont (VT)	Green Mtn. State	Montpelier (7,372) Burlington (42,819)	March 4, 1791 (14)	623,989 (49)	9,616 (45)
Virginia (VA)	Old Dominion	Richmond (230,436) Virginia Beach (449,974)	June 25, 1788 (10)	8,535,519 (12)	42,775 (35)
Washington (WA)	Evergreen State	Olympia (52,882) Seattle (753,675)	Nov. 11, 1889 (42)	7,614,893 (13)	71,298 (18)
West Virginia (WV)	Mountain State	Charleston (46,536)	June 20, 1863 (35)	1,792,147 (39)	24,230 (41)
Wisconsin (WI)	Badger State	Madison (259,680) Milwaukee (590,157)	May 29, 1848 (30)	5,822,434 (20)	65,496 (23)
Wyoming (WY)	Equality State	Cheyenne (64,235)	July 10, 1890 (44)	578,759 (50)	97,813 (10)

The District of Columbia, which encloses Washington City, is a federal district independent of any state. It elects a non-voting delegate to the US House of Representatives. The district measures 68 square miles and contains a population of 705,749.

Largest Cities by Population

1	New York	NY	8,336,817		49	Arlington	TX	398,854
2	Los Angeles	CA	3,979,576		50	New Orleans	LA	390,144
3	Chicago	IL	2,693,976		51	Wichita	KS	389,938
4	Houston	TX	2,320,268		52	Bakersfield	CA	384,145
5	Phoenix	AZ	1,680,992		53	Cleveland	OH	381,009
6	Philadelphia	PA	1,584,064		54	Aurora	CO	379,289
7	San Antonio	TX	1,547,253		55	Anaheim	CA	350,365
8	San Diego	CA	1,423,851		56	Honolulu	HI	345,064
9	Dallas	TX	1,343,573		57	Santa Ana	CA	332,318
10	San Jose	CA	1,021,795		58	Riverside	CA	331,360
11	Austin	TX	978,908		59	Corpus Christi	TX	326,586
12	Jacksonville	FL	911,507		60	Lexington	KY	323,152
13	Fort Worth	TX	909,585		61	Henderson	NV	320,189
14	Columbus	OH	898,553		62	Stockton	CA	312,697
15	Charlotte	NC	885,708		63	Saint Paul	MN	308,096
16	San Francisco	CA	881,549		64	Cincinnati	OH	303,940
17	Indianapolis	IN	876,384		65	St. Louis	MO	300,576
18	Seattle	WA	753,675		66	Pittsburgh	PA	300,286
19	Denver	CO	727,211		67	Greensboro	NC	296,710
20	Washington	DC	705,749		68	Lincoln	NE	289,102
21	Boston	MA	692,600		69	Anchorage	AK	288,000
22	El Paso	TX	681,728		70	Plano	TX	287,677
23	Nashville	TN	670,820		71	Orlando	FL	287,442
24	Detroit	MI	670,031		72	Irvine	CA	287,401
25	Oklahoma City	OK	655,057		73	Newark	NJ	282,011
26	Portland	OR	654,741		74	Durham	NC	278,993
27	Las Vegas	NV	651,319		75	Chula Vista	CA	274,492
28	Memphis	TN	651,073		76	Toledo	OH	272,779
29	Louisville	KY	617,638		77	Fort Wayne	IN	270,402
30	Baltimore	MD	593,490		78	St. Petersburg	FL	265,351
31	Milwaukee	WI	590,157		79	Laredo	TX	262,491
32	Albuquerque	NM	560,513		80	Jersey City	NJ	262,075
33	Tucson	AZ	548,073		81	Chandler	AZ	261,165
34	Fresno	CA	531,576		82	Madison	WI	259,680
35	Mesa	AZ	518,012		83	Lubbock	TX	258,862
36	Sacramento	CA	513,624		84	Scottsdale	AZ	258,069
37	Atlanta	GA	506,811		85	Reno	NV	255,601
38	Kansas City	MO	495,327		86	Buffalo	NY	255,284
39	Colorado Springs	CO	478,221		87	Gilbert	AZ	254,114
40	Omaha	NE	478,192		88	Glendale	AZ	252,381
41	Raleigh	NC	474,069		89	North Las Vegas	NV	251,974
42	Miami	FL	467,963		90	Winston-Salem	NC	247,945
43	Long Beach	CA	462,628		91	Chesapeake	VA	244,835
44	Virginia Beach	VA	449,974		92	Norfolk	VA	242,742
45	Oakland	CA	433,031		93	Fremont	CA	241,110
46	Minneapolis	MN	429,606		94	Garland	TX	239,928
47	Tulsa	OK	401,190		95	Irving	TX	239,798
48	Tampa	FL	399,700		96	Hialeah	FL	233,339

#	City	State	Population
97	Richmond	VA	230,436
98	Boise	ID	228,959
99	Spokane	WA	222,081
100	Baton Rouge	LA	220,236
101	Tacoma	WA	217,827
102	San Bernardino	CA	215,784
103	Modesto	CA	215,196
104	Fontana	CA	214,547
105	Des Moines	IA	214,237
106	Moreno Valley	CA	213,055
107	Santa Clarita	CA	212,979
108	Fayetteville	NC	211,657
109	Birmingham	AL	209,403
110	Oxnard	CA	208,881
111	Rochester	NY	205,695
112	Port St. Lucie	FL	201,846
113	Grand Rapids	MI	201,013
114	Huntsville	AL	200,574
115	Salt Lake City	UT	200,567
116	Frisco	TX	200,490
117	Yonkers	NY	200,370
118	Amarillo	TX	199,371
119	Glendale	CA	199,303
120	Huntington Beach	CA	199,223
121	McKinney	TX	199,177
122	Montgomery	AL	198,525
123	Augusta	GA	197,888
124	Aurora	IL	197,757
125	Akron	OH	197,597
126	Little Rock	AR	197,312
127	Tempe	AZ	195,805
128	Columbus	GA	195,769
129	Overland Park	KS	195,494
130	Grand Prairie	TX	194,543
131	Tallahassee	FL	194,500
132	Cape Coral	FL	194,495
133	Mobile	AL	188,720
134	Knoxville	TN	187,603
135	Shreveport	LA	187,112
136	Worcester	MA	185,428
137	Ontario	CA	185,010
138	Vancouver	WA	184,463
139	Sioux Falls	SD	183,793
140	Chattanooga	TN	182,799
141	Brownsville	TX	182,781
142	Fort Lauderdale	FL	182,437
143	Providence	RI	179,883
144	Newport News	VA	179,225
145	Rancho Cucamonga	CA	177,603
146	Santa Rosa	CA	176,753
147	Peoria	AZ	175,961
148	Oceanside	CA	175,742
149	Elk Grove	CA	174,775
150	Salem	OR	174,365
151	Pembroke Pines	FL	173,591
152	Eugene	OR	172,622
153	Garden Grove	CA	171,644
154	Cary	NC	170,282
155	Fort Collins	CO	170,243
156	Corona	CA	169,868
157	Springfield	MO	167,882
158	Jackson	MS	160,628
159	Alexandria	VA	159,428
160	Hayward	CA	159,203
161	Clarksville	TN	158,146
162	Lakewood	CO	157,935
163	Lancaster	CA	157,601
164	Salinas	CA	155,465
165	Palmdale	CA	155,079
166	Hollywood	FL	154,817
167	Springfield	MA	153,606
168	Macon	GA	153,159
169	Kansas City	KS	152,960
170	Sunnyvale	CA	152,703
171	Pomona	CA	151,691
172	Killeen	TX	151,666
173	Escondido	CA	151,625
174	Pasadena	TX	151,227
175	Naperville	IL	148,449
176	Bellevue	WA	148,164
177	Joliet	IL	147,344
178	Murfreesboro	TN	146,900
179	Midland	TX	146,038
180	Rockford	IL	145,609
181	Paterson	NJ	145,233
182	Savannah	GA	144,464
183	Bridgeport	CT	144,399
184	Torrance	CA	143,592
185	McAllen	TX	143,268
186	Syracuse	NY	142,327
187	Surprise	AZ	141,664
188	Denton	TX	141,541
189	Roseville	CA	141,500
190	Thornton	CO	141,464
191	Miramar	FL	141,191
192	Pasadena	CA	141,029
193	Mesquite	TX	140,937
194	Olathe	KS	140,545
195	Dayton	OH	140,407
196	Carrollton	TX	139,248
197	Waco	TX	139,236
198	Orange	CA	138,669
199	Fullerton	CA	138,632
200	Charleston	SC	137,566

US Armed Forces

The United States armed forces date to 1775, when America needed a defense force to protect the original 13 colonies from a British invasion. Today, there are six branches:

- The **United States Army** is the oldest (established June 14, 1775) and largest of the branches. Soldiers are responsible for performing land-based military operations. The US Army Military Academy is located at West Point, NY.

- The **United States Navy** mainly operates from the waters (seas and oceans) providing protection both in the water and in the air. The Continental Navy was created by Congress on Oct. 13, 1775. The US Naval Academy is located at Annapolis, Md.

- The modern-day **United States Air Force** was established Sept. 18, 1947, replacing the US Army Air Corps. Before the modern-day Air Force was created, it was an arm of the U.S. Army, dating to 1907. Airmen are responsible for carrying out aerial military operations. The US Air Force Academy is located at Colorado Springs, Colo.

- The **United States Marine Corps** is the smallest of the four branches under the Department of Defense. Marines provide both land and sea support to the Army, Navy, Air Force, and, in times of war, Coast Guard. The USMC was founded on Nov. 10, 1775.

- The **United States Coast Guard** is the only branch that falls under the Department of Homeland Security. The Coast Guard is multi-functional, with many peacetime missions, including maritime search and rescue, maritime law enforcement, marine environmental protection, and ports, waterways, and coastal security. Founded Aug. 4, 1790 as the Revenue-Marine.

- The **U.S. Space Force** was established on Dec. 20, 2019, within the Department of the Air Force. The Secretary of the Air Force has overall responsibility for the USSF, under the guidance and direction of the Secretary of Defense. The USSF is a military service that organizes, trains, and equips space forces to protect U.S. and allied interests in space and to provide space capabilities to the joint force. USSF responsibilities include developing military space professionals, acquiring military space systems, maturing the military doctrine for space power, and organizing space forces to present to our Combatant Commands.

Unlike active duty, **Reserve Soldiers** serve part time, allowing them to earn an extra paycheck, go to school, or work a civilian job while still maintaining many of the benefits of military service. The Reserves are the military's pool of extra resources and personnel. Reserve Soldiers perform critical jobs on a part-time basis.

The **National Guard** has a unique dual mission. Domestically, it serves at the state level to protect local communities. The Guard's federal mission is to support active-duty military forces in responding to threats abroad and humanitarian disasters. Army National Guard Soldiers hold civilian jobs or attend school while maintaining their military training part-time and are always ready to serve their community in the event of an emergency.

Land of the Free, Home of the Brave

US Army Bases and Facilities

Alabama
Anniston Army Depot
Fort Rucker
Redstone Arsenal
Alaska
Fort Greely
Fort Wainwright
Joint Base Elmendorf–Richardson
Arizona
Camp Navajo (Army National Guard)
Davis-Monthan AFB
Fort Huachuca
Yuma Proving Ground
Luke AFB
Arkansas
Robinson Maneuver Training Center (ARNG)
Fort Chaffee Maneuver Training Center (ARNG)
Pine Bluff Arsenal
California
Camp Beale
Camp Cooke
Camp Haan
Camp Roberts (ARNG)
Camp San Luis Obispo (ARNG)
Camp Pendleton
Fort Hunter Liggett
Fort Irwin
Los Alamitos Joint Forces Training Base
Los Angeles AFB
Military Ocean Terminal Concord
Naval Air Station North Island
Parks Reserve Forces Training Area
Presidio of Monterey
San Joaquin Depot
Sharpe Facility
Stockton's Rough & Ready Island
Tracy Facility
Sierra Army Depot
Colorado
Peterson AFB
Fort Carson
Fort Logan National Cemetery
Pueblo Chemical Depot
Rocky Mountain Arsenal
Connecticut
Camp Niantic (ARNG)
Delaware
Bethany Beach Training Site (ARNG)
District of Columbia
Fort Lesley J. McNair
Florida
Camp Blanding (ARNG)
Eglin Air Force Base
MacDill Air Force Base
Patrick Air Force Base
Hurlburt Field
Tyndall Air Force Base
Georgia
Camp Frank D. Merrill
Fort Benning
Fort Gordon
Fort Stewart
Hunter Army Airfield
Hawaii
Fort DeRussy (MWR Resort)
Hale Koa Hotel
Fort Shafter
Kunia Field Station
Pohakuloa Training Area
Schofield Barracks
Tripler Army Medical Center
Wheeler Army Airfield
Idaho
MTA Gowen Field Boise (ARNG)
Orchard Range TS Boise (ARNG)
TS Edgemeade Mountain Home (ARNG)
Illinois
Charles M. Price Support Center
Rock Island Arsenal
Camp Lincoln (ARNG)
Indiana
Camp Atterbury (ARNG)
Fort Benjamin Harrison
Muscatatuck Urban Training Center
Iowa
Camp Dodge
Fort Des Moines (ARNG)
Iowa Army Ammunition Plant
Kansas
Fort Leavenworth
Fort Riley
Great Plains Joint Training Area (ARNG)
Kansas Regional Training Institute (ARNG)
Nickel Hall Barracks (ARNG)
Smoky Hill Weapons Range (ANG)
Kentucky
Blue Grass Army Depot
Fort Campbell
Fort Knox
Louisiana
Barksdale Air Force Base
Camp Beauregard
Fort Polk
Peason Ridge Artillery Range
Maine
MTA Deepwoods (ARNG)
MTA Riley-Bog Brook (ARNG)
TS Caswell (ARNG)
TS Hollis Plains (ARNG)
Maryland
Aberdeen Proving Ground
Camp Fretterd Military Reservation (ARNG)
Fort Detrick
Fort George G. Meade
Massachusetts
Camp Curtis Guild (ARNG)
Camp Edwards (ARNG)
Fort Devens
Natick Army Soldiers Systems Center
Michigan
Camp Grayling (ARNG)
Detroit Arsenal
Fort Custer (ARNG)
Minnesota
Camp Ripley (ARNG)

Land of the Free, Home of the Brave

US Army Bases and Facilities

Fort Snelling (USAR)

Mississippi
Camp McCain (ARNG)
Camp Shelby
Mississippi Ordnance Plant

Missouri
Camp Clark (ARNG)
Fort Leonard Wood

Montana
Fort William Henry Harrison (ARNG)

Nebraska
Camp Ashland (ARNG)

Nevada
Hawthorne Army Ammunition Depot

New Hampshire
Center Strafford Training Site (ARNG)

New Jersey
Fort Dix (part of Joint Base McGuire)
Picatinny Arsenal
US Coast Guard Training Center Cape May

New Mexico
Kirtland AFB
Los Alamos Demolition Range
White Sands Missile Range

New York
Camp Smith (ARNG)
Fort Drum
Fort Hamilton
United States Military Academy
Watervliet Arsenal

North Carolina
Camp Butner (ARNG)
Camp Davis
Camp Mackall
Fort Bragg
Military Ocean Terminal Sunny Point

North Dakota
Camp Grafton (ARNG)

Ohio
Camp Perry (ARNG)
Camp Ravenna Joint Military Training Center (ARNG)
Camp Sherman (ARNG)

Oklahoma
Camp Gruber (ARNG)
Fort Sill
McAlester Army Ammunition Plant

Oregon
Camp Rilea (ARNG)

Pennsylvania
Carlisle Barracks
Fort Indiantown Gap (ARNG)
Harrisburg Military Post (ARNG)
Letterkenny Army Depot
New Cumberland Army Depot
Tobyhanna Army Depot

Rhode Island
Camp Fogarty (ARNG)
Fort Greene (USAR)
Camp Varnum (ARNG)

South Carolina
Fort Jackson
McEntire Joint National Guard Base (ARNG/ANG)

South Dakota
Fort Meade (ARNG)

Tennessee
Holston Army Ammunition Plant
Kingston Demolition Range
Milan Army Ammunition Plant

Texas
Camp Bowie
Camp Bullis
Camp Mabry
Camp Maxey
Camp Swift
Camp Stanley
Fort Wolters (ARNG)
Corpus Christi Army Depot
Fort Bliss
Fort Hood
Fort Sam Houston, part of Joint Base San Antonio
Martindale Army Airfield

Red River Army Depot

Utah
Camp W. G. Williams (ARNG)
Dugway Proving Ground
Fort Douglas (USAR)
Tooele Army Depot

Vermont
Camp Ethan Allen Training Site (ARNG)

Virginia
Camp Pendleton State Military Reservation (ARNG)
Fort A.P. Hill
Fort Belvoir
Fort Eustis, part of Joint Base Langley-Eustis
Fort Lee
Fort McNair (part of Joint Base Myer–Henderson Hall)
Fort Myer (also part of JBM-HH)
Fort Pickett (ARNG)
Judge Advocate General's Legal Center
Quantico Military Reservation
National Ground Intelligence Center
Radford Army Ammunition Plant
Warrenton Training Center

Washington
Camp Murray (ANG/ARNG)
Fort Lewis, part of Joint Base Lewis-McChord
Yakima Training Center

West Virginia
Camp Dawson Training Area (ARNG)

Wisconsin
Fort McCoy
Camp Williams (ARNG)

Wyoming
Guernsey Maneuver Area (ARNG)

Land of the Free, Home of the Brave

US Naval Bases and Facilities

California
NAWS China Lake
NB Coronado
NAS Lemoore
NPS Monterey
NAS North Island
NB Point Loma
NB Ventura County-NAS Point Mugu
NB Ventura County-NCBC Port Hueneme
Naval Base San Diego

Connecticut
NSB New London

Washington, D.C.
Washington Naval Yard
United States Naval Research Laboratory

Florida
Corry Station NTTC
NAS Jacksonville
NAS Key West
NS Mayport
NSA Orlando
NSA Panama City
NAS Pensacola
NAS Whiting Field

Georgia
Gen. Lucius D. Clay National Guard Center
NSB Kings Bay
Dobbins ARB

Guam
Naval Base Guam
Andersen Air Force Base

Hawaii
NS Barking Sands
Joint Base Pearl Harbor Hickam

Illinois
NS Great Lakes

Indiana
NSWC Crane Division

Louisiana
NASJRB New Orleans

Maine
Portsmouth NS

Maryland
Cryptologic Warfare Group Six
(Fort Meade)
NSA Annapolis
NAS Patuxent River
NSF Thurmont
United States Naval Academy
Indian Head Naval Surface Warfare Center
(in Maryland, but a part of NSASP of Dahlgren, Virginia)
Joint Base Andrews (USN/USAF)

Mississippi
NCBC Gulfport
NAS Meridian
NS Pascagoula

Nevada
NAS Fallon

New Jersey
NWS Earle
NAES Lakehurst

New York
NSA Saratoga Springs

Pennsylvania
NAS Willow Grove

Rhode Island
NS Newport

South Carolina
NSA Charleston

Tennessee
NSA Mid-South

Texas
NAS Corpus Christi
NAS JRB Fort Worth
NAS Kingsville

Virginia
Chesapeake NSGA
Naval Support Activity South Potomac
Training Support Center Hampton Roads
NAB Little Creek
NS Norfolk
NAS Oceana
Wallops Island ASCS
NWS Yorktown

Washington
NBK Bangor
NBK Bremerton
NAS Whidbey Island
NS Everett

West Virginia
NIOC Sugar Grove

Land of the Free, Home of the Brave

US Air Force Bases and Facilities

Alabama
Maxwell Air Force Base

Alaska
Clear Air Force Station
Eielson Air Force Base
Joint Base Elmendorf Richardson

Arizona
Davis–Monthan Air Force Base
Luke Air Force Base

Arkansas
Little Rock Air Force Base

California
Beale Air Force Base
Edwards Air Force Base
Los Angeles Air Force Base
March Joint Air Reserve Base
Travis Air Force Base
Vandenberg Air Force Base

Colorado
Buckley Air Force Base
Schriever Air Force Base
Peterson Air Force Base
United States Air Force Academy

Delaware
Dover Air Force Base

Washington, D.C.
Bolling Air Force Base

Florida
Cape Canaveral Air Force Station
Eglin Air Force Base
Hurlburt Field
MacDill Air Force Base
Patrick Air Force Base
Tyndall Air Force Base

Georgia
Moody Air Force Base
Robins Air Force Base

Hawaii
Joint Base Pearl Harbor Hickam

Idaho
Mountain Home Air Force Base

Illinois
Scott Air Force Base

Indiana
Grissom Joint Air Reserve Base

Kansas
McConnell Air Force Base

Louisiana
Barksdale Air Force Base
New Orleans Joint Reserve Base

Maryland
Joint Base Andrews

Massachusetts
Hanscom Air Force Base
Westover Joint Air Reserve Base

Michigan
Selfridge Air National Guard Base

Mississippi
Columbus Air Force Base
Keesler Air Force Base

Missouri
Whiteman Air Force Base

Montana
Malmstrom Air Force Base

Nebraska
Offutt Air Force Base

Nevada
Nellis Air Force Base

New Jersey
Joint Base McGuire-Dix-Lakehurst

New Mexico
Cannon Air Force Base
Holloman Air Force Base
Kirtland Air Force Base

North Carolina
Pope Air Force Base
Seymour Johnson Air Force Base

North Dakota
Grand Forks Air Force Base
Minot Air Force Base

Ohio
Wright-Patterson Air Force Base

Oklahoma
Altus Air Force Base
Tinker Air Force Base
Vance Air Force Base

South Carolina
Charleston Air Force Base
Shaw Air Force Base

South Dakota
Ellsworth Air Force Base

Tennessee
Arnold Air Force Base

Texas
Brooks City-Base
Dyess Air Force Base
Goodfellow Air Force Base
Lackland Air Force Base
Laughlin Air Force Base
Randolph Air Force Base
Sheppard Air Force Base

Utah
Hill Air Force Base

Virginia
Langley Air Force Base

Washington
Fairchild Air Force Base
JBLM McChord Field, Joint Base Lewis-McChord

Wyoming
Francis E. Warren Air Force Base

US Marine Corps Bases and Facilities

Arizona
MCAS Yuma

California
MCLB Barstow
MCB Camp Pendleton
MCAS Miramar
MCRD San Diego
Mountain Warfare Training Center
MCAGCC 29 Palms

Florida
MCSF Blount Island

Georgia
MCLB Albany

Hawaii
MCB Hawaii

North Carolina
MCAS Cherry Point
MCAS New River
MCB Camp Lejeune

South Carolina
MCAS Beaufort
MCRD Parris Island

Virginia
Henderson Hall
MCB Quantico

Washington, D.C.
Marine Barracks, Washington, D.C.

Abbreviations:
AFB   Air Force Base
ANG   Air National Guard
ARNG   Army National Guard

MCAS   Marine Corps Air Station
MCAGCC   Marine Corps Air Ground Combat Center
MCB   Marine Corps Base
MCLB   Marine Corps Logistics Base
MCRD   Marine Corps Recruit Depot
MCSF   Marine Corps

MWR   Morale Welfare Recreation

NAB   Naval Amphibious Base
NAS   Naval Air Station
NASJRB   Naval Air Station Joint Reserve Base
NAWS   Naval Air Weapons Station
NB   Naval Base
NIOC   Naval Information Operations Command
NSA   Naval Support Activity
NSB   Naval Submarine Base
NSF   Naval Support Facility
NSWC   Naval Surface Warfare Center
NWS   Naval Weapons Station

— Land of the Free, Home of the Brave —

Highest-Ranking US Military Officers

Seniority Order / Rank

		Officer	Service	Highest Rank	Date of Rank

1 1 George Washington   U.S. Army   General of the Armies   4 Jul 1776
Declared by a Congressional Act in 1976 to be the most senior United States officer of all time. Held the rank of lieutenant general in the United States Army during his lifetime, as well as a special rank of "General and Commander-in-Chief" of the Continental Army during the American Revolutionary War (originally commissioned to him by the Continental Congress on June 19, 1775).

2 1 John J. Pershing   U.S. Army   General of the Armies   3 Sep 1919
Only person to hold the rank of General of the Armies on active duty.

3 1 George Dewey   U.S. Navy   Admiral of the Navy   2 Mar 1899
Inaugural and sole holder of rank.

4 4 Winfield Scott   U.S. Army   Lieutenant general   29 Mar 1847
Second person in American history to hold the rank of lieutenant general after George Washington. Senior officer of the U.S. military during the Mexican-American War as well as the opening months of the American Civil War.

5 3 Ulysses S. Grant   U.S. Army   General of the Army   25 Jul 1866
Inaugural holder of the rank, which was a 19th-century equivalent to a modern-day four-star general (this differed from the 20th century rank of the same name which was clearly a five-star position).

6 3 David G. Farragut   U.S. Navy   Admiral   25 Jul 1866
Inaugural holder of the rank, granted by Congress due to services rendered as senior officer of the navy during the American Civil War.

7 3 William T. Sherman   U.S. Army   General of the Army   4 Mar 1869
Second holder of the rank "General of the Army". Grant, Sherman, and Sheridan wore four stars and held ranks equivalent to current four-star generals and admirals, one step higher than the Civil War-era rank of lieutenant general. This special version of the title General of the Army of the United States, Act of US Congress July 25, 1866, indicated that Congress intended only one person to have it at a time.

8 3 David D. Porter   U.S. Navy   Admiral   25 Jul 1866
Second person in the history of the United States Navy to hold the rank of admiral.

9 4 Stephen C. Rowan   U.S. Navy   Vice admiral   1 Aug 1870
Longest serving officer in the history of the United States Navy with 63 years of service and retirement at the age of 80.

10 3 Philip H. Sheridan   U.S. Army   General of the Army   1 Jun 1888
Final person in U.S. Army history to hold the Civil War-era rank "General of the Army". The rank was discontinued upon Sheridan's death and was not reactivated until World War II, then as a five-star position.

11 4 John Schofield   U.S. Army   Lieutenant general   5 Feb 1895
First Commanding General of the United States Army following the disestablishment of the rank General of the Army and first peacetime promotion to the permanent rank of lieutenant general.

12 4 Nelson A. Miles   U.S. Army   Lieutenant general   6 Jun 1900
Last Commanding General of the United States Army. Succeeded by Samuel Baldwin Marks Young, who became the first Chief of Staff. After this point in time, the Chief of Staff was by default considered the most senior officer of the United States Army.

13 3 Tasker H. Bliss   U.S. Army   General   6 Oct 1917
Second person promoted to the four-star rank of General in the 20th century (the other was John Pershing) for service in the National Army during the First World War.

Highest-Ranking US Military Officers

Seniority Order / *Rank*

		Officer	Service	Highest Rank	Date of Rank
14	2	**William D. Leahy**	U.S. Navy	Fleet Admiral	15 Dec 1944

First five-star officer appointed during the Second World War

15	2	**George C. Marshall**	U.S. Army	General of the Army	16 Dec 1944

Second officer promoted to five-stars. The initial promotion of these officers was spaced over a period of one week so as to match the original seniority held by the officers at the four-star level.

16	2	**Ernest J. King**	U.S. Navy	Fleet Admiral	17 Dec 1944

Third officer promoted to five-star rank

17	2	**Douglas MacArthur**	U.S. Army	General of the Army	18 Dec 1944

Fourth officer to hold five-star rank and second within the United States Army (after George Marshall). MacArthur was further considered for promotion to the "six star" position of General of the Armies, both during and following the Second World War.

18	2	**Chester W. Nimitz**	U.S. Navy	Fleet Admiral	19 Dec 1944

Fifth officer to hold five-star rank and the third within the United States Navy. Served as the first post-World War II Chief of Naval Operations.

19	2	**Dwight D. Eisenhower**	U.S. Army	General of the Army	20 Dec 1944

Later served as President of the United States. Required to resign his commission as a five-star officer during his term; five-star rank was reinstated after leaving office by President John F. Kennedy.

20	2	**Henry H. "Hap" Arnold**	U.S. Army	General of the Army	21 Dec 1944

Last of the initial five-star appointments during the Second World War.

——		**Henry H. "Hap" Arnold**	U.S. Air Force	General of the Air Force	7 May 1949

Five-star rank was converted to that of General of the Air Force in 1949. No other officer has held the Air Force five-star version since Arnold.

21	2	**William F. Halsey**	U.S. Navy	Fleet Admiral	11 Dec 1945

First of two post World War II promotions to five-star rank (the other being Omar Bradley).

22	2	**Omar Bradley**	U.S. Army	General of the Army	20 Sep 1950

Most recent officer in U.S. history to be promoted to five-star rank.

23	3	**Raymond A. Spruance**	U.S. Navy	Admiral	4 Feb 1944

A close contender for the rank of Fleet Admiral, his promotion was consistently blocked by Congressman Carl Vinson, but he was granted the full pay of an admiral on the retirement list in July 1948. The Spruance-class destroyer is named in his honor.

24	3	**George S. Patton**	U.S. Army	General	14 Apr 1945

Generally regarded as the most successful U.S. combat commander in Europe in World War II. A possible contender for the rank of General of the Army, he was killed in an automobile accident in 1945 before any such consideration.

25	3	**Matthew Ridgway**	U.S. Army	General	11 May 1951

Replaced Douglas MacArthur as senior officer during the Korean War, after MacArthur was relieved by Harry S. Truman. Later served as Chief of Staff of the United States Army.

Source: Wikipedia, based on Dept of the Army, U.S. Army Leadership Handbook: Skills, Tactics, and Techniques for Leading in Any Situation, Skyhorse Publishing; 1st edition (March 1, 2012) and Hearn, Chester, Navy: An Illustrated History: The U.S. Navy from 1775 to the 21st Century, Zenith Press; 1st edition (May 15, 2007)

US Medals and Honors

Civilian Medals and Honors

The Presidential Medal of Freedom - As the highest civilian award in the United States, the Presidential Medal of Freedom is given for an especially meritorious contribution to the security or national interests of the U.S., to world peace, or to cultural or other significant public or private endeavors. It may also be awarded to members of the military and non-citizens. First awarded in 1963, the medal can be additionally awarded "With Distinction" for especially important service.

The Congressional Gold Medal - The Congressional Gold Medal is the highest civilian award given by Congress. It is awarded for achievements that have a major impact on American history or culture. Awardees can be civilian or military personnel and are not required to be citizens. This medal is also given in silver and bronze. This medal was first awarded to Founding Father George Washington by the Second Continental Congress in 1776.

The National Medal of Arts - This is the highest award given to artists and arts patrons by the United States government. The National Medal of Arts is awarded to individuals or groups who "are deserving of special recognition by reason of their outstanding contributions to the excellence, growth, support, and availability of the arts in the United States." Recipients are selected by the National Endowment for The Arts. This medal was first awarded in 1984.

The Kennedy Center Honors - Awarded by the Kennedy Center's Board of Trustees, which is headed by the First Lady, this award is given by the President to honor outstanding contributions to U.S. art, music, theatre, film, and culture. This award was first given in 1978.

The National Medal of Science - The National Medal of Science was established by the 86th Congress in 1959 as a presidential award to be given to individuals "deserving of special recognition by reason of their outstanding contributions to knowledge in the physical, biological, mathematical, or engineering sciences." In 1980, Congress expanded this recognition to include the social and behavioral sciences.

The National Humanities Medal - This award honors individuals or groups whose work has "deepened the nation's understanding of the humanities and broadened our citizens' engagement with history, literature, languages, philosophy, and other humanities subjects." This medal succeeds the Charles Frankel Prize and was first awarded in 1997.

The National Medal of Technology and Innovation - This medal is awarded by the President of the United States to American inventors and innovators who have made significant contributions to the development of new and important technology. The award may be granted to a specific person, to a group of people, or to an entire organization or corporation. This medal was first awarded in 1985 as the National Medal of Technology.

Military Medals

Medal of Honor - The Medal of Honor is the nation's highest military award, bestowed upon members of the U.S. armed forces for acts of valor in combat. It's presented by the President in the name of Congress and was signed into law by President Abraham Lincoln in December 1861. There are three different designs for the Medal of Honor award: Army, Air Force, and Navy versions. (The Navy MOH can also be presented to Marines and Coast Guard members.) The award is given based on "conspicuous gallantry and intrepidity at the risk of life above and beyond the call of duty."

US Medals and Honors

The Army's Distinguished Service Cross, the Navy Cross, and the Air Force Cross - The military cross awards are presented to U.S. military members for extraordinary heroism in combat. In each branch, they are the second-highest military service awards. The Navy Cross can be presented to Marines and to Coast Guard members serving under the Department of the Navy. A new Coast Guard Cross was created by Congress in 2010 for extraordinary heroism in action while not operating under the Navy.

Silver Star - Awarded for gallantry in action, the Silver Star is the third-highest award for members of the armed forces in the U.S. It was first established in 1918 as the Citation Star but in 1932 it was replaced by a new design.

Distinguished Flying Cross - Established by the Air Corps Act in 1926, the Distinguished Flying Cross is awarded for "heroism or extraordinary achievement while participating in an aerial flight." The first award was given to Captain Charles Lindbergh in 1927 for his transatlantic flight from New York to Paris.

Purple Heart - The act of giving U.S. military awards was established by General George Washington on August 7, 1782, when he created the Badge of Military Merit, the predecessor of the Purple Heart, which was established in 1932. The Purple Heart is given to soldiers, sailors, airmen, Marines, and Coast Guard members wounded or killed in action in defense of the nation.

Wars Ranked by Military Combat Deaths			
1	World War II	1941-45	291,557
2	Civil War	1861-65	214,938
3	World War I	1917-18	53,402
4	Vietnam War	1955-75	47,424
5	Korean War	1950-53	33,686
6	Revolutionary War	1775-83	8,000
7	Iraq War	2003-2011	3,836
8	War of 1812	1812-15	2,260
9	War in Afghanistan	2001-present	1,833
10	Mexican-American War	1846-49	1,733

US Military Casualties by War

War	Dates	Deaths Combat	Deaths Other	Deaths Total	Casualties Wounded	Casualties Total	Missing
Revolutionary War	1775-83	8,000	17,000	25,000	25,000	50,000	
War of 1812	1812-15	2,260	12,740	15,000	4,505	20,000	
Creek War	1813-14			575		575	
First Seminole War	1817-18	47	0	47	36	83	
Black Hawk War	1832	47	258	305	85	390	
Second Seminole War	1835-42	328	1,207	1,535		1,535	
Mexican-American War	1846-48	1,733	11,550	13,283	4,152	17,435	
Third Seminole War	1855-58	26		26	27	53	
Civil War: Total	1861-65	214,938	450,000	655,000			
Civil War - U.S. Army		140,414	224,097	364,511	281,881	646,392	
Civil War - Confederate		94,000	195,000	290,000	194,026	483,026	
Indian Wars	1865-98	919			1,025	1,944	
Spanish-American War	1898	385	2,061	2,446	1,622	4,068	
Philippine-US War	1898-1913	1,020	3,176	4,196	2,930	7,126	
World War I	1914-18	53,402	63,114	116,516	204,002	320,518	3,350
World War II	1941-45	291,557	113,842	405,399	670,846	1,076,245	30,314
Korean War	1950-53	33,686	2,830	36,516	92,134	128,650	4,759
U.S.S.R. Cold War	1947-91	32		32	12	44	
China Cold War	1950-72	16		16		16	
Vietnam War	1955-75	47,424	10,785	58,209	153,303	211,454	1,587
Gulf War	1990-91	149	145	294	849	1,143	
Bosnia-Herzegovina	1995-2004	1	11	12		12	
Kosovo War	1998-99	4	14	18	N/A	18	2
War in Afghanistan	2001-present	1,833	383	2,216	20,050	22,266	
Iraq War	2003-11	3,836	961	4,497	32,222	36,710	2
Totals	1775-2019	666,441	673,929	1,354,664	1,498,240	2,852,901	40,031

Arlington National Cemetery

Arlington National Cemetery, across the Potomac River from Washington, D.C., is the final resting place for our country's finest leaders and most courageous heroes. Situated on 624 rolling, grassy acres, the cemetery holds 400,000 interments, contains 28 major and 142 minor monuments and memorials, and enshrines 396 Medal of Honor recipients. The Tomb of the Unknown Soldier stands on a hillside, constructed of 79 tons of Colorado marble, and opened to the public in 1932. The tomb contains the remains of soldiers from both World Wars and the Korean War, their identities known only to God. The Tomb of the Unknown Soldier has been perpetually guarded since July 2, 1937, by the U.S. Army. The 3rd U.S. Infantry Regiment ("The Old Guard") began guarding the Tomb on April 6, 1948.

On July 16, 1862, Congress passed legislation authorizing the government to purchase land for national cemeteries for military dead, and put the U.S. Army Quartermaster General in charge of this program. In May 1864, Union forces suffered large numbers of dead in the Battle of the Wilderness. Quartermaster General Montgomery C. Meigs determined that the Arlington Estate, former home of Confederate Gen. Robert E. Lee, was a most suitable location for a new cemetery. The first military burial at Arlington, for William Henry Christman, was made on May 13, 1864.

Five state funerals have been held at Arlington — Presidents William Howard Taft and John F. Kennedy, his two brothers, Senator Robert F. Kennedy and Senator Edward "Ted" Kennedy, and General of the Armies John J. Pershing.

US astronauts John Glenn, Gus Grissom, and Roger Chaffee are buried at Arlington. Memorials to the Space Shuttle *Challenger* crew, lost in 1986, and the Space Shuttle *Columbia* crew, lost in 2003, have been dedicated there. Five of the 14 lost shuttle astronauts are buried there.

Another famous memorial is the USS Maine Mast Memorial, which commemorates the 266 men who lost their lives aboard the *USS Maine* in Havana harbor in 1898.

The Victims of Terrorist Attack on the Pentagon Memorial covers a group burial site and commemorates the victims of the Pentagon, which was struck by terrorists on Sept. 11, 2001. The names of the 115 Pentagon employees and 10 contractors in the building, as well as the 53 passengers and six crew members aboard American Airlines Flight 77 (which crashed into the building), are inscribed on the memorial.

Arlington National Cemetery encapsulates America's history — a living tribute to our Nation's past and how it continues to thrive through the service and sacrifice of those willing to dedicate their life to its ideals.

American Battle Monuments Commission

The ABMC administers, operates, and maintains 26 permanent American military cemeteries, and 30 federal memorials, monuments, and markers, which are located in 17 foreign countries, the U.S. Commonwealth of the Northern Mariana Islands, and the British dependency of Gibraltar; three of the memorials are located within the US (Honolulu, New York City, San Francisco). These cemeteries and memorials are among the most beautiful and meticulously maintained shrines in the world.

In addition to grave sites, the World War I and II cemeteries, together with the three memorials on U.S. soil, also commemorate by name those U.S. service members who were missing in action, or lost or buried at sea during World War I, World War II, the Korean War, and the Vietnam War. There are 207,621 U.S. war dead from World War I and World War II commemorated at ABMC sites; this includes 30,973 interments and 4,456 memorializations for World War I, and 92,958 interments and 78,985 memorializations for World War II. Additionally, the names of 8,209 individuals listed as missing from the Korean War and 2,504 individuals from the Vietnam War are memorialized at ABMC's Honolulu Memorial. ABMC also administers Mexico City National Cemetery, Corozal American Cemetery in Panama, and Clark Veterans Cemetery in the Philippines. More than 15,000 members of the armed forces, veterans, and others are interred there.

―――――― Land of the Free, Home of the Brave ――――――

National Cemeteries

The Department of Veterans Affairs' (VA) National Cemetery Administration maintains 143 national cemeteries in 40 states (and Puerto Rico) as well as 33 soldier's lots and monument sites.

ALABAMA
Alabama National Cemetery
3133 Highway 119
Montevallo, AL 35115

Fort Mitchell National Cemetery
553 Highway 165
Ft. Mitchell, AL 36856

Mobile National Cemetery
1202 Virginia Street
Mobile, AL 36604

ALASKA
Fort Richardson National Cemetery
Bldg 58-512 Davis Hwy
Fort Richardson, AK 99505

Sitka National Cemetery
803 Sawmill Creek Road
Sitka, AK 99835

ARIZONA
National Memorial Cemetery of Arizona
23029 North Cave Creek Road
Phoenix, AZ 85024

Prescott National Cemetery
500 Highway 89 North
Prescott, AZ 86313

ARKANSAS
Fayetteville National Cemetery
700 Government Avenue
Fayetteville, AR 72701

Fort Smith National Cemetery
522 Garland Aveand South 6th St
Fort Smith, AR 72901

Little Rock National Cemetery
2523 Springer Boulevard
Little Rock, AR 72206

CALIFORNIA
Bakersfield National Cemetery
30338 East Bear Mountain Blvd.
Arvin, CA 93203

Fort Rosecrans National Cemetery
Cabrillo Memorial Drive
San Diego, CA 92106

Golden Gate National Cemetery
1300 Sneath Lane
San Bruno, CA 94066

Los Angeles National Cemetery
950 S Sepulveda Blvd.
Los Angeles, CA 90049

Miramar National Cemetery
5795 Nobel Drive
San Diego, CA 92122

Riverside National Cemetery
22495 Van Buren Blvd.
Riverside, CA 92518

Sacramento Valley National Cemetery
5810 Midway Road
Dixon, CA 95620

San Francisco National Cemetery
1 Lincoln Boulevard
Presidio of San Francisco
San Francisco, CA 94129

San Joaquin Valley National Cemetery
32053 W McCabe Rd.
Santa Nella, CA 95322

COLORADO
Fort Logan National Cemetery
4400 W. Kenyon Ave.
Denver, CO 80236

Fort Lyon National Cemetery
15700 County Road HH
Las Animas, CO 81054

Pikes Peak National Cemetery
10545 Drennan Road
Colorado Springs, CO 80925

DISTRICT OF COLUMBIA
Congressional Cemetery
Government Lots
1801 E Street, SE
Washington, DC 20003

FLORIDA
Barrancas National Cemetery
1 Cemetery Road
Pensacola, FL 32508

Bay Pines National Cemetery
10000 Bay Pines Boulevard North
St. Petersburg, FL 33708

Cape Canaveral National Cemetery
5525 U.S. Highway 1
Mims, FL 32754

Florida National Cemetery
6502 S.W. 102nd Avenue
Bushnell, FL 33513

Jacksonville National Cemetery
4083 Lannie Road
Jacksonville, FL 32218

Sarasota National Cemetery
9810 State Road 72
Sarasota, FL 34241

South Florida National Cemetery
6501 S. State Road 7
Lake Worth, FL 33449

St. Augustine National Cemetery
104 Marine Street
St. Augustine, FL 32084

Tallahassee National Cemetery
5015 Apalachee Parkway
Tallahassee, FL 32311

GEORGIA
Georgia National Cemetery
1080 Scott Hudgens Drive
Canton, GA 30114

Marietta National Cemetery
500 Washington Avenue
Marietta, GA 30060

HAWAII
National Memorial Cemetery
of the Pacific
2177 Puowaina Drive
Honolulu, HI 96813

IDAHO
Snake River Canyon National Cemetery
1585 East Elm Street (E 4150 N)
Buhl, ID 83316

ILLINOIS
Abraham Lincoln National Cemetery
20953 W. Hoff Road
Elwood, IL 60421

Alton National Cemetery
600 Pearl Street
Alton, IL 62002

Camp Butler National Cemetery
5063 Camp Butler Road
Springfield, IL 62707-9722

Danville National Cemetery
1900 East Main Street
Danville, IL 61832

Fort Sheridan National Cemetery
Vatner Road
Fort Sheridan, IL 60037

Mound City National Cemetery
141 State Highway 37
Mound City, IL 62963

Quincy National Cemetery
36th & Maine Street
Quincy, IL 62301

Rock Island National Cemetery
Bldg 118 Rock Island Arsenal
Rock Island, IL 61299

--- Land of the Free, Home of the Brave ---

National Cemeteries

Confederate Mound
Oak Woods Cemetery
1035 E 67th St
Chicago, IL 60637

North Alton Confederate Cemetery
635 Rozier Street
Alton, IL 62003

Rock Island Confederate Cemetery
Rodman Avenue
Rock Island Arsenal
Rock Island, IL 61299

INDIANA
Crown Hill National Cemetery
700 West 38th Street
Indianapolis, IN 46208

Marion National Cemetery
1700 East 38th Street
Marion, IN 46952

New Albany National Cemetery
1943 Ekin Avenue
New Albany, IN 47150

Crown Hill Cemetery
Confederate Plot
700 West 38th Street
Indianapolis, IN 46208

Woodlawn Monument Site
North 3rd Street and 4th Avenue
Terre Haute, IN 47802

IOWA
Keokuk National Cemetery
1701 J Street
Keokuk, IA 52632

Oakdale Cemetery Soldiers' Lot
Oakdale Memorial Gardens
2501 Eastern Avenue
Davenport, IA 52807

KANSAS
Fort Leavenworth National Cemetery
395 Biddle Boulevard
Fort Leavenworth, KS 66027

Fort Scott National Cemetery
900 East National Avenue
Fort Scott, KS 66701

Leavenworth National Cemetery
150 Muncie Road
Leavenworth, KS 66048

Baxter Springs City Soldiers' Lot
Baxter Springs City Cemetery
Baxter Springs, KS 66713

Mound City Cemetery Soldiers' Lot
Woodland Cemetery
Mound City, KS 66506

KENTUCKY
Camp Nelson National Cemetery
6980 Danville Road
Nicholasville, KY 40356

Cave Hill National Cemetery
701 Baxter Avenue
Louisville, KY 40204

Danville National Cemetery
277 North First Street
Danville, KY 40422

Lebanon National Cemetery
20 Hwy 208
Lebanon, KY 40033

Lexington National Cemetery
833 West Main Street
Lexington, KY 40508

Mill Springs National Cemetery
9044 West Highway 80
Nancy, KY 42544

Zachary Taylor National Cemetery
4701 Brownsboro Road
Louisville, KY 40207

Evergreen Cemetery Soldiers' Lot
25 South Alexandria Pike
Southgate, KY 41071

LOUISIANA
Alexandria National Cemetery
209 East Shamrock Street
Pineville, LA 71360

Baton Rouge National Cemetery
220 North 19th Street
Baton Rouge, LA 70806

Louisiana National Cemetery
303 W. Mount Pleasant Road
Zachary, LA 70791

Port Hudson National Cemetery
20978 Port Hickey Road
Zachary, LA 70791

MAINE
Togus National Cemetery
VA Medical & Regional Office Center
Togus, ME 4330

Mount Pleasant Cemetery
Soldiers' Lot
North Street
Augusta, ME 04330

MARYLAND
Annapolis National Cemetery
800 West Street
Annapolis, MD 21401

Baltimore National Cemetery
5501 Frederick Avenue
Baltimore, MD 21228

Loudon Park National Cemetery
3445 Frederick Avenue
Baltimore, MD 21228

Point Lookout Confederate Cemetery
Point Lookout
Ridge, MD 20680

MASSACHUSETTS
Massachusetts National Cemetery
Connery Avenue
Bourne, MA 02532

Woodlawn Cemetery Soldiers' Lot
Harvard Street
Ayer, MA 01432

MICHIGAN
Fort Custer National Cemetery
15501 Dickman Rd.
Augusta, MI 49012

Great Lakes National Cemetery
4200 Belford Road
Holly, MI 48442

Fort Mackinac Post Cemetery
Mackinac State Park
Mackinac Island, MI 49757

Lakeside Cemetery Soldiers' Lot
3781 Gratiot Street
Port Huron, MI 48060

MINNESOTA
Fort Snelling National Cemetery
7601 34th Avenue South
Minneapolis, MN 55450

MISSISSIPPI
Biloxi National Cemetery
400 Veterans Ave Bldg 1001
Biloxi, MS 39531

Corinth National Cemetery
1551 Horton Street
Corinth, MS 38834

Natchez National Cemetery
41 Cemetery Road
Natchez, MS 39120

MISSOURI
Jefferson Barracks National Cemetery
2900 Sheridan Road
St. Louis, MO 63125

Jefferson City National Cemetery
1024 E. McCarty Street
Jefferson City, MO 65101

Springfield National Cemetery
1702 East Seminole Street
Springfield, MO 65804

Land of the Free, Home of the Brave

National Cemeteries

Union Confederate Monument Site
227 E. 28th Street Terrace
Kansas City, MO 64108

MONTANA
Fort Missoula Post Cemetery
Guardsman Lane
Missoula, MT 59804

Yellowstone National Cemetery
55 Buffalo Trail Road
Laurel, MT 59044

NEBRASKA
Fort McPherson National Cemetery
12004 South Spur 56A
Maxwell, NE 69151

Omaha National Cemetery
14250 Schram Road
Omaha, NE 68138

Forest Lawn Cemetery Soldiers' Lot
Forest Lawn Memorial Park
7909 Mormon Bridge Road
Omaha, NE 68112

NEW JERSEY
Beverly National Cemetery
916 Bridgeboro Road
Beverly, NJ 08010

Finn's Point National Cemetery
454 Fort Mott Road
Pennsville, NJ 08070

NEW MEXICO
Fort Bayard National Cemetery
200 Camino De Paz
Fort Bayard, NM 88036

Santa Fe National Cemetery
501 North Guadalupe Street
Santa Fe, NM 87501

NEW YORK
Bath National Cemetery
San Juan Avenue
Bath, NY 14810

Calverton National Cemetery
210 Princeton Boulevard
Calverton, NY 11933

Cypress Hills National Cemetery
625 Jamaica Avenue
Brooklyn, NY 11208

Gerald B. H. Solomon Saratoga
National Cemetery
200 Duell Road
Schuylerville, NY 12871

Long Island National Cemetery
2040 Wellwood Avenue
Farmingdale, NY 11735

Woodlawn National Cemetery
1825 Davis Street
Elmira, NY 14901

Albany Rural Cemetery Soldiers' Lot
Cemetery Avenue
Albany, NY 12204

NORTH CAROLINA
New Bern National Cemetery
1711 National Avenue
New Bern, NC 28560

Raleigh National Cemetery
501 Rock Quarry Road
Raleigh, NC 27610

Salisbury National Cemetery
501 Statesville Boulevard
Salisbury, NC 28144

Wilmington National Cemetery
2011 Market Street
Wilmington, NC 28403

NORTH DAKOTA
Fargo National Cemetery
8709 40th Ave. N, County Road 20
Harwood, ND 58042

OHIO
Dayton National Cemetery
4400 West Third Street
Dayton, OH 45428

Ohio Western Reserve National
Cemetery
10175 Rawiga Road
Seville, OH 44273

Camp Chase Confederate Cemetery
2900 Sullivant Avenue
Columbus, OH 43204

Confederate Stockade Cemetery
Johnson's Island
Sandusky, OH 44870

Woodland Cemetery Soldiers' Lot
6901 Woodland Avenue
Cleveland, OH 44104

OKLAHOMA
Fort Gibson National Cemetery
1423 Cemetery Road
Ft. Gibson, OK 74434

Fort Sill National Cemetery
2648 NE Jake Dunn Road
Elgin, OK 73538

OREGON
Eagle Point National Cemetery
2763 Riley Rd.
Eagle Point, OR 97524

Roseburg National Cemetery
913 NW Garden Valley Blvd
Roseburg, OR 97471

Willamette National Cemetery
11800 SE Mt. Scott Blvd.
Portland, OR 97086

PENNSYLVANIA
Indiantown Gap National Cemetery
Indiantown Gap Rd.
Annville, PA 17003

National Cemetery of the Alleghenies
1158 Morgan Road
Bridgeville, PA 15017

Philadelphia National Cemetery
Haines St. and Limekiln Pike
Philadelphia, PA 19138

Washington Crossing National
Cemetery
830 Highland Road
Newtown, PA 18940

Allegheny Cemetery Soldiers' Lot
4734 Butler Street
Pittsburgh, PA 15201

Ashland Cemetery Soldiers' Lot
630 South Hanover Street
Carlisle, PA 17013

Mount Moriah Cemetery Soldiers' Lot
62nd Street and Kingsessing Ave.
Philadelphia, PA 19142

Mount Moriah Cemetery Naval Plot
62nd Street and Kingsessing Ave.
Philadelphia, PA 19142

Prospect Hill Cemetery Soldiers' Lot
700 North George Street
York, PA 17404

PUERTO RICO
Puerto Rico National Cemetery
Avenue Cementerio Nacional #50
Bayamon, PR 00961

SOUTH CAROLINA
Beaufort National Cemetery
1601 Boundary St.
Beaufort, SC 29902

Florence National Cemetery
803 E National Cemetery Rd.
Florence, SC 29501

Fort Jackson National Cemetery
4170 Percival Road
Columbia, SC 29229

SOUTH DAKOTA
Black Hills National Cemetery
20901 Pleasant Valley Drive
Sturgis, SD 57785

Fort Meade National Cemetery
Old Stone Rd.
Sturgis, SD 57785

Land of the Free, Home of the Brave

National Cemeteries

Hot Springs National Cemetery
VA Medical Center
Hot Springs, SD 57747

TENNESSEE
Chattanooga National Cemetery
1200 Bailey Ave.
Chattanooga, TN 37404

Knoxville National Cemetery
939 Tyson St. NW
Knoxville, TN 37917

Memphis National Cemetery
3568 Townes Ave.
Memphis, TN 38122

Mountain Home National Cemetery
215 Heroes Drive
Mountain Home, TN 37684

Nashville National Cemetery
1420 Gallatin Rd. S
Madison, TN 37115

TEXAS
Dallas-Fort Worth National Cemetery
2000 Mountain Creek Parkway
Dallas, TX 75211

Fort Bliss National Cemetery
5200 Fred Wilson Rd.
El Paso, TX 79906

Fort Sam Houston National Cemetery
1520 Harry Wurzbach Rd.
San Antonio, TX 78209

Houston National Cemetery
10410 Veterans Memorial Dr.
Houston, TX 77038

Kerrville National Cemetery
3600 Memorial Blvd.
Kerrville, TX 78028

San Antonio National Cemetery
517 Paso Hondo Street
San Antonio, TX 78202

UTAH
Fort Douglas Post Cemetery
405 Chipeta Way
Salt Lake City, UT 84108

VERMONT
Green Mount Cemetery Soldiers' Lot
250 State Street
Montpelier, VT 05602

Prospect Hill Cemetery Soldiers' Lot
94 South Main Street
Brattleboro, VT 05301

VIRGINIA
Alexandria National Cemetery
1450 Wilkes St.
Alexandria, VA 22314

Ball's Bluff National Cemetery
Rt. 7
Leesburg, VA 22075

City Point National Cemetery
10th Ave. and Davis St.
Hopewell, VA 23860

Cold Harbor National Cemetery
6038 Cold Harbor Road
Mechanicsville, VA 23111

Culpeper National Cemetery
305 US Ave.
Culpeper, VA 22701

Danville National Cemetery
721 Lee St.
Danville, VA 24541

Fort Harrison National Cemetery
8620 Varina Rd.
Richmond, VA 23231

Glendale National Cemetery
8301 Willis Church Rd.
Richmond, VA 23231

Hampton National Cemetery
1 Cemetery Rd.
Hampton, VA 23669

Hampton National Cemetery (VAMC)
VA Medical Center
Emancipation Drive
Hampton, VA 23667

Quantico National Cemetery
18424 Joplin Rd.
Triangle, VA 22172

Richmond National Cemetery
1701 Williamsburg Rd.
Richmond, VA 23231

Seven Pines National Cemetery
400 E Williamsburg Rd.
Sandston, VA 23150

Staunton National Cemetery
901 Richmond Ave.
Staunton, VA 24401

Winchester National Cemetery
401 National Ave.
Winchester, VA 22601

WASHINGTON
Fort Lawton Post Cemetery
Texas Way
Seattle, WA 98199

Tahoma National Cemetery
18600 SE 240th Street
Kent, WA 98042

Vancouver Barracks National Cemetery
1455 E 4th Plain Blvd.
Vancouver, WA 98663

WEST VIRGINIA
Grafton National Cemetery
431 Walnut St.
Grafton, WV 26354

West Virginia National Cemetery
42 Veterans Memorial Lane
Grafton, WV 26354

WISCONSIN
Wood National Cemetery
5000 W National Ave. Bldg. 1301
Milwaukee, WI 53295

Fort Winnebago Cemetery Soldiers' Lot
Highway EE
Portage, WI 53901

Forest Hill Cemetery Soldiers' Lot
One Speedway Road
Madison, WI 53705

Forest Home Cemetery Soldiers' Lot
2405 West Forest Home Avenue
Milwaukee, WI 53215

Fort Crawford Cemetery Soldiers' Lot
413 South Beaumont Road
Prairie du Chien, WI 53821

Mound Cemetery Soldiers' Lot
1147 West Boulevard
Racine, WI 53405

Big Battles, Minor Wars, Old Forts, Military Museums

Shiloh National Military Park
Off the beaten path on the Tennessee River, Shiloh (or Pittsburg Landing) is probably the nation's most pristine battlefield. It was here April 6-7, 1862 that nearly 110,000 untested troops clashed in a bloody battle that resulted in 23,746 casualties. It was the first mass-casualty battle of the Civil War. The quiet, scenic 4,200-acre site features a visitors center, national cemetery, 156 monuments, 217 cannons, more than 650 interpretive markers, and a 10-mile self-guided driving tour.

Gettysburg National Military Park
The largest battle in North America, fought July 1-3, 1863, at a small town in Pennsylvania, marked the high tide of the Confederacy. Up to that point, General Robert E. Lee had seemed invincible. He admitted he asked too much of his Army of Northern Virginia. George Meade's Federals held their ground and halted Lee's invasion. Later, President Lincoln would give his famous speech at the dedication of the Gettysburg cemetery. The massive park, which attracts one million visitors each year, features a modern visitors center, 1,328 monuments, markers, and memorials.

River Raisin National Battlefield Park
On Jan. 22, 1813, British forces and their Indian allies attacked the US camp at Frenchtown (present-day Monroe, Michigan). When US commanding general James Winchester was captured he surrendered, even though his left wing was still engaged. The British pledged to protect the wounded but withdrew during the night, leaving the disabled to be slaughtered by the Indians. Nine months later, US cavalry liberated Frenchtown and advanced into Canada, where they defeated Shawnee Chief Tecumseh's men, rallying to the cry, "Remember the Raisin!"

Battle of Fort Sanders
During his campaign to capture Knoxville, Tenn., Confederate Gen. James Longstreet's forces attacked small Fort Sanders, part of the city's defenses under Gen. Ambrose Burnside, on Nov. 29, 1863. The battle was a deadly comedy of errors, with the Federals fending off the attack and losing only eight men killed versus 813 Confederates killed, wounded, or captured. Longstreet withdrew and headed back to Virginia. Today, all traces of the fort are gone, marked only by a street-corner stone monument.

Kings Mountain National Military Park
Threatened by Major Patrick Ferguson, bands of Overmountain men journeyed to South Carolina to confront him and his Loyalist troops. The American victory Oct. 7, 1780 at Kings Mountain was a turning point in the Revolutionary War's southern campaign. Ferguson and all of his men were either killed or captured by the loosely organized Patriots. Except for Ferguson, the lopsided, one-hour battle was fought entirely by Americans. Nearby, Cowpens National Battlefield celebrates Gen. Daniel Morgan's Jan. 17, 1781 victory over bloodthirsty British cavalry chieftain Col. Banestre Tarleton.

Mabila
The Spanish conquistador Hernando de Soto and 600 men wandered for three years (1539-43) throughout the Southeast US in search of gold and treasure. On Oct. 18, 1540 the Spaniards battled Muskogee warriors under Chief Tuskaloosa at the fortified village of Mabila, believed to be located in the vicinity of present-day Selma, Ala. Approximately 3,000 Indians were killed and the village burned down, one of the deadliest battles of North America. DeSoto died later along the Mississippi River; his men wandered further into Texas and Mexico.

Yorktown Battlefield
With the help of the French, US troops under Gen. George Washington defeated the British army under General Lord Cornwallis, who surrendered on Oct. 19, 1781, effectively ending the War for Independence. The Treaty of Paris was signed two years later. Nearby attractions include Colonial Williamsburg, the Jamestown site, numerous Civil War battle sites, and the historic sites of Norfolk, Va.

Chalmette Battlefield
One of the greatest victories in US military history was earned on the plains of Chalmette, near New Orleans, La., over what was considered a vastly superior force of highly trained British troops under Gen. William Packenham. On Jan. 8, 1815, the British attacked a defensive line manned by the ragtag army of Gen. Andrew Jackson, including frontier riflemen, pirate artillerymen, freedmen of color, local militia, and others. The British were soundly defeated and suffered massive casualties. The Treaty of Ghent, ending the War of 1812, had been signed a month earlier but did not take effect until US ratification in mid-February.

Big Battles, Minor Wars, Old Forts, Military Museums

Battle of the Wabash
The greatest defeat of the US Army by Native-Americans occurred Nov. 4, 1791 at the headwaters of the Wabash River near the Indiana-Ohio border. Nine tribal bands organized into battle formation and attacked at dawn the camp of Gen. Arthur St. Clair. The fighting turned into a rout and massacre, with more than 900 casualties. The Indian warriors were led by Little Turtle of the Miamis, Blue Jacket of the Shawnees, and Buckongahelas of the Delawares. On Aug. 20, 1794, Major General "Mad Anthony" Wayne's Legion of the United States exacted revenge at the Battle of Fallen Timbers near modern-day Toledo.

Battle of Tippecanoe
On Nov. 7, 1811, forces under Indiana Territorial Gov. William Henry Harrison attacked and destroyed the Indian village known as Prophetstown at the Wabash and Tippecanoe rivers. The Prophet, a religious leader, was the brother of Shawnee leader Tecumseh, who was away recruiting. Harrison later became President; Tecumseh was killed at the Battle of the Thames in Canada in October 1813; the Prophet died in 1836.

Battle of Point Pleasant
In what has been described as the first battle of the War for Independence, the Battle of Point Pleasant (Kanawha) was fought on Oct. 10, 1774 between Virginia militia and Shawnee and Mingo warriors. Forces under the Shawnee Chief Cornstalk attacked Virginia militia under Colonel Andrew Lewis, hoping to halt Lewis' advance into the Ohio Valley. After a furious day-long battle, Cornstalk retreated. The Virginians, along with a second force led by Lord Dunmore, the Royal Governor of Virginia, marched into the Ohio Valley and compelled Cornstalk to agree to a treaty, ending Lord Dunmore's War.

Ox Hill Battlefield Park
The small 4.8-acre park nestled among the suburban office buildings of Fairfax, Va. tells the story of the Sept. 1, 1862 battle (also called Chantilly) between Federal Gens. Kearny and Stevens and Confederate Gens. Jackson and Stuart. The park, which includes less than five percent of the actual battlefield, holds the graves of Kearny and Stevens, both killed in the inconclusive battle. The well-designed park features extensive interpretive signage and a self-guided loop walkway (roughened to prevent skaters).

Horseshoe Bend National Military Park
At this bend in the Tallapoosa River in central Alabama, forces under Major Gen. Andrew Jackson, including David Crockett and Sam Houston, defeated the rebel Creek warriors known as Red Sticks on March 27, 1814. The battle ended the Creek War, resulted in a land cession of 23 million acres to the US, and created a national hero of Jackson.

Parker's Crossroads Battlefield
When Confederate forces were attacked in front and rear at this crossroads in West Tennessee on Dec. 31, 1862, Confederate cavalry commander Gen. Nathan Bedford Forrest responded by ordering, "Charge 'em both ways!" Eventually, the rebel forces were able to withdraw from the site and fight another day.

Black Patch War
In 1904-09, raisers of dark-fired tobacco in Kentucky and Tennessee, known as the Planters' Protective Association (PPA), fought with agents of the American Tobacco Company (ATC) owned by James B. Duke, one of the largest U.S. industrial monopolies. Farmers engaged in vigilante violence, with Night Riders raiding the Kentucky towns of Princeton, Hopkinsville, and Russellville, destroying tobacco stores. The war ended with the arrests of several raid leaders by the Kentucky State Guard. Growers received higher prices for their crops, and the tobacco trust was broken up.

Hoo Doo War
The Mason County, Texas war was ignited by an increase in cattle rustling in 1875-76 and involved mob lynchings and retaliatory murders. At least a dozen were killed, and the Texas Rangers got involved. The war was aggravated by hostilities among the settlers, German immigrants, and Native-Americans. In 1877, the county courthouse burned to the ground. Hoo Doo refers to masked members of a vigilance committee.

Coal Creek War
In 1891-92, coal miners in Anderson County, Tenn. struck against the Tennessee Coal, Iron and Railway Co. over its use of supervised convicts in the mines. The miners attacked company stockades and mines, with 27 miners killed and dozens of company personnel killed or wounded. The war ended when Governor Buchanan dispatched hundreds of militiamen under the command of General Samuel T. Carnes to East Tennessee. As a result, in 1896, the state refused to

Big Battles, Minor Wars, Old Forts, Military Museums

renew its labor contracts with the company.

Whiskey Rebellion
Hundreds of west Pennsylvania farmers and whiskey makers rebelled against new taxes by the federal government. In 1794, a tax inspector's home was attacked by a mob. After talks failed, President George Washington rode at the head of 13,000 militiamen from Virginia, Maryland, New Jersey, and Pennsylvania. The rebels scattered before the militia arrived. Resistance continued, but the "war" demonstrated that the new federal government was willing to use force to enforce its laws.

War of the Regulation
In 1765-71, colonists on the North Carolina frontier rose up against corrupt British colonial power centered in New Bern, resulting in the Battle of Alamance, May 16, 1771, in which Governor William Tyron's forces crushed the Regulators. Nine fatalities were suffered by each side. Six Regulators were later hanged.

Shay's Rebellion
Shay's Rebellion was an armed uprising in 1786-87 in western Massachusetts led by former soldier Daniel Shays. The protest, involving 4,000 rebels, contested taxes and economic policy. The rebels tried unsuccessfully to seize the Springfield armory. The rebellion was shut down by state militia. Six rebels were killed, and two were hanged. The struggle contributed to the rejection of the national Articles of Confederation.

King Philip's War
In 1675-78, war raged between New England colonists and indigenous peoples, resulting in 4,000 casualties and half the towns in Plymouth Colony attacked. The deadliest war in colonial America—a militia victory—was named for the Wampanoag chief who had adopted a European name.

Utah War
In 1857-58, President James Buchanan proclaimed Utah to be in rebellion and sent government troops to fight Mormon settlers, members of the Church of Latter-Day Saints, which had been persecuted for many years. The Mormon war generated no real battles and led to a temporary decline in Mormon influence, at least until Utah was declared a state in 1896.

LST 325
This historic WWII landing craft (Landing Ship-Tank) can be toured at its mooring on the Ohio River at Evansville, Ind. The cargo ship participated in the Normandy landings, among others. During the war, Evansville shipyards produced 167 of the massive ships. Trucks, P-47 Thunderbolt fighters, and .45-caliber ammunition were also produced in Evansville, in addition to Sherman tank overhauls. Ironically, *LST 325* was built at the Philadelphia, Pa. shipyards.

USS Alabama
This decommissioned WWII battleship (BB-60), along with the *USS Drum* submarine, can be toured at the memorial park in Mobile Bay, Ala. The massive 680-ft-long ship carried 1,793 officers and crew and boasted nine 16-in. guns, along with many smaller weapons. She frequently bombarded Japanese positions in support of amphibious assaults, and took part in the Mariana and Palau Islands campaigns, the Philippines campaign, and the Battle of Okinawa.

USS Yorktown
One of 24 Essex-class aircraft carriers built during WWII, her name commemorates the loss of the original *USS Yorktown* carrier at Midway. She served with distinction in the Korean and Vietnam wars, and was a recovery ship for the Apollo 8 space mission. Today she is a museum ship and National Historic Landmark moored at Patriots Point in Mount Pleasant, S.C., along with other warships and aircraft displays.

USS Cairo
Among the multitude of sites to see comprising the 1863 Vicksburg Campaign is the exhibit of the *USS Cairo* ironclad gunboat at Vicksburg National Military Park. Sunk by a mine on the nearby Yazoo River in 1862, the 180-foot-long behemoth was discovered and recovered during the 1960s. The gunboat, one of the City Class ironclads, was partially reconstructed, to include heavy guns and its steam boilers and engines. Hundreds of artifacts found during the recovery are displayed, telling the story of the life of a Federal sailor during the Civil War.

National Naval Aviation Museum
Located on a naval base in Pensacola, Fla., this top-flight museum covers the entire history of US naval aviation, from the early World War I-era aircraft

Big Battles, Minor Wars, Old Forts, Military Museums

carriers and flying boats to the War in the Pacific, 1941-45, to the age of modern jets. Featured are outstanding displays of 150 artifacts and aircraft, indoors and out, plus videos on the giant high-resolution screen, the new Apollo 11 experience, flight simulators, trainers, and demonstrations by the world-famous Blue Angels naval aviators.

Steven F. Udvar-Hazy Center
Part of the Smithsonian system but located at Washington Dulles International Airport, this huge museum displays hundreds of aircraft, both commercial and military, from all eras, including the Space Shuttle *Discovery*, a Concorde airliner, and the B-29 bomber that dropped the first atomic bomb. In addition, the National Air and Space Museum on the National Mall in downtown Washington, D.C. has thousands of objects on display, including the 1903 Wright Flyer and Neil Armstrong's Apollo 11 spacesuit.

Virgil I. Grissom Memorial Museum
Located in Spring Mill State Park, Indiana, this small museum covers the legacy of astronaut Gus Grissom, who flew into space during the Mercury and Gemini projects and was tragically killed in the Apollo I fire. Of particular interest is the *Molly Brown* Gemini capsule and the corned-beef sandwich stowed during the Gemini 3 flight. Also, there is the Grissom Monument in Mitchell, Ind. and the Grissom Air Museum in Peru, Ind. The Neil Armstrong Air and Space Museum is located in Wapakoneta, Ohio.

NRA National Firearms Museum
The National Rifle Association museum in Fairfax, Va. displays a huge collection of historic firearms, including 15 galleries comprising 85 exhibit cases housing 3,000 firearms. The Robert E. Petersen Gallery displays firearms masterpieces, while another gallery shows guns used in Hollywood movies.

National Atomic Testing Museum
This Smithsonian affiliate not far off the Las Vegas Strip showcases 70 years of nuclear weapons testing, especially at the nearby Nevada Test Site. Back in the Fifties, tourists could view atomic mushroom clouds from casino row. See a replica of the Control Point where the countdown was conducted before each nuclear detonation and experience a Ground Zero Theater simulation of an above-ground test.

National WWII Museum
The huge site in downtown New Orleans, La. includes a giant video experience, galleries of aircraft, vehicles, and boats, and two giant exhibit halls — one covering the European Theater, the war against Germany and Italy; and one on the Pacific Theater war against Japan. There's even an official host hotel and convention center on site.

National WWI Museum and Memorial
Located in Kansas City, Mo., the Liberty Memorial was constructed in 1926 and recently renovated. In 2006, the new museum opened with 80,000-sq.-ft. of exhibit space and 330,000 artifacts. The Liberty Memorial Tower rises 217 feet above the main courtyard, and is designated a National Historic Landmark.

George Rogers Clark National Historic Park
Located along the Wabash River in Vincennes, Ind., the round classical temple-like memorial features a bronze statue of Clark and seven murals depicting his hazardous journey into the Illinois Territory to capture the British fort at Sackville in 1779. This victory led to the settlement of what is now the modern Midwest. Also in town is Grouseland, the frontier home of William Henry Harrison, governor of the Indiana Territory and future US President.

Jefferson Davis Memorial State Historic Site
Located near his birthplace in Fairview, Ky., the small site features a 351-ft.-tall obelisk, the tallest unreinforced concrete structure in the world and fourth-tallest monument in the USA. There is an observation deck at the top and a visitors center at the bottom, commemorating the President of the Confederate States of America, 1861-65.

National D-Day Memorial
This museum, much of it outdoors on 88 acres, is located in the Blue Ridge mountains of Bedford, Va., home of the famous Bedford Boys. The memorial commemorates the June 6, 1944 invasion and landings at Normandy, France. A guided walking tour is included with admission.

Fort Pulaski National Monument and Fort McAlister State Historic Park
Brick versus sand. Located at the mouth of the Savannah River, the monumental Fort Pulaski was captured in 1862 by Federal forces in 30 hours through use of rifled cannon to demolish the brick structure.

Big Battles, Minor Wars, Old Forts, Military Museums

Nearby is Old Fort Jackson, built in 1808 and manned during the War of 1812. Located on the south bank of the Great Ogeechee River, Fort McAlister is the most well-preserved earthwork fortification of the Confederacy. The sand and mud earthworks were attacked seven times by Federal ironclads but did not fall until captured in 1864 by Gen. William T. Sherman.

Fort Sumter National Monument
The Civil War commenced in April 1861 when Confederate artillery fired upon Fort Sumter (built in 1829) in Charleston Harbor. A day later, Major Robert Anderson surrendered the fort. Now a major tourist attraction, the island fort is accessible only by boat.

Fort Negley and Fortress Rosecrans
Fort Negley, a European-style fortress designed by Gen. James St. Clair Morton, was the largest stone fortification built during the Civil War. It was the showpiece of the extensive Nashville, Tenn. fortifications. A modern visitors center interprets the impressive ruins. Built in 1863 at nearby Murfreesboro, Fortress Rosecrans (named for the Federal commanding general) was a massive fortified supply depot along the railroad to Chattanooga and Atlanta. Some earthworks have been preserved.

Old Stone Fort State Archaeological Park
Initially believed to be a fort built by a lost civilization, this structure was built during the Middle Woodland Period, 1,500-2,000 years ago, by Native Americans. The ceremonial grounds, used for 500 years, are ringed by stone walls and an intricate entrance port. The site near Manchester, Tenn. features a visitors center and recreational facilities.

Fort Necessity National Battlefield
The battle at Fort Necessity in 1754 in southwest Pennsylvania was the opening action of the French and Indian War. The conflict forced out the French and set the stage for the Revolutionary War. The site includes an interpretive center, reconstructed fort, Fort Washington Tavern, and the gravesite of British General Braddock.

Forts Henry and Donelson
The 1862 capture of Fort Henry on the Tennessee River and Fort Donelson on the Cumberland River paved the way for the Federal army-navy invasion of the Mid-South and capture of Nashville. Fort Donelson National Battlefield features reconstructed river batteries and a visitors center; Fort Henry, however, is now underwater.

Fort Monroe National Monument
The Casemate Museum (1951) is located within the moat area of Fort Monroe (1822-47), America's largest stone fort. The fort at Hampton, Va. remained a major Union stronghold throughout the Civil War. It bore witness in 1862 to the first battle between ironclad gunboats, the *USS Monitor* and the *CSS Virginia*. Confederate President Jefferson Davis was imprisoned here after the war. The site totals 565 acres and includes 170 historic buildings.

Castillo de San Marcos National Monument
Located in St. Augustine, Fla., the colonial Spanish stone fortress was built 1672-95 and sits on 2.5 acres. St. Mark's Castle is the oldest masonry fort in the USA, built when Florida was part of the Spanish empire. Its works were built with coquina, stone made from shells. To the north, in Jacksonville, Fort Caroline was a settlement built by the French in 1564.

Natural Bridge
Perhaps the nation's first tourist attraction, this 215-foot-tall limestone gorge carved out by Cedar Creek in Virginia was once explored by George Washington and Thomas Jefferson. The National Historic Landmark in Rockbridge County is now the center of extensive tourist attractions.

Fort Jefferson National Monument
Fort Jefferson (1846) is a massive but unfinished coastal fortress, the largest brick masonry structure in the USA. The fort is located on Garden Key in the lower Florida Keys within the Dry Tortugas National Park, 68 miles west of the island of Key West. It is accessible only by boat.

Shot Tower State Park
Overlooking the New River in Virginia, the rectangular stone shot tower was built more than 200 years ago to make ammunition for the early settlers. Lead from the nearby Austinville Mines was melted in a kettle atop the 75-foot tower and poured through a sieve, falling through the tower and an additional 75-foot shaft beneath the tower into a kettle of water. Tourists can ascend the tower, which is on the National Register of Historic Places.

Old Hickory Smokeless Gunpowder Plant
The world's largest smokeless gunpowder plant was

Big Battles, Minor Wars, Old Forts, Military Museums

built well within a year by E.I. du Pont de Nemours & Company for the federal government at Hadley's Bend, Nashville, Tenn. At the time of the Nov. 11, 1918 armistice, the plant was 90 percent complete and producing almost one million pounds of gunpowder per day. In addition to the plant, housing for the thousands of workers had to be built, plus a village of houses for the plant workers, both labor and management. At the end of WWI, the plant was shut down; no gunpowder was ever shipped overseas. Eventually the gunpowder inventory exploded, with fire consuming half the abandoned plant. A dam and reservoir in the 1950s covered more of the site, which today is occupied mainly by an auto auction lot.

Clinton Engineer Works

The Manhattan Project during WWII built a huge processing facility on a secret, guarded 58-sq.-mile reservation in the hollers of East Tennessee with the sole purpose of enriching enough uranium to fuel an atomic bomb. To hedge their bets, Army engineers tried four different processes, with gaseous diffusion and electro-magnetic separation most successful. Tourists today can see the X-10 Graphic Reactor (test project for producing plutonium), and sites at the Y-12 and K-25 complexes. At one time, the K-25 site was the largest building in the world.

Arnold Engineering Development Complex

Built during the Cold War, this aerospace testing and simulation facility near Tullahoma, Tenn. features wind-tunnel and projectile testing, metallurgical testing, space chamber simulations, and jet-engine and rocket test cells. Nearly all modern jet engines, aircraft (military and commercial), missile stores, and small rocket engines were tested at some phase here. During WWII, Camp Forrest here housed prisoners of war and detainees, and hosted the training of Army Rangers and maneuvers for Gen. Patton's tank crews. Tours are by appointment only.

George C. Marshall Space Flight Center

Site of the Redstone Arsenal, this NASA facility in Huntsville, Ala. saw former German rocket scientist Werner von Braun and associates design and test the massive Saturn V rocket booster and its powerful F-1 engines that sent US astronauts to the Moon. It is best known today for the US Space and Rocket Center and its popular Space Camp.

Project Pluto

This US military project (1957-64) sought to develop a nuclear-powered ramjet that would power a cruise missile, called SLAM (Supersonic Low Altitude Missile). Although tests were conducted in Nevada, the "atomic crowbar" concept was deemed too catastrophic to complete, as the missile would spew radioactive waste wherever it flew; it could stay aloft indefinitely; and there was no means by which to shoot it down. Efforts to develop nuclear-powered military aircraft also proved unsuccessful and too dangerous.

Gladiators of the Gridiron

On the rim of the southeastern deck of Neyland Stadium in Knoxville, Tenn. are the names of four Tennessee Volunteers who made the ultimate sacrifice in World War Two — Bill Nowling, Rudy Klarer, Willis Tucker, and Clyde Fuson. At a street-level concourse is a bronze statue of famed Tennessee football coach General Robert Neyland. Among other honors, Neyland coached teams that won four national championships and completed nine undefeated seasons (in one seven-year stretch his teams lost two games and tied five). Neyland was a West Point graduate and excellent athlete — boxing champion three years in a row, all-star baseball pitcher (20 consecutive wins), and member of Army's national football champions. During WWII, Neyland, who was an engineer (he designed Neyland Stadium), supervised military logistics operations in Calcutta, India. At that same time, a former Vols player and U.S. Marine, Austin Shofner, was participating in the breakout from the Japanese prison camp at Davao, The Philippines, which housed the survivors of the Bataan Death March. When the escapees were on the verge of collapse, Shofner, recalling the maxims learned from Coach Neyland, inspired the fugitives to carry on. Long story short, the escapees were rescued by submarine and were able to reveal the horrors of the Bataan Death March to US officials and eventually the world. Shofner taught at Camp Lejeune and returned to combat duty in The Philippines. He died in 1999, at the rank of brigadier general. Brig. Gen. Neyland died in 1962, having been inducted into the National Football Hall of Fame in 1956.

HISTORY OF US SPACE PROGRAM

National Aeronautics and Space Administration (NASA)

Project Mercury (1958-63)

There were 20 unmanned missions, several of them failures. On Jan. 31, 1961, a chimpanzee named Ham went aloft for 16 min. The launch vehicles were the Mercury Atlas and the Mercury Redstone.

On May 5, 1961, Alan Shepard in Freedom 7 was the first American launched into space, from Cape Canaveral (later Cape Kennedy), Florida. He flew for 15 min., 22 sec. (The Soviets had launched cosmonaut Yuri Gagarin for a single orbit on April 12th.)

On July 21, astronaut Gus Grissom flew for 15 min. in Liberty Bell 7, the capsule lost upon ocean splash-down. It was later recovered.

The next year, on Feb. 20, John Glenn orbited the Earth three times in Friendship 7. He would later become a US Senator from Ohio, and ride on the Space Shuttle.

On May 24, 1962, Scott Carpenter flew for 3 orbits in Aurora 7.

Wally Schirra orbitted six times in Sigma 7 on Oct. 3, 1962.

The final Mercury mission was Faith 7 in which Gordon Cooper completed 22 orbits on May 15, 1963. The mission lasted more than 34 hours.

The other original Mercury 7 astronaut was Deke Slayton, who did not fly due to medical conditions but served ably as Director of Flight Crew Operations.

The Mercury capsules can be viewed at:

Freedom 7	JFK Library and Museum, Boston
Liberty Bell 7	Kansas Cosmosphere and Space Center, Hutchinson
Friendship 7	National Air and Space Museum, Washington, D.C.
Aurora 7	Museum of Science and Industry, Chicago
Sigma 7	US Astronaut Hall of Fame, Kennedy Space Center
Faith 7	Johnson Space Center, NASA, Houston

Project Gemini (1961-66)

The launch vehicle for all missions was the Titan II, a modified ICBM. The command pilot is listed first. The first two missions were unmanned in order to test heat shield and other components.

On March 23, 1965, Gemini 3 flew 3 orbits, manned by Grissom and John Young.

On June 3-7, 1965, Jim McDivitt and Ed White flew Gemini IV for 4 days, including a space walk by White.

On Aug. 21-29, 1965, Gemini V completed 120 orbits with Cooper and Pete Conrad onboard.

On Dec. 4-18, 1965, Gemini VII was aloft with Frank Borman and Jim Lovell for 14 days, and used Gemini VI-A (Schirra and Thomas Stafford) as a docking rendezvous target. Gemini VI was cancelled after the launch of the Agena docking target failed. Gemini VI-A was aloft for little more than one day.

HISTORY OF US SPACE PROGRAM

On March 16-17, 1966, Gemini VIII accomplished first docking with another space vehicle, an uncrewed Agena. While docked, a Gemini spacecraft thruster malfunction caused near-fatal tumbling of the craft, which, after undocking, Neil Armstrong was able to overcome; the first emergency landing of a crewed U.S. space mission. David Scott was the secondary pilot.

On June 3-6, 1966, Gemini IX-A with Stafford and Gene Cernan completed 44 orbits but failed to dock because the shroud on the docking vehicle did not deploy.

On July 18-21, 1966, Gemini X did 43 orbits, with Young commanding and Mike Collins performing a 49-min. space walk.

On Sept. 12-15, 1966, Gemini XI went 44 obits, with Conrad commanding and Richard Gordon making two space walks.

Finally, on Nov. 11-15, 1966, Lovell and Buzz Aldrin aboard Gemini XII docked with Agena and performed space walk (5.5 hrs.) while attached.

The Gemini capsules can be viewed at:

Gemini 1	Intentionally disintegrated upon re-entry into the atmosphere
Gemini 2	Air Force Space and Missile Museum, Cape Canaveral Air Force Station
Gemini III	Grissom Memorial, Spring Mill State Park, Mitchell, Ind.
Gemini IV	National Air and Space Museum, Washington, D.C.
Gemini V	Johnson Space Center, NASA, Houston
Gemini VI	Stafford Air & Space Museum, Weatherford, Okla.
Gemini VII	Steven F. Udvar-Hazy Center, Chantilly, Va.
Gemini VIII	Armstrong Air and Space Museum, Wapakoneta, Ohio
Gemini IX	Kennedy Space Center, NASA, Merritt Island, Fla.
Gemini X	Kansas Cosmosphere and Space Center, Hutchinson
Gemini XI	California Museum of Science and Industry, Los Angeles
Gemini XII	Adler Planetarium, Chicago

Project Apollo

Three unmanned flights of the Saturn IB (a smaller version of the Saturn V) were flown in 1966.

Apollo I was not flown, following a fire on the launch pad Jan. 27, 1967 in which all three astronauts—Grissom, White, and Roger Chaffee—were killed. An intensive investigation followed, with three unmanned flights of the Saturn V rocket (Apollo 4-5-6) occurring in Nov. 1967 and January and April 1968.

Apollo 7: On Oct. 11-22, 1968, Schirra, Walt Cunningham, and Donn Eisele went up in a Saturn IB and performed first live TV transmission and flew 163 orbits in 10 days.

Apollo 8: On Dec. 21-27, 1968, Borman, Lovell, and Bill Anders flew the first Saturn V rocket mission, and the first crewed flight to the Moon, during Christmas-time, orbitting the Moon 10 times before returning home.

HISTORY OF US SPACE PROGRAM

Apollo 9: On March 3-13, 1969, McDivitt, Scott, and Rusty Schweickart tested the lunar lander in Earth orbit.

Apollo 10: On May 18-26, 1969, Stafford, Young, and Cernan rehearsed the lunar landing, flying in the lander to within 50,000 ft. of the lunar surface.

Apollo 11: On July 16-24, 1969, Armstrong, Aldrin, and Collins flew to the Moon, and on July 20th, Armstrong and Aldrin landed in the Eagle on the lunar surface at Tranquility Base while Collins orbited the Moon in Columbia. The astronauts performed experiments on the Moon for 2.5 hrs. The first to step on the Moon, Armstrong said, "That's one small step for [a] man, one giant leap for mankind." Beating the Soviets to the Moon was a significant goal of the Cold War, fulfilling President Kennedy's promise in 1961.

Apollo 12: On Nov. 14-24, 1969, Conrad and Gordon spent 7:45 hrs. on the lunar surface while Alan Bean manned the Command Module.

Apollo 13: Lovell, Jack Swigert, and Fred Haise launched on April 11, 1970 but had to return to Earth early (April 17th) due to an explosion aboard their Service Module. They orbited the Moon and then used the Lunar Module (lander) as a "lifeboat" to survive until splashdown.

Apollo 14: On Jan. 31-Feb. 9, 1971, Shepard and Stuart Roosa walked on the moon for 9:21 hr., with Edgar Mitchell as Command Module pilot. Shepard hit a golf ball while on the Moon.

Apollo 15: July 26-Aug. 7, 1971. Scott and James Irwin walked on the Moon, with Alfred Worden circling above. First use of Lunar Roving Vehicle. Set multiple records for duration.

Apollo 16: April 16-27, 1972. Young and Charlie Duke spent three days on the Moon, drove 16 miles, and collected 200 lbs. of lunar samples while Ken Mattingly flew the Command Module.

Apollo 17: Dec. 7-19, 1972. Cernan and Harrison Schmitt, a geologist spent 22 hrs. on the Moon and collected 243 lbs. of soil and rocks. Ronald Evans was the Command Module Pilot.

The Apollo Command Modules can be viewed at:

Apollo 1 Command Module	NASA Langley Research Center, Hampton
Apollo 7 Command Module	Frontiers of Flight Museum, Dallas
Apollo 8 Command Module	Museum of Science and Industry, Chicago
Apollo 9 Command Module "Gumdrop"	San Diego Air & Space Museum
Apollo 10 Command Module "Charlie Brown"	Science Museum, London, England
Apollo 11 Command Module "Columbia"	National Air and Space Museum, Washington, DC
Apollo 12 Command Module "Yankee Clipper"	Virginia Air & Space Center, Hampton
Apollo 13 Command Module "Odyssey"	Kansas Cosmosphere and Space Center
Apollo 14 Command Module "Kitty Hawk"	Kennedy Space Center, Florida
Apollo 15 Command Module "Endeavour"	National Museum of the US Air Force, Dayton
Apollo 16 Command Module "Casper"	US Space & Rocket Center, Huntsville
Apollo 17 Command Module "America"	Johnson Space Center, Houston

HISTORY OF US SPACE PROGRAM

Skylab was the first US space station, launched by NASA, occupied for about 24 weeks between May 1973 and February 1974, by three separate three-astronaut crews. Major operations included an orbital workshop, a solar observatory, Earth observation, and hundreds of experiments. Unable to be re-boosted by the Space Shuttle, which was not ready until the early 1980s, Skylab's orbit decayed and it burned up in the atmosphere on July 11, 1979, over the Indian Ocean.

The **Space Shuttle** (Space Transportation System or STS) was a partially reusable low Earth orbital spacecraft system operated by NASA from 1981 to 2011. Five complete Space Shuttle orbiter vehicles were built and flown on a total of 135 missions, launched from the Kennedy Space Center (KSC) in Florida. Operational missions launched numerous satellites, interplanetary probes, and the Hubble Space Telescope (HST); conducted science experiments in orbit; and participated in construction and servicing of the International Space Station.

Four fully operational orbiters were initially built: *Columbia, Challenger, Discovery,* and *Atlantis*. Of these, two were lost in mission accidents: *Challenger* on Jan. 28, 1986 during an explosion 73 sec. after launch (civilian schoolteacher Christa McAuliffe was one of the crew); and *Columbia* during re-entry on Feb. 1, 2003, with a total of 14 astronauts killed. A fifth operational orbiter, *Endeavour,* was built in 1991 to replace *Challenger*. The *Enterprise* performed flight tests but was not capable of spaceflight. The Space Shuttle was retired from service following *Atlantis'* final flight on July 21, 2011. The U.S. relied on the Russian Soyuz spacecraft to transport astronauts to the International Space Station from the last Shuttle flight until the first Commercial Crew Development launch on May 30, 2020.

The Space Shuttles can be viewed at:

Shuttle *Atlantis*	Kennedy Space Center Visitor Complex
Shuttle *Discovery*	Steven F. Udvar-Hazy Center
Shuttle *Endeavour*	California Science Center
Shuttle *Enterprise*	Intrepid Sea, Air & Space Museum, NYC

MONUMENTS, ENGINEERING MARVELS OF THE USA

The USA is a land of massive engineering projects and innovative structures, some defying possibilities and imagination. Monuments have been built that memorialize significant persons and achievements. There are 247 Historic Civil Engineering Landmarks in the USA, as designated by the American Society of Civil Engineers.

Erie Canal, New York
When it was completed in 1825, the 363-mile canal, connecting the Great Lakes with the Atlantic Seaboard, was the second longest in the world. Canal fever swept most of the nation, e.g., the Chesapeake & Delaware Canal.

Holland Tunnel, New York City
Opened in 1927, the tunnel designed by Clifford Holland was the longest continuous underwater vehicular tunnel in the world, connecting lower Manhattan with New Jersey. Also, the first to use a mechanical ventilation system. The Lincoln Tunnel also serves the city. Other notable tunnels are the Detroit-Windsor Tunnel; the Boston Big Dig tunnels; the Cumberland Gap tunnel; the Eisenhower-Johnson Memorial Tunnel in the Colorado Rockies; Chesapeake Bay Bridge-Tunnel; the Cowan (Tenn.) Railroad Tunnel (1852); and the Narrows of the Harpeth (290-ft. diversion tunnel built 1818 with slave labor and gunpowder). Also notable are subway systems of major cities such as New York City and Washington, DC.

Brooklyn Bridge, New York City
John and Washington Roebling's masterpiece spanned the East River, connecting Manhattan with Brooklyn. The beautiful suspension bridge (1870-83) measures 1,595 feet, the longest suspension bridge in the world at the time of its opening. The structure cost $15 million and required 600 workers. The innovative bridge is a National Historic Landmark.

John A. Roebling Suspension Bridge, Cincinnati
Roebling's first bridge, linking Cincinnati and Covington, Kentucky. With a span of 1,057 feet, it was the longest suspension bridge in the world when it was completed in 1867 over the Ohio River.

Eads Bridge, St. Louis
The first steel-truss bridge in the world was built in 1874, spanning the Mississippi River, allowing uninterrupted travel. The engineer, James Buchanan Eads, was one of the country's most brilliant.

Golden Gate Bridge, San Francisco
Completed in 1937 and designed by Joseph Strass, this beautiful and graceful suspension bridge spans the Golden Gate between the San Francisco Bay and the Pacific Ocean, a length of 1.7 miles. At the time of its opening, it was the tallest bridge at 746 feet. Often covered by fog, the orange-painted structure is probably the most photographed bridge in the world.

Transcontinental Railroad
The Central Pacific and the Union Pacific railroads met in 1869, marking the completion of tracks from Sacramento, Calif. to the Missouri River with a golden spike at Promontory, Utah. The railroads were built, mostly by Chinese laborers, in five years over rugged mountains and the Great Plains.

Hoover Dam, Nevada
A group called Six Companies employed thousands of men (100 lost their lives) and spent $48 million to build this massive dam (1931-36), once called Boulder Dam, on the Colorado River. A National Historic Landmark, the Art Deco structure draws 1 million tourists each year. The dam provides irrigation, hydroelectric power, and flood prevention. At 726 feet tall and 1,244 feet in length, the dam created 247-sq-mile Lake Mead.

Colorado River Aqueduct, California
Engineers built the 242-mile-long Colorado River Aqueduct in 1930 to redirect water from the Colorado River to the Los Angeles area. Water passes through open canals, tunnels, and pump systems that bring it up and over the mountains.

New Orleans Hurricane & Storm Damage Risk Reduction System
Built by the U.S. Army Corps of Engineers following the devastation of Hurricane Katrina in 2005, the project saw the construction of a two-mile 26-foot-high barrier, and a revamped canal system, as well as the addition of new pump stations.

Reversal of the Chicago River
It was determined that the Chicago River's flow could be reversed to prevent contamination of drinking water. En-

MONUMENTS, ENGINEERING MARVELS OF THE USA

gineers dug the Chicago Sanitary and Ship Canal to drain the polluted water away from the city, using a series of locks to redirect and reverse the flow of water to a man-made river. The river now flows to the Mississippi River instead of Lake Michigan.

Lake Pontchartrain Causeway, Louisiana
One of the world's longest bridges, the causeway spans nearly 28 miles of Lake Pontchartrain in Louisiana, including a stretch of 8 miles where land is not visible. The span requires 9,500 concrete pilings. The roadway lies 15 feet above the water's surface. Two lanes opened in 1956; four lanes in 1969.

Interstate Highway System
The Federal-Aid Highway Act of 1956 under President Eisenhower began 35 years of construction for the original 41,000-mile-long system costing $114 billion. Now the system covers more than 46,000 miles, providing long-haul truck shipping and speedy passenger travel between major cities.

Tennessee Valley Authority
During the Depression of the 1930s, the TVA built dams on the Tennessee River that created jobs, reservoirs and navigation, and rural electrification. Today, the federally owned electric utility operates 29 hydroelectric dams and provides electricity to 10 million consumers through local utilities.

Manhattan Project
Begun in 1942 during World War II, this super-secret Army project spent $2.0 billion and employed 130,000 people to produce the first atomic weapons, two of which were dropped on Japan to end the war. The main facilities were at Oak Ridge, Tenn. (enriching uranium), Hanford, Wash. (producing plutonium), and Los Alamos, NM (design, production, and testing of the weapons). The bombs were delivered to Japan by newly built Boeing B-29 Superfortresses, a separate US project of nearly similar size, cost, and difficulty.

Apollo Program
Fulfilling President Kennedy's pledge to reach the moon by 1970, the National Aeronautics and Space Agency (NASA) spent more than $25 billion to land men on the moon in July 1969, plus five more lunar landing missions. The biggest obstacle was designing and building the massive three-stage Saturn V booster rocket, which stood 363 feet high. Its five F-1 main-stage rockets produced 7.6 million pounds of force.

Empire State Building, New York City
Completed in 1931 in record time during the Depression, the National Historic Landmark in Manhattan rises 102 stories (85 stories of office space) and 1,454 feet high, topped by an observation deck. The Art Deco building was the tallest in the world until 1970. In 1945, a B-25 bomber hit the 80th floor, killing 14 people. The building was climbed by King Kong in the movies. The Empire State Building surpassed the nearby Chrysler Building, which opened in 1930.

Statue of Liberty, New York City
The copper statue of Lady Liberty was designed by sculptor Frédéric Auguste Bartholdi and built by Gustave Eiffel as a symbol of friendship between the USA and France. After its 1886 dedication, the statue, 305 feet high, became a welcome sight to immigrants sailing to New York.

Bunker Hill Monument, Boston
The massive granite obelisk dedicated to the 1775 battle actually fought at Breed's Hill was completed in 1842. The British won the battle but paid a heavy cost in lives. The Marquis de Lafayette set the cornerstone for the 221-foot-tall monument in 1825.

Historic Heroic Statuary
Washington, DC and the entire USA is filled with remarkable statuary, including the massive Iwo Jima Memorial at Arlington National Cemetery, also called the US Marine Corps Memorial; the Andrew Jackson equestrian statues by Clark Mills found at the White House, Jackson Square in New Orleans, and the Tennessee State Capitol (also a replica in downtown Jacksonville, Fla.); and the Grant Memorial by Henry Shrady in D.C., one of the most impressive cast-bronze statues anywhere. The Standing Soldiers monuments, 2,000 in all, were erected in the late 1800s in towns across the USA to commemorate the Civil War soldier, either North or South. The statues, mostly identical, could be ordered from a catalog.

Lincoln Memorial, Washington, D.C.
Built in 1922, the Lincoln Memorial was part of an ex-

MONUMENTS, ENGINEERING MARVELS OF THE USA

pansion of the National Mall. Architect Henry Bacon was inspired by Greek temples for the building housing the massive marble sculpture of the 16th president, created by Daniel Chester French. The temple contains inscriptions of two of the most well-known Lincoln speeches, the Gettysburg Address, and his second inaugural address. Also impressive are the Thomas Jefferson Memorial, World War Two Memorial, Korean War Memorial and other monuments in our nation's capital.

Washington Monument, Washington, DC
The 555-foot-tall memorial to our first President was begun in 1843 and finished in 1884. The centerpiece of Washington City, it was designed by Robert Mills and consists of 36,000 marble and granite blocks. It is the tallest obelisk in the world.

Mount Rushmore, South Dakota
Sculptor Gutzon Borglum carved the faces of four Presidents (Washington, Lincoln, Theodore Roosevelt, and Jefferson) onto this gigantic Black Hills edifice. Each granite head is 60 feet high. Officially completed on Oct. 31, 1941, Mount Rushmore draws more than 2.6 million visitors per year. Nearby is the gigantic stone carving of Chief Crazy Horse of the Oglala Lakota tribe.

Gateway Arch, Saint Louis
Designed by Eero Saarinen, the Gateway Arch (1965) is a monument to Thomas Jefferson and westward expansion. The 1965 structure near the Mississippi River stands 630 feet high, clad in gleaming stainless steel, the world's tallest arch. Tourists can ride a tram to an observation deck at the top.

Vietnam Veterans Memorial, Washington, DC
The memorial (1982) consists of two 246-ft-long walls of polished black granite listing the names of 58,318 soldiers and sailors who died during the Vietnam War. The controversial design was created by Yale architecture undergraduate Maya Lin. The Three Servicemen bronze sculpture was added in 1984, and the Vietnam Women's Memorial in 1993.

Oklahoma City National Memorial
On April 19, 1995 a terrorist detonated a bomb at the Alfred P. Murrah Federal Building, killing 168 people, including 19 children, the deadliest terror attack in America until 2001. The memorial (2000) includes a field of 168 empty chairs, one for each of the victims; a reflecting pool; and a section of the damaged wall from the building inscribed with the names of survivors.

Seattle Space Needle
Designed for the 1962 World's Fair by Edward E. Carlson, the 605-foot-tall structure has come to represent Seattle. It contains an observation deck, restaurant, elevators, and surrounding grounds. It was the tallest structure west of the Mississippi for many years.

Stratosphere Tower, Las Vegas
The 1,149-ft-tall Stratosphere Tower (1996), the tallest freestanding observation tower in the US and the second-tallest in the Western Hemisphere (2nd to the CN Tower in Toronto), looms over the Las Vegas Strip. Now called The Strat, the tower features thrill rides at the top. The Strip also features replicas of the Eiffel Tower, Roman palaces, the Egyptian Sphinx and Giza Pyramid, Venetian waterways, the powerful Bellagio water fountains, and the impressive 550-ft-tall High Roller, a Ferris wheel with 28 40-person cabins.

Grand Central Station, New York City
The passenger rail terminal (1913) in Manhattan covers 48 acres and has 44 platforms, more than any other railroad station in the world. Tourists totaling 21 million per year admire its Beaux-Arts architecture and monumental details. Penn Station (1910), also in Manhattan, actually serves more passengers per year.

Chicago Skyscrapers
In 1884 the Home Insurance Building, 10 stories on an innovative skeletal steel frame, was the first modern skyscraper. The John Hancock Tower (1968) was the tallest building in the world at the time. Today the tallest Chicago skyscrapers are the 110-story Willis Tower (formerly the Sears Tower), Trump Tower (98 floors), Vista Tower (101 floors), Aon Center (83 stories), and 875 N Michigan Ave (formerly John Hancock Center).

The Pentagon, Arlington, Virginia
The largest office building in the world at 6.5 million sq. ft., the seven-floor Pentagon (1941-43) is the headquarters of the US Dept. of Defense. It contains 7.5 miles of corridors and encloses a central plaza of 5 acres.

DISASTERS AND CATASTROPHES

Even in the USA, bad things happen. Back in the day, disease, famine and poor nutrition, polluted drinking water, and fires were the major concerns. Flooding, droughts, blizzards and heat waves were regular occurrences. Earthquakes, hurricanes, wildfires, tornado outbreaks, and even a volcanic eruption have caused widespread damage and casualties. All kinds of explosions—coal mine, wartime munitions, steamship boilers, natural gas—have created havoc. Ships wreck, trains collide, spacecraft explode, and aircraft fall to the earth. Enemy attacks, civil unrest, and mass shootings continue to shock. The world is a dangerous place. Here are some of the more famous US disasters (the list includes only events in the US and is not comprehensive by any measure. Many fatality figures are estimates; property damage is historic, not adjusted for inflation).

Year	Event	Deaths	Damage	Location
2020	Covid-19 Pandemic	165,000	—	United States (as of August 2020)
2018	Camp Fire Wildfires	18	$16.5B	California
2018	Hurricane Florence	54	$24.2B	East Coast (southern)
2017	Hurricane Maria	5,740	$91.6B	Florida, Puerto Rico
2017	Hurricane Irma	134	$64.8B	Florida, South Carolina, Georgia, Puerto Rico
2017	Hurricane Harvey	107	$125B	Texas, Louisiana, Alabama
2017	Mass Shooting	59	—	Las Vegas, Nevada
2016	Smoky Mountain Wildfires	14	$990M	Tennessee
2016	Hurricane Matthew	49	$15.0B	Florida, Georgia, Carolinas
2016	Blizzard	55	$500M	Eastern Coast
2015	Okanogan Fire	3	$8.0B	Washington
2015	Flood	46	—	Texas, Kansas, Oklahoma
2014	Snowstorm	24	—	New York, Great Lakes
2014	Tornados	35	$1.0B	Nebraska, Louisiana, Oklahoma, Illinois, Florida, N. Carolina
2014	Mudslide	43	—	Oslo, Washington
2013-14	Cold Wave	21	—	Eastern US
2013	Tornado	24	$2.0B	Oklahoma
2012	Hurricane Sandy	147	$75B	Eastern Coast
2012	School Shooting	28	—	Sandy Hook, Connecticut
2011	Tornado	160	$3.0B	Joplin, Missouri
2011	Tornado Outbreak	346	$11.0B	Southern US
2010	Flood	31	$2.3B	Tennessee, Kentucky, Mississippi
2008	Tornado Outbreak	59	$1.2B	Tennessee, Arkansas, Kentucky, Alabama, Illinois
2007	Mass Shooting	33	—	Blacksburg, Virginia
2005	Hurricane Katrina	1,836	$125B	Gulf Coast
2005	Hurricane Rita	120	$10.0B	Louisiana, Texas
2004	Hurricane Ivan	124	$19.0B	Texas, Florida, East Coast
2004	Hurricane Frances	49	$9.0B	Florida
2002	Tropical Storm Allison	41	$5.5B	Texas, Louisiana, Pennsylvania
2003	Space Shuttle Accident	7	$1.6B	Over Texas, Louisiana, Arkansas
2001	Aircraft Crash	265	—	Queens, New York

DISASTERS AND CATASTROPHES

Year	Event	Deaths	Damage	Location
2001	9/11 Terrorism Attacks	2,996	$10B	New York City, Washington DC, Pennsylvania
1999	Heat Wave	271	—	Midwest, Northeast
1999	School Shooting	15	—	Columbine, Colorado
1999	Tornado Outbreak	48	$1.5B	Oklahoma, Kansas, Texas, Tennessee
1996	Aircraft Accident	230	—	Long Island, New York
1995	Terrorism Explosion	168	—	Oklahoma City, Oklahoma
1995	Heat Wave	739	—	Chicago, Illinois
1994	Earthquake	57	$23.0B	Los Angeles, California area
1993	Blizzard	318	$6.6B	East Coast
1993	Flooding	50	$15.0B	Midwest
1992	Hurricane Andrew	26	$25.0B	Florida, Louisiana
1992	Urban Riots	58	$1.0B	Los Angeles, California
1991	Oakland Hills Wildfire	25	$1.5B	San Francisco Bay, California
1990	Arson-Building	87	—	New York, New York
1989	Loma Prieta Earthquake	69	$6.0B	San Francisco Bay, California
1986	Space Shuttle Explosion	7	$1.6B	Cape Canaveral, Florida
1981	Hotel Walkway Collapse	114	—	Kansas City, Missouri
1980	Heat Wave	1,700	$20.0B	Central, Southern US
1980	Ship-Bridge Wreck	35	—	St. Petersburg, Florida
1980	Volcanic Eruption	57	$1.1B	Mount St. Helens, Washington
1979	Aircraft Crash	273	—	Chicago, Illinois
1978	Construction Accident	51	—	Willow Island, West Virginia
1977	Fire-Supper Club	165	—	Southgate, Kentucky
1977	County Jail Fire	42	—	Columbia, Tennessee
1975	Shipwreck	29	$24M	Lake Superior-*SS Edmund Fitzgerald*
1972	London Flu	1,027	—	United States
1969	Hurricane Camille	256	$1.4B	Mississippi, Alabama, Virginia
1964	Earthquake	143	$116M	Anchorage, Alaska
1963	Submarine *Thresher*	129	—	Off coast of Massachusetts
1960	Hurricane Donna	157	$491.0M	East Coast
1958	Nuclear Bomb Lost	0	—	Savannah, Georgia
1950	Blizzard	353	$66.7M	Eastern US
1947	Explosion-Ship	581	—	Texas City, Texas
1947	Coal Mine	111	—	Centralia, Illinois
1944	Explosion-Ship	320	—	Port Chicago, California
1942	Fire-Nightclub	492	—	Boston, Massachusetts

DISASTERS AND CATASTROPHES

Year	Event	Deaths	Damage	Location
1941	Naval Air Attack	2,467	—	Pearl Harbor, Hawaii
1938	Hurricane	600	$306M	New England
1937	Flooding	385	$5.0B	Ohio, Kentucky, Indiana, Illinois
1937	*Hindenburg* Zeppelin	36	$10M	Lakehurst, New Jersey
1936	Flooding	69	$3,0B	Pittsburgh, Pennsylvania
1931-39	Great Dust Bowl	7,000	$1.0T	Great Plains
1927	Flooding	246	$400M	Mississippi River Valley (lower)
1927	Mass Murder-School	45	—	Bath Township, Michigan
1924-25	Smallpox Epidemic	500	—	Minnesota
1921	Race Riot	300	—	Tulsa, Oklahoma
1920	Anarchist Bombing	38	—	Wall Street, New York, NY
1919	Hurricane	600	—	Florida Keys, Texas
1919	Molasses Flood	21	—	Boston, Massachusetts
1918	Influenza Pandemic	675,000	—	United States
1918	Train Collision	101	—	Nashville, Tennessee
1915	Shipwreck-Capsize	844	—	Chicago, Illinois
1911	Fire-Workshop	146	—	New York, New York
1910	Avalanche	96	—	Wellingston, Washington
1909	Tunnel Fire	60	—	Chicago, Illinois
1907	Coal Mine	362	—	Monogah, West Virginia
1906	Earthquake-Fire	3,000	$500M	San Francisco, California
1900	Bubonic Plague	119	—	San Francisco, California
1900	Hurricane	10,000	$28M	Galveston, Texas
1899	Hurricane	3,389	$20M	Puerto Rico, East Coast
1889	Flooding-Dam Failure	2,295	$17M	Johnstown, Pennsylvania
1888	Blizzard	400	—	Northeast US
1883	Coal Mine Explosion	74	—	Diamond, Illinois
1871	Wildfire	2,000	1.2M acres	Pestigo, Wisconsin
1871	Fire	300	$222M	Chicago, Illinois
1865	Shipwreck-Boiler Explosion	1,700	—	Mississippi River, *USS Sultana*
1863	Race Riot	112	$4.0M	New York, New York
1832-49	Cholera Epidemics	150,000	—	Western US
1820	Yellow Fever	700	—	Savannah, Georgia
1811-12	Earthquakes	500	—	New Madrid Seismic Zone

TOP USA TOURIST ATTRACTIONS

Rank	Attraction	Location	Annual Visitation
1	Times Square	New York City	42 million
2	Central Park	New York City	40 million
3	Union Station	Washington DC	36 million
4	Las Vegas Strip	Las Vegas	29 million
5	Millennium Park	Chicago	25 million
6	Grand Central Terminal	New York City	22 million
7	Lincoln Park	Chicago	20 million
8	Magic Kingdom, Walt Disney World	Orlando	17 million
9	Disneyland Resort	Anaheim CA	16 million
10	Golden Gate Bridge	San Francisco	15 million
11	Faneuil Hall	Boston	15 million
12	Golden Gate Park	San Francisco	13 million
13	Balboa Park	San Diego	13 million
14	Epcot, Walt Disney World	Orlando	11 million
15	Pike Place Market	Seattle	10 million
16	Animal Kingdom, Walt Disney World	Orlando	10 million
17	Hollywood Studios, Walt Disney World	Orlando	10 million
18	Great Smoky Mountains National Park	Tennessee	9 million
19	South Street Seaport	New York City	9 million
20	Mackinac Bridge	Michigan	9 million

National Park System Properties

Alabama
Birmingham Civil Rights National Monument
Freedom Riders National Monument
Horseshoe Bend National Military Park
Little River Canyon National Preserve
Russell Cave National Monument
Tuskegee Airmen National Historic Site
Tuskegee Institute National Historic Site

Alaska
Alagnak Wild River
Aniakchak National Monument
Aniakchak National Preserve
Bering Land Bridge National Preserve
Cape Krusenstern National Monument
Denali National Park
Denali National Preserve
Gates of the Arctic National Park
Gates of the Arctic National Preserve
Glacier Bay National Park
Glacier Bay National Preserve
Katmai National Park
Katmai National Preserve
Kenai Fjords National Park
Klondike Gold Rush National Historical Park
Kobuk Valley National Park
Lake Clark National Park
Lake Clark National Preserve
Noatak National Preserve
Sitka National Historical Park
Wrangell-St. Elias National Park
Wrangell-St. Elias National Preserve
Yukon-Charley Rivers National Preserve

Arizona
Canyon De Chelly National Monument
Casa Grande Ruins National Monument
Chiricahua National Monument
Coronado National Memorial
Fort Bowie National Historic Site
Glen Canyon National Recreation Area
Grand Canyon National Park
Hohokam Pima National Monument
Hubbell Trading Post National Historic Site
Montezuma Castle National Monument
Navajo National Monument
Organ Pipe Cactus National Monument
Petrified Forest National Park
Pipe Spring National Monument
Saguaro National Park
Sunset Crater Volcano National Monument
Tonto National Monument
Tumacacori National Historical Park
Tuzigoot National Monument
Walnut Canyon National Monument
Wupatki National Monument

Arkansas
Arkansas Post National Memorial
Buffalo National River
Fort Smith National Historic Site
Hot Springs National Park
Little Rock Central High School National Historic Site
Pea Ridge National Military Park
President Clinton Birthplace Home National Historic Site

California
Cabrillo National Monument
Castle Mountains National Monument
César E. Chávez National Monument
Channel Islands National Park
Death Valley National Park
Devils Postpile National Monument
Eugene O'Neill National Historic Site
Fort Point National Historic Site
Golden Gate National Recreation Area
John Muir National Historic Site
Joshua Tree National Park
Kings Canyon National Park
Lassen Volcanic National Park
Lava Beds National Monument
Manzanar National Historic Site
Mojave National Preserve
Muir Woods National Monument
Pinnacles National Park
Point Reyes National Seashore
Port Chicago Naval Magazine National Memorial
Redwood National Park
Rosie the Riveter/World War II Home Front National Historical Park
San Francisco Maritime National Historical Park
Santa Monica Mountains National Recreation Area
Sequoia National Park
Tule Lake National Monument
Whiskeytown-Shasta-Trinity National Recreation Area
Yosemite National Park

Land of the Free, Home of the Brave

National Park System Properties

Colorado
Bent's Old Fort National Historic Site
Black Canyon of the Gunnison National Park
Colorado National Monument
Curecanti National Recreation Area
Dinosaur National Monument
Florissant Fossil Beds National Monument
Great Sand Dunes National Park
Great Sand Dunes National Preserve
Hovenweep National Monument
Mesa Verde National Park
Rocky Mountain National Park
Sand Creek Massacre National Historic Site
Yucca House National Monument

Connecticut
Weir Farm National Historic Site

Delaware
First State National Historical Park

Florida
Big Cypress National Preserve
Biscayne National Park
Canaveral National Seashore
Castillo de San Marcos National Monument
De Soto National Memorial
Dry Tortugas National Park
Everglades National Park
Fort Caroline National Memorial
Fort Matanzas National Monument
Gulf Islands National Seashore
Timucuan Ecological and Historic Preserve

Georgia
Andersonville National Historic Site
Appalachian National Scenic Trail (to Maine)
Chattahoochee River National Recreation Area
Chickamauga and Chattanooga National Military Park
Cumberland Island National Seashore
Fort Frederica National Monument
Fort Pulaski National Monument
Jimmy Carter National Historic Site
Kennesaw Mountain National Battlefield Park
Martin Luther King, Jr. National Historic Site
Ocmulgee Mounds National Historical Park

Hawaii
Haleakala National Park
Hawaii Volcanoes National Park
Honouliuli National Historic Site
Kalaupapa National Historical Park
Kaloko-Honokohau National Historical Park
Pearl Harbor National Memorial
Pu'uhonua O Honaunau National Historical Park
Pu'ukohola Heiau National Historic Site

Idaho
City of Rocks National Reserve
Craters of the Moon National Monument
Craters of the Moon National Preserve
Hagerman Fossil Beds National Monument
Minidoka National Historic Site
Nez Perce National Historical Park

Illinois
Lincoln Home National Historic Site
Pullman National Monument

Indiana
George Rogers Clark National Historical Park
Indiana Dunes National Park
Lincoln Boyhood National Memorial

Iowa
Effigy Mounds National Monument
Herbert Hoover National Historic Site

Kansas
Brown vs. Board of Education National Historic Site
Fort Larned National Historic Site
Fort Scott National Historic Site
Nicodemus National Historic Site
Tallgrass Prairie National Preserve

Kentucky
Abraham Lincoln Birthplace National Historical Park
Camp Nelson Heritage National Monument
Cumberland Gap National Historical Park
Mammoth Cave National Park

Louisiana
Cane River Creole National Historical Park
Jean Lafitte National Historical Park and Preserve
New Orleans Jazz National Historical Park

― Land of the Free, Home of the Brave ―

National Park System Properties

Poverty Point National Monument

Maine
Acadia National Park
Appalachian National Scenic Trail (to Georgia)
Katahdin Woods and Waters National Monument
Saint Croix Island International Historic Site

Maryland
Antietam National Battlefield
Assateague Island National Seashore
Catoctin Mountain Park
C&O Canal National Historical Park
Clara Barton National Historic Site
Fort McHenry National Monument & Historic Shrine
Fort Washington Park
Greenbelt Park
Hampton National Historic Site
Harriet Tubman Underground Railroad National Historical Park
Monocacy National Battlefield
Piscataway Park
Potomac Heritage National Scenic Trail
Thomas Stone National Historic Site

Massachusetts
Adams National Historical Park
Boston African American National Historic Site
Boston Harbor Islands National Recreation Area
Boston National Historical Park
Cape Cod National Seashore
Frederick Law Olmsted National Historic Site
John F. Kennedy National Historic Site
Longfellow House–Washington's Headquarters National Historic Site
Lowell National Historical Park
Minute Man National Historical Park
New Bedford Whaling National Historical Park
Salem Maritime National Historic Site
Saugus Iron Works National Historic Site
Springfield Armory National Historic Site

Michigan
Isle Royale National Park
Keweenaw National Historical Park
Pictured Rocks National Lakeshore
River Raisin National Battlefield Park
Sleeping Bear Dunes National Lakeshore

Minnesota
Grand Portage National Monument
Mississippi National River and Recreation Area
Pipestone National Monument
Voyageurs National Park

Mississippi
Brices Cross Roads National Battlefield Site
Natchez National Historical Park
Natchez Trace Parkway
Natchez Trace National Scenic Trail
Tupelo National Battlefield
Vicksburg National Military Park

Missouri
Gateway Arch National Park
George Washington Carver National Monument
Harry S Truman National Historic Site
Ozark National Scenic Riverways
Ulysses S. Grant National Historic Site
Wilson's Creek National Battlefield

Montana
Big Hole National Battlefield
Bighorn Canyon National Recreation Area
Glacier National Park
Grant-Kohrs Ranch National Historic Site
Little Bighorn Battlefield National Monument

Nebraska
Agate Fossil Beds National Monument
Homestead National Monument of America
Missouri National Recreational River
Niobrara National Scenic River
Scotts Bluff National Monument

Nevada
Great Basin National Park
Lake Mead National Recreation Area
Tule Springs Fossil Beds National Monument

New Hampshire
Saint-Gaudens National Historical Park

New Jersey
Delaware Water Gap National Recreation Area
Great Egg Harbor Scenic and Recreational River
Morristown National Historical Park

National Park System Properties

Paterson Great Falls National Historical Park
Thomas Edison National Historical Park

New Mexico
Aztec Ruins National Monument
Bandelier National Monument
Capulin Volcano National Monument
Carlsbad Caverns National Park
Chaco Culture National Historical Park
El Malpais National Monument
El Morro National Monument
Fort Union National Monument
Gila Cliff Dwellings National Monument
Manhattan Project National Historical Park
Pecos National Historical Park
Petroglyph National Monument
Salinas Pueblo Missions National Monument
Valles Caldera National Preserve
White Sands National Park

New York
African Burial Ground National Monument
Castle Clinton National Monument
Eleanor Roosevelt National Historic Site
Federal Hall National Memorial
Fire Island National Seashore
Fort Stanwix National Monument
Gateway National Recreation Area
General Grant National Memorial
Governors Island National Monument
Hamilton Grange National Memorial
Harriet Tubman National Historical Park
Home of Franklin D. Roosevelt National Historic Site
Martin Van Buren National Historic Site
Saint Paul's Church National Historic Site
Sagamore Hill National Historic Site
Saratoga National Historical Park
Statue of Liberty National Monument
Stonewall National Monument
Theodore Roosevelt Birthplace National Historic Site
Theodore Roosevelt Inaugural National Historic Site
Vanderbilt Mansion National Historic Site
Women's Rights National Historical Park

North Carolina
Blue Ridge Parkway
Cape Hatteras National Seashore
Cape Lookout National Seashore

Carl Sandburg Home National Historic Site
Fort Raleigh National Historic Site
Guilford Courthouse National Military Park
Moores Creek National Battlefield
Wright Brothers National Memorial

North Dakota
Fort Union Trading Post National Historic Site
Knife River Indian Villages National Historic Site
Theodore Roosevelt National Park

Ohio
Charles Young Buffalo Soldiers National Monument
Cuyahoga Valley National Park
Dayton Aviation Heritage National Historical Park
First Ladies National Historic Site
Hopewell Culture National Historical Park
James A. Garfield National Historic Site
Perry's Victory and International Peace Memorial
William Howard Taft National Historic Site

Oklahoma
Chickasaw National Recreation Area
Washita Battlefield National Historic Site

Oregon
Crater Lake National Park
Lewis and Clark National Historical Park
John Day Fossil Beds National Monument
Oregon Caves National Monument and Preserve

Pennsylvania
Allegheny Portage Railroad National Historic Site
Edgar Allan Poe National Historic Site
Eisenhower National Historic Site
Flight 93 National Memorial
Fort Necessity National Battlefield
Friendship Hill National Historic Site
Gettysburg National Military Park
Hopewell Furnace National Historic Site
Independence National Historical Park
Johnstown Flood National Memorial
Middle Delaware National Scenic River
Steamtown National Historic Site
Thaddeus Kosciuszko National Memorial
Upper Delaware Scenic and Recreational River
Valley Forge National Historical Park

Land of the Free, Home of the Brave

National Park System Properties

Puerto Rico
San Juan National Historic Site

Rhode Island
Blackstone River Valley National Historical Park
Roger Williams National Memorial

South Carolina
Charles Pinckney National Historic Site
Congaree National Park
Cowpens National Battlefield
Fort Sumter & Fort Moultrie National Historical Park
Kings Mountain National Military Park
Ninety Six National Historic Site
Reconstruction Era National Historical Park

South Dakota
Badlands National Park
Jewel Cave National Monument
Minuteman Missile National Historic Site
Mount Rushmore National Memorial
Wind Cave National Park

Tennessee
Andrew Johnson National Historic Site
Big South Fork National River and Recreation Area
Fort Donelson National Battlefield
Great Smoky Mountains National Park
Manhattan Project National Historical Park
Natchez Trace Parkway
Obed Wild and Scenic River
Shiloh National Military Park
Stones River National Battlefield

Texas
Alibates Flint Quarries National Monument
Amistad National Recreation Area
Big Bend National Park
Big Thicket National Preserve
Chamizal National Memorial
Fort Davis National Historic Site
Guadalupe Mountains National Park
Lake Meredith National Recreation Area
Lyndon B. Johnson National Historical Park
Padre Island National Seashore
Palo Alto Battlefield National Historical Park
Rio Grande Wild and Scenic River
San Antonio Missions National Historical Park

Waco Mammoth National Monument

Utah
Arches National Park
Bryce Canyon National Park
Canyonlands National Park
Capitol Reef National Park
Cedar Breaks National Monument
Golden Spike National Historical Park
Natural Bridges National Monument
Rainbow Bridge National Monument
Timpanogos Cave National Monument
Zion National Park

Vermont
Marsh-Billings-Rockefeller National Historical Park

Virgin Islands
Buck Island Reef National Monument
Christiansted National Historic Site
Salt River Bay National Historical Park and Ecological Preserve
Virgin Islands National Park
Virgin Islands Coral Reef National Monument

Virginia
Appomattox Court House National Historical Park
Arlington House, The Robert E. Lee Memorial
Booker T. Washington National Monument
Cedar Creek & Belle Grove National Historical Park
Colonial National Historical Park
Fort Monroe National Monument
Fredericksburg and Spotsylvania National Military Park
George Washington Birthplace National Monument
George Washington Memorial Parkway
Maggie L. Walker National Historic Site
Manassas National Battlefield Park
Petersburg National Battlefield
Prince William Forest Park
Richmond National Battlefield Park
Shenandoah National Park
Wolf Trap National Park for the Performing Arts

Washington
Ebey's Landing National Historical Reserve
Fort Vancouver National Historic Site
Lake Chelan National Recreation Area
Lake Roosevelt National Recreation Area

National Park System Properties

Manhattan Project National Historical Park
Mount Rainier National Park
North Cascades National Park
Olympic National Park
Ross Lake National Recreation Area
San Juan Island National Historical Park
Whitman Mission National Historic Site

Washington DC
Belmont-Paul Women's Equality National Monument
Carter G. Woodson Home National Historic Site
Constitution Gardens
Ford's Theatre National Historic Site
Franklin D. Roosevelt Memorial
Frederick Douglass National Historic Site
Korean War Veterans Memorial
Lincoln Memorial
Lyndon Baines Johnson Memorial Grove on the Potomac
Martin Luther King, Jr. Memorial
Mary McLeod Bethune Council House National Historic Site
National Capital Parks
National Mall
Pennsylvania Avenue National Historic Site
Rock Creek Park
Theodore Roosevelt Island
Thomas Jefferson Memorial
Vietnam Veterans Memorial
Washington Monument
White House and President's Park
World War I Memorial
World War II Memorial

West Virginia
Bluestone National Scenic River
Gauley River National Recreation Area
Harpers Ferry National Historical Park
New River Gorge National River

Wisconsin
Apostle Islands National Lakeshore
Saint Croix National Scenic Riverway

Wyoming
Devils Tower National Monument
Fort Laramie National Historic Site
Fossil Butte National Monument
Grand Teton National Park
John D. Rockefeller Memorial Parkway
Yellowstone National Park

―――― Land of the Free, Home of the Brave ――――

Historic Sites in the USA

In addition to the NPS sites, there are tens of thousands of sites listed on the National Register of Historic Places, including 2,500 National Historic Landmarks. Each state maintains historic signage and markers. Each county and town features its own historic sites. Sites include museums, monuments, statues, historic districts, cemeteries, forts, buildings, churches, industrial facilities, battlefields, even ancient villages. This is but a small sampling of USA historic sites open to the public.

National Archives, Washington, DC

Library of Congress, US Capitol, Lincoln Memorial, Washington Memorial, Jefferson Memorial, Rev. Martin Luther King Memorial, Franklin D. Roosevelt Memorial, Smithsonian Institution Museums, Ford's Theater, World War Two Memorial, Vietnam Veterans Memorial, Korean War Memorial, White House, US Capitol.

Presidential Birthplaces, Homeplaces, and Burial Sites (e.g., Mount Vernon, Monticello, The Hermitage, Grant's Tomb)

Arlington National Cemetery, National Cemeteries, and Historic Cemeteries

State Capitols in all 50 State Capitals
Mount Rushmore, Keystone, S.D.
National Civil Rights Museum, Memphis, Tenn.
9/11 Memorial and Museum, New York, NY

US Naval Academy, Annapolis, Md.
US Army Academy, West Point, NY
US Air Force Academy, Colorado Springs, Colo.

Castillo de San Marcos, St. Augustine, Fla.
Canyonlands National Park
Navajo National Monument
Tuzigoot
Montezuma Castle
Hohokam Piman
Casa Grande Ruins
Canyon de Chelly
Hovenweep
Mesa Verde National Park
Clovis
Folsom
Knife River Indian villages
Effigy Mounds
Cahokia Mounds
Poverty Point

Hopewell Culture
Indian Serpent Mound
Etowah Mounds
Pinson Mounds
Old Stone Fort

Trinity Church
Washington National Cathedral
Mormon Tabernacle
Old Ship Church
San Miguel Mission
Abyssinian Baptist Church
Jamestown Church
St. Patrick's Cathedral
Old Sheldon Church

George Rogers Clark Historic Park, Vincennes, Ind.
Tippecanoe Battlefield Site, Battle Ground, Ind.
Battle of the Wabash, Fort Recovery, Ohio
Fallen Timbers Battlefield, Maumee, Ohio
River Raisin National Battlefield, Monroe, Mich.
Tu-Endie-Wei State Park, Point Pleasant, WVa
Alamance Battleground, Burlington, NC
Fort Loudoun State Historic Area, Vonore, Tenn.
Horseshoe Bend National Military Park, Dadeville, Ala.

Historic Sites in the USA

Little Bighorn Battlefield, Crow Agency, Mont.
Plimoth Plantation, Plymouth, Mass.
Colonial National Historic Park, Williamsburg, Va.
Jamestown, Williamsburg, Va.
Independence Hall and Liberty Bell Center
Museum of the American Revolution, Philadelphia, Pa.

Revolutionary and War of 1812 Battlefields (e.g., Lexington and Concord, Bunker Hill Monument, Paul Revere House, Freedom Trail, Faneuil Hall, Valley Forge, Kings Mountain, Cowpens, Yorktown, Fort McHenry, New Orleans).

Civil War National Battlefields and National Military Parks (e.g., Fort Sumter, Gettysburg, Antietam, Harper's Ferry, Richmond and Petersburg, Fredricksburg, Appomattox, Shiloh, Vicksburg, Chickamagua and Chattanooga, Stones River, Pea Ridge, Wilson's Creek, Old Fort Jackson, Fort Pulaski, Fort McAlister, Fort Negley, and many more)

Museum of the Confederacy, New Orleans, La.
Confederate White House, Montgomery, Ala.
Windsor Ruins
Destrehan Plantation
Jekyll Island Historic District
Biltmore Estate, Asheville, NC
Belle Meade Plantation, Nashville, TN

National WWI Museum & Memorial, Kansas City, Mo.
Alvin York State Historic Site, Tenn.
National WWII Museum, New Orleans, La.
US Marine Corps Museum, Quantico, Va.
National Museum of the Pacific War, Fredericksburg, Texas
Pearl Harbor and USS Arizona Memorial, Honolulu
National D-Day Memorial, Bedford, Va.
George C. Marshall Museum, Lexington, Va.

National Museum of the US Air Force, Dayton, Ohio
National Naval Aviation Museum, Pensacola, Fla.
US Holocaust Memorial Museum, Washington, DC
Manhattan Project Sites-Oak Ridge, Tenn., Hanford, Wash., Los Alamos, NM
National Atomic Testing Museum, Las Vegas, Nev.
Wright Brothers National Museum, Dayton, Ohio
Wright Bros. National Memorial, Kill Devil Hills, NC
Museum of Science and Technology, Chicago, Ill.
Henry Ford Museum of American Innovation, Dearborn, Mich.
Thomas Edison National Historic Park, NJ
Railroad Museum of Pennsylvania
Hopewell Iron Furnace, Pa.
Shot Tower State Park, Va.

Kennedy Space Center, Cape Canaveral, Fla.
Udvar-Hazy National Air and Space Museum, Va.
Gus Grissom Memorial, Spring Mill Park, Ind.
Neil Armstrong Air and Space Museum, Ohio

The King Center, Atlanta, Ga.
National Civil Rights Museum, Memphis, Tenn.

Natural Bridge State Park, Natural Bridge, Va.
Niagra Falls State Park, Niagra Falls, NY
Gateway Arch National Park, St. Louis, Mo.
Newport Historic Districts, Newport, R.I.
The Alamo, San Antonio, Texas
Ellis Island, New York, NY
Statue of Liberty, New York, NY
Alcatraz Island, San Francisco Bay
Hoover Dam, Boulder City, Nev.
La Brea Tar Pits and Museum, Los Angeles, Calif.
Golden Gate Bridge, San Francisco, Calif.

―― Land of the Free, Home of the Brave ――

Historic Sites in the USA

Historic Ships and Warships:
USS Yorktown, Mt. Pleasant, S.C.
USS Intrepid, New York, NY
USS Hornet, Alameda, Calif.
USS Lexington, Corpus Christi, Texas
USS Midway, San Diego, Calif.
USS Alabama, Mobile, Ala.
USS Arizona, Pearl Harbor, Hawaii
USS Iowa, San Pedro, Calif.
USS Massachusetts, Fall River, Mass.
USS Missouri, Pearl Harbor, Hawaii
USS New Jersey, Camden, NJ
USS North Carolina, Wilmington, NC
USS Texas, La Porte, Texas
USS Wisconsin, Norfolk, Va.
USS Constitution, Charlestown, Mass.
USS Constellation, Baltimore, Md.
USS Nautilus, Groton, Conn.
USS Olympia, Philadelphia, Pa.
USS Cairo, Vicksburg, Miss.
U-505, Chicago, Ill.
HL Hunley, North Charleston, SC
USS Monitor, Newport News, Va.
USS LST-325, Evansville, Ind.
PT 305, New Orleans, La.

Historic Route 66 (numerous sites)
Country Music Hall of Fame and Museum, Nashville, Tenn.
Rock and Roll Hall of Fame, Cleveland, Ohio
Graceland, Memphis, Tenn.

Pro Football Hall of Fame, Canton, Ohio
College Football Hall of Fame, Atlanta, Ga.
National Baseball Hall of Fame and Museum, Cooperstown, NY
World Golf Hall of Fame, St. Augustine, Fla.
Women's Basketball Hall of Fame, Knoxville, Tenn.

Jack Daniel's Distillery, Lynchburg, Tenn.
Jim Beam American Stillhouse, Clermont, Ky.
Oscar Getz Museum of Whiskey History, Bardstown, Ky.
Kentucky Bourbon Trail
Tennessee Whiskey Trail
George Washington's Distillery at Mt. Vernon
Rheingeist Brewery, Cincinnati, Ohio
Appalachian Brewing Co., Harrisburg, Pa.

and many, many more!

MLB WORLD SERIES RESULTS

2019	Washington Nationals (NL) over Houston Astros (AL) in 7.
2018	Boston Red Sox (AL) over Los Angeles Dodgers (NL) in 5.
2017	Houston Astros (AL) over Los Angeles Dodgers (NL) in 7.
2016	Chicago Cubs (NL) over Cleveland Indians (AL) in 7.
2015	Kansas City Royals (AL) over New York Mets (NL) in 5.
2014	San Francisco Giants (NL) over Kansas City Royals (AL) in 7.
2013	Boston Red Sox (AL) over St. Louis Cardinals (NL) in 6.
2012	San Francisco Giants (NL) over Detroit Tigers (AL) in 4.
2011	St. Louis Cardinals (NL) over Texas Rangers (AL) in 7.
2010	San Francisco Giants (NL) over Texas Rangers (AL) in 5.
2009	New York Yankees (AL) over Philadelphia Phillies (NL) in 6.
2008	Philadelphia Phillies (NL) over Tampa Bay Rays (AL) in 5.
2007	Boston Red Sox (AL) over Colorado Rockies (NL) in 4.
2006	St. Louis Cardinals (NL) over Detroit Tigers (AL) in 5.
2005	Chicago White Sox (AL) over Houston Astros (NL) in 4.
2004	Boston Red Sox (AL) over St. Louis Cardinals (NL) in 4.
2003	Florida Marlins (NL) over New York Yankees (AL) in 6.
2002	Anaheim Angels (AL) over San Francisco Giants (NL) in 7.
2001	Arizona Diamondbacks (NL) over New York Yankees (AL) in 7.
2000	New York Yankees (AL) over New York Mets (NL) in 5.
1999	New York Yankees (AL) over Atlanta Braves (NL) in 4.
1998	New York Yankees (AL) over San Diego Padres (NL) in 4.
1997	Florida Marlins (NL) over Cleveland Indians (AL) in 7.
1996	New York Yankees (AL) over Atlanta Braves (NL) in 6.
1995	Atlanta Braves (NL) over Cleveland Indians (AL) in 6.
1994	No World Series due to players' strike
1993	Toronto Blue Jays (AL) over Philadelphia Phillies (NL) in 6.
1992	Toronto Blue Jays (AL) over Atlanta Braves (NL) in 6.
1991	Minnesota Twins (AL) over Atlanta Braves (NL) in 7.
1990	Cincinnati Reds (NL) over Oakland Athletics (AL) in 4.
1989	Oakland Athletics (AL) over San Francisco Giants (NL) in 4.
1988	Los Angeles Dodgers (NL) over Oakland Athletics (AL) in 5.
1987	Minnesota Twins (AL) over St. Louis Cardinals (NL) in 7.
1986	New York Mets (NL) over Boston Red Sox (AL) in 7.
1985	Kansas City Royals (AL) over St. Louis Cardinals (NL) in 7.
1984	Detroit Tigers (AL) over San Diego Padres (NL) in 5.
1983	Baltimore Orioles (AL) over Philadelphia Phillies (NL) in 5.
1982	St. Louis Cardinals (NL) over Milwaukee Brewers (AL) in 7.
1981	Los Angeles Dodgers (NL) over New York Yankees (AL) in 6.

MLB WORLD SERIES RESULTS

1980	Philadelphia Phillies (NL) over Kansas City Royals (AL) in 6.
1979	Pittsburgh Pirates (NL) over Baltimore Orioles (AL) in 7.
1978	New York Yankees (AL) over Los Angeles Dodgers (NL) in 6.
1977	New York Yankees (AL) over Los Angeles Dodgers (NL) in 6.
1976	Cincinnati Reds (NL) over New York Yankees (AL) in 4.
1975	Cincinnati Reds (NL) over Boston Red Sox (AL) in 7.
1974	Oakland Athletics (AL) over Los Angeles Dodgers (NL) in 5.
1973	Oakland Athletics (AL) over New York Mets (NL) in 7.
1972	Oakland Athletics (AL) over Cincinnati Reds (NL) in 7.
1971	Pittsburgh Pirates (NL) over Baltimore Orioles (AL) in 7.
1970	Baltimore Orioles (AL) over Cincinnati Reds (NL) in 5.
1969	New York Mets (NL) over Baltimore Orioles (AL) in 5.
1968	Detroit Tigers (AL) over St. Louis Cardinals (NL) in 7.
1967	St. Louis Cardinals (NL) over Boston Red Sox (AL) in 7.
1966	Baltimore Orioles (AL) over Los Angeles Dodgers (NL) in 4.
1965	Los Angeles Dodgers (NL) over Minnesota Twins (AL) in 7.
1964	St. Louis Cardinals (NL) over New York Yankees (AL) in 7.
1963	Los Angeles Dodgers (NL) over New York Yankees (AL) in 4.
1962	New York Yankees (AL) over San Francisco Giants (NL) in 7.
1961	New York Yankees (AL) over Cincinnati Reds (NL) in 5.
1960	Pittsburgh Pirates (NL) over New York Yankees (AL) in 7.
1959	Los Angeles Dodgers (NL) over Chicago White Sox (AL) in 6.
1958	New York Yankees (AL) over Milwaukee Braves (NL) in 7.
1957	Milwaukee Braves (NL) over New York Yankees (AL) in 7.
1956	New York Yankees (AL) over Brooklyn Dodgers (NL) in 7.
1955	Brooklyn Dodgers (NL) over New York Yankees (AL) in 7.
1954	New York Giants (NL) over Cleveland Indians (AL) in 4.
1953	New York Yankees (AL) over Brooklyn Dodgers (NL) in 6.
1952	New York Yankees (AL) over Brooklyn Dodgers (NL) in 7.
1951	New York Yankees (AL) over New York Giants (NL) in 6.
1950	New York Yankees (AL) over Philadelphia Phillies (NL) in 4.
1949	New York Yankees (AL) over Brooklyn Dodgers (NL) in 5.
1948	Cleveland Indians (AL) over Boston Braves (NL) in 6.
1947	New York Yankees (AL) over Brooklyn Dodgers (NL) in 7.
1946	St. Louis Cardinals (NL) over Boston Red Sox (AL) in 7.
1945	Detroit Tigers (AL) over Chicago Cubs (NL) in 7.
1944	St. Louis Cardinals (NL) over St. Louis Browns (AL) in 6.
1943	New York Yankees (AL) over St. Louis Cardinals (NL) in 5.
1942	St. Louis Cardinals (NL) over New York Yankees (AL) in 5.

MLB WORLD SERIES RESULTS

1941 New York Yankees (AL) over Brooklyn Dodgers (NL) in 5.
1940 Cincinnati Reds (NL) over Detroit Tigers (AL) in 7.
1939 New York Yankees (AL) over Cincinnati Reds (NL) in 4.
1938 New York Yankees (AL) over Chicago Cubs (NL) in 4.
1937 New York Yankees (AL) over New York Giants (NL) in 5.
1936 New York Yankees (AL) over New York Giants (NL) in 6.
1935 Detroit Tigers (AL) over Chicago Cubs (NL) in 6.
1934 St. Louis Cardinals (NL) over Detroit Tigers (AL) in 7.
1933 New York Giants (NL) over Washington Senators (AL) in 5.
1932 New York Yankees (AL) over Chicago Cubs (NL) in 4.
1931 St. Louis Cardinals (NL) over Philadelphia Athletics (AL) in 7.
1930 Philadelphia Athletics (AL) over St. Louis Cardinals (NL) in 6.
1929 Philadelphia Athletics (AL) over Chicago Cubs (NL) in 5.
1928 New York Yankees (AL) over St. Louis Cardinals (NL) in 4.
1927 New York Yankees (AL) over Pittsburgh Pirates (NL) in 4.
1926 St. Louis Cardinals (NL) over New York Yankees (AL) in 7.
1925 Pittsburgh Pirates (NL) over Washington Senators (AL) in 7.
1924 Washington Senators (AL) over New York Giants (NL) in 7.
1923 New York Yankees (AL) over New York Giants (NL) in 6.
1922 New York Giants (NL) over New York Yankees (AL) in 4-0-1.
1921 New York Giants (NL) over New York Yankees (AL) in 5-3.
1920 Cleveland Indians (AL) over Brooklyn Robins (NL) in 5-2.
1919 Cincinnati Reds (NL) over Chicago White Sox (AL) in 5-3.
1918 Boston Red Sox (AL) over Chicago Cubs (NL) in 6.
1917 Chicago White Sox (AL) over New York Giants (NL) in 6.
1916 Boston Red Sox (AL) over Brooklyn Robins (NL) in 5.
1915 Boston Red Sox (AL) over Philadelphia Phillies (NL) in 5.
1914 Boston Braves (NL) over Philadelphia Athletics (AL) in 4.
1913 Philadelphia Athletics (AL) over New York Giants (NL) in 5.
1912 Boston Red Sox (AL) over New York Giants (NL) in 4-3-1.
1911 Philadelphia Athletics (AL) over New York Giants (NL) in 6.
1910 Philadelphia Athletics (AL) over Chicago Cubs (NL) in 5.
1909 Pittsburgh Pirates (NL) over Detroit Tigers (AL) in 7.
1908 Chicago Cubs (NL) over Detroit Tigers (AL) in 5.
1907 Chicago Cubs (NL) over Detroit Tigers (AL) in 4-0-1.
1906 Chicago White Sox (AL) over Chicago Cubs (NL) in 6.
1905 New York Giants (NL) over Philadelphia Athletics (AL) in 5.
1904 No World Series
1903 Boston Americans (AL) over Pittsburgh Pirates (NL) in 5-3.

SUPER BOWL - NATIONAL FOOTBALL LEAGUE

Number	Date	Teams, Result, Site
LIV (54)	02-02-2020	Kansas City Chiefs (AFC) over San Francisco 49ers (NFC), 31-20, at Hard Rock Stadium, Miami Gardens, FL
LIII (53)	02-03-2019	New England Patriots (AFC) over Los Angeles Rams (NFC), 13-3, at Mercedes-Benz Stadium, Atlanta, GA
LII (52)	02-04-2018	Philadelphia Eagles (NFC) over New England Patriots (AFC), 41-33, at US Bank Stadium, Minneapolis, MN
LI (51)	02-05-2017	New England Patriots (AFC) over Atlanta Falcons (NFC), 34-28 (OT) at NRG Stadium, Houston, TX
50	02-07-2016	Denver Broncos (AFC) over Carolina Panthers (NFC), 24-10, at Levi's Stadium, Santa Clara, CA
XLIX (49)	02-01-2015	New England Patriots (AFC) over Seattle Seahawks (NFC), 28-24, at U. of Phoenix Stadium, Glendale, AZ
XLVIII (48)	02-02-2014	Seattle Seahawks (NFC) over Denver Broncos (AFC), 43-8, at MetLife Stadium, E. Rutherford, NJ
XLVII (47)	02-03-2013	Baltimore Ravens (AFC) over San Francisco 49ers (NFC), 34-31, at Mercedes-Benz Superdome, New Orleans, LA
XLVI (46)	02-05-2012	New York Giants (NFC) over New England Patriots (AFC), 21-17, at Lucas Oil Stadium, Indianapolis, IN
XLV (45)	02-06-2011	Green Bay Packers (NFC) over Pittsburgh Steelers (AFC), 31-25, at Cowboys Stadium, Arlington, TX
XLIV (44)	02-07-2010	New Orleans Saints (NFC) over Indianapolis Colts (AFC), 31-17, at Sun Life Stadium, Miami Gardens, FL
XLIII (43)	02-01-2009	Pittsburgh Steelers (AFC) over Arizona Cardinals (NFC), 27-23, at Raymond James Stadium, Tampa, FL
XLII (42)	02-03-2008	New York Giants (NFC) over New England Patriots (AFC), 17-14, at U. of Phoenix Stadium, Glendale, AZ
XLI (41)	02-04-2007	Indianapolis Colts (AFC) over Chicago Bears (NFC), 29-17, at Dolphin Stadium, Miami Gardens, FL
XL (40)	02-05-2006	Pittsburgh Steelers (AFC) over Seattle Seahawks (NFC), 21-10, at Ford Field, Detroit, MI
XXXIX (39)	02-06-2005	New England Patriots (AFC) over Philadelphia Eagles (NFC), 24-21, at Alltel Stadium, Jacksonville, FL
XXXVIII (38)	02-01-2004	New England Patriots (AFC) over Carolina Panthers, 32-29, at Reliant Stadium, Houston, TX
XXXVII (37)	01-26-2003	Tampa Bay Buccaneers (NFC) over Oakland Raiders (AFC), 48-21, at Qualcomm Stadium, San Diego, CA
XXXVI (36)	02-03-2002	New England Patriots (AFC) over St. Louis Rams (NFC), 20-17, at Louisiana Superdome, New Orleans, LA
XXXV (35)	01-28-2001	Baltimore Ravens (AFC) over New York Giants (NFC), 34-7, at Raymond James Stadium, Tampa, FL
XXXIV (34)	01-30-2000	St. Louis Rams (NFC) over Tennessee Titans (AFC), 23-16, at Georgia Dome, Atlanta, GA
XXXIII (33)	01-31-1999	Denver Broncos (AFC) over Atlanta Falcons (NFC), 34-19, at Pro Player Stadium, Miami, FL
XXXII (32)	01-25-1998	Denver Broncos (AFC) over Green Bay Packers (NFC), 31-24, at Qualcomm Stadium, San Diego, CA
XXXI (31)	01-26-1997	Green Bay Packers (NFC) over New England Patriots (AFC), 35-21, at Louisiana Superdome, New Orleans, LA
XXX (30)	01-28-1996	Dallas Cowboys (NFC) over Pittsburgh Steelers (AFC), 27-17, at Sun Devil Stadium, Tempe, AZ
XXIX (29)	01-29-1995	San Francisco 49ers (NFC) over San Diego Chargers (AFC), 49-26, at Joe Robbie Stadium, Miami, FL
XXVIII (28)	01-30-1994	Dallas Cowboys (NFC) over Buffalo Bills (AFC), 30-13, at Georgia Dome, Atlanta, GA
XXVII (27)	01-31-1993	Dallas Cowboys (NFC) over Buffalo Bills (AFC), 52-17, at Rose Bowl, Pasadena, CA

SUPER BOWL - NATIONAL FOOTBALL LEAGUE

Number	Date	Teams, Result, Site
XXVI (26)	01-26-1992	Washington Redskins (NFC) over Buffalo Bills (AFC), 37-24, at Metrodome, Minneapolis, MN
XXV (25)	01-27-1991	New York Giants (NFC) over Buffalo Bills (AFC), 20-19, at Tampa Stadium, Tampa, FL
XXIV (24)	01-28-1990	San Francisco 49ers (NFC) over Denver Broncos (AFC), 55-10, at Louisiana Superdome, New Orleans, LA
XXIII (23)	01-22-1989	San Francisco 49ers (NFC) over Cincinnati Bengals (AFC), 20-16, at Joe Robbie Stadium, Miami, FL
XXII (22)	01-31-1988	Washington Redskins (NFC) over Denver Broncos (AFC), 42-10, at Jack Murphy Stadium, San Diego, CA
XXI (21)	01-25-1987	New York Giants (NFC) over Denver Broncos (AFC), 39-20, at Rose Bowl, Pasadena, CA
XX (20)	01-26-1986	Chicago Bears (NFC) over New England Patriots (AFC), 46-10, at Louisiana Superdome, New Orleans, LA
XIX (19)	01-20-1985	San Francisco 49ers (NFC) over Miami Dolphins (AFC), 38-16, at Stanford Stadium, Stanford, CA
XVIII (18)	01-22-1984	Los Angeles Raiders (AFC) over Washington Redskins (NFC), 38-9, at Tampa Stadium, Tampa, FL
XVII (17)	01-30-1983	Washington Redskins (NFC) over Miami Dolphins (AFC), 27-17, at Rose Bowl, Pasadena, CA
XVI (16)	01-24-1982	San Francisco 49ers (NFC) over Cincinnati Bengals (AFC), 26-21, at Pontiac Silverdome, Pontiac, MI
XV (15)	01-25-1981	Oakland Raiders (AFC) over Philadelphia Eagles (NFC), 27-10, at Louisiana Superdome, New Orleans, LA
XIV (14)	01-20-1980	Pittsburgh Steelers (AFC) over Los Angeles Rams (NFC), 31-19, at Rose Bowl, Pasadena, CA
XIII (13)	01-21-1979	Pittsburgh Steelers (AFC) over Dallas Cowboys (NFC), 35-31, at Orange Bowl, Miami, FL
XII (12)	01-15-1978	Dallas Cowboys (NFC) over Denver Broncos (AFC), 27-10, at Louisiana Superdome, New Orleans, LA
XI (11)	01-09-1977	Oakland Raiders (AFC) over Minnesota Vikings (NFC), 32-14, at Rose Bowl, Pasadena, CA
X (10)	01-18-1976	Pittsburgh Steelers (AFC) over Dallas Cowboys (NFC), 21-17, at Orange Bowl, Miami, FL
IX (9)	01-12-1975	Pittsburgh Steelers (AFC) over Minnesota Vikings (NFC), 16-6, at Tulane Stadium, New Orleans, LA
VIII (8)	01-13-1974	Miami Dolphins (AFC) over Minnesota Vikings (NFC), 24-7, at Rice Stadium, Houston, TX
VII (7)	01-14-1973	Miami Dolphins (AFC) over Washington Redskins (NFC), 14-7, at Memorial Coliseum, Los Angeles, CA
VI (6)	01-16-1972	Dallas Cowboys (NFC) over Miami Dolphins (AFC), 24-3, at Tulane Stadium, New Orleans, LA
V (5)	01-17-1971	Baltimore Colts (AFC) over Dallas Cowboys (NFC), 16-13, at Orange Bowl, Miami, FL
IV (4)	01-11-1970	Kansas City Chiefs (AFL) over Minnesota Vikings (NFL), 23-7, at Tulane Stadium, New Orleans, LA
III (3)	01-12-1969	New York Jets (AFL) over Baltimore Colts (NFL), 16-7, at Orange Bowl, Miami, FL
II (2)	01-14-1968	Green Bay Packers (NFL) over Oakland Raiders (AFL), 33-14, at Orange Bowl, Miami, FL
I (1)	01-15-1967	Green Bay Packers (NFL) over Kansas City Chiefs (AFL), 35-10, at Memorial Coliseum, Los Angeles, CA

Super Bowls I-IV were AFL/NFL World Championship Games

STANLEY CUP - NATIONAL HOCKEY LEAGUE

Season	Winner	Runner-Up	Games
2019	St. Louis Blues	Boston Bruins	4-3
2018	Washington Capitals	Vegas Golden Knights	4-1
2017	Pittsburgh Penguins	Nashville Predators	4-2
2016	Pittsburgh Penguins	San Jose Sharks	4-2
2015	Chicago Black Hawks	Tampa Bay Lightning	4-2
2014	Los Angeles Kings	New York Rangers	4-1
2013	Chicago Black Hawks	Boston Bruins	4-2
2012	Los Angeles Kings	New Jersey Devils	4-2
2011	Boston Bruins	Vancouver Canucks	4-3
2010	Chicago Black Hawks	Philadelphia Flyers	4-2
2009	Pittsburgh Penguins	Detroit Red Wings	4-3
2008	Detroit Red Wings	Pittsburgh Penguins	4-2
2007	Anaheim Ducks	Ottawa Senators	4-1
2006	Carolina Hurricanes	Edmonton Oilers	4-3
2005	No Stanley Cup-Season Cancelled		
2004	Tampa Bay Lightning	Calgary Flames	4-3
2003	New Jersey Devils	Mighty Ducks of Anaheim	4-3
2002	Detroit Red Wings	Carolina Hurricanes	4-1
2001	Colorado Avalanche	New Jersey Devils	4-3
2000	New Jersey Devils	Dallas Stars	4-2
1999	Dallas Stars	Buffalo Sabres	4-2
1998	Detroit Red Wings	Washington Capitals	4-0
1997	Detroit Red Wings	Philadelphia Flyers	4-0
1996	Colorado Avalanche	Florida Panthers	4-0
1995	New Jersey Devils	Detroit Red Wings	4-0
1994	New York Rangers	Vancouver Canucks	4-3
1993	Montreal Canadiens	Los Angeles Kings	4-1
1992	Pittsburgh Penguins	Chicago Black Hawks	4-0
1991	Pittsburgh Penguins	Minnesota North Stars	4-2
1990	Edmonton Oilers	Boston Bruins	4-1
1989	Calgary Flames	Montreal Canadiens	4-2
1988	Edmonton Oilers	Boston Bruins	4-0
1987	Edmonton Oilers	Philadelphia Flyers	4-3
1986	Montreal Canadiens	Calgary Flames	4-1
1985	Edmonton Oilers	Philadelphia Flyers	4-1
1984	Edmonton Oilers	New York Islanders	4-1
1983	New York Islanders	Edmonton Oilers	4-0
1982	New York Islanders	Vancouver Canucks	4-0
1981	New York Islanders	Minnesota North Stars	4-1
1980	New York Islanders	Philadelphia Flyers	4-2
1979	Montreal Canadiens	New York Rangers	4-1
1978	Montreal Canadiens	Boston Bruins	4-2
1977	Montreal Canadiens	Boston Bruins	4-0
1976	Montreal Canadiens	Philadelphia Flyers	4-0
1975	Philadelphia Flyers	Buffalo Sabres	4-2
1974	Philadelphia Flyers	Boston Bruins	4-2
1973	Montreal Canadiens	Chicago Black Hawks	4-2
1972	Boston Bruins	New York Rangers	4-2
1971	Montreal Canadiens	Chicago Black Hawks	4-3
1970	Boston Bruins	St. Louis Blues	4-0
1969	Montreal Canadiens	St. Louis Blues	4-0
1968	Montreal Canadiens	St. Louis Blues	4-0
1967	Toronto Maple Leafs	Montreal Canadiens	4-2
1966	Montreal Canadiens	Detroit Red Wings	4-2
1965	Montreal Canadiens	Chicago Black Hawks	4-2
1964	Toronto Maple Leafs	Detroit Red Wings	4-3
1963	Toronto Maple Leafs	Detroit Red Wings	4-1
1962	Toronto Maple Leafs	Chicago Black Hawks	4-2
1961	Chicago Black Hawks	Detroit Red Wings	4-2
1960	Montreal Canadiens	Toronto Maple Leafs	4-0
1959	Montreal Canadiens	Toronto Maple Leafs	4-1
1958	Montreal Canadiens	Boston Bruins	4-2
1957	Montreal Canadiens	Boston Bruins	4-1
1956	Montreal Canadiens	Detroit Red Wings	4-1
1955	Detroit Red Wings	Montreal Canadiens	4-3
1954	Detroit Red Wings	Montreal Canadiens	4-3
1953	Montreal Canadiens	Boston Bruins	4-1
1952	Detroit Red Wings	Montreal Canadiens	4-0
1951	Toronto Maple Leafs	Montreal Canadiens	4-1
1950	Detroit Red Wings	New York Rangers	4-3
1949	Toronto Maple Leafs	Detroit Red Wings	4-0
1948	Toronto Maple Leafs	Detroit Red Wings	4-0
1947	Toronto Maple Leafs	Montreal Canadiens	4-2
1946	Montreal Canadiens	Boston Bruins	4-1
1945	Toronto Maple Leafs	Detroit Red Wings	4-2
1944	Montreal Canadiens	Chicago Black Hawks	4-0
1943	Detroit Red Wings	Boston Bruins	4-0
1942	Toronto Maple Leafs	Detroit Red Wings	4-3
1941	Boston Bruins	Detroit Red Wings	4-0
1940	New York Rangers	Toronto Maple Leafs	4-2
1939	Boston Bruins	Toronto Maple Leafs	4-1
1938	Chicago Black Hawks	Toronto Maple Leafs	3-1
1937	Detroit Red Wings	New York Rangers	3-2
1936	Detroit Red Wings	Toronto Maple Leafs	3-1
1935	Montreal Maroons	Toronto Maple Leafs	3-0
1934	Chicago Black Hawks	Detroit Red Wings	3-1
1933	New York Rangers	Toronto Maple Leafs	3-1
1932	Toronto Maple Leafs	New York Rangers	3-0
1931	Montreal Canadiens	Chicago Black Hawks	3-2
1930	Montreal Canadiens	Boston Bruins	2-0
1929	Boston Bruins	New York Rangers	2-0

FINALS - NATIONAL BASKETBALL LEAGUE

Year	Winner-Runner-up	Games
2019	Toronto Raptors (E) over Golden State Warriors (W)	4-2
2018	Golden State Warriors (W) over Cleveland Cavaliers (E)	4-0
2017	Golden State Warriors (W) over Cleveland Cavaliers (E)	4-1
2016	Cleveland Cavaliers (E) over Golden State Warriors (W)	4-3
2015	Golden State Warriors (W) over Cleveland Cavaliers (E)	4-2
2014	San Antonio Spurs (W) over Miami Heat (E)	4-1
2013	Miami Heat (E) over San Antonio Spurs (W)	4-3
2012	Miami Heat (E) over Oklahoma City Thunder (W)	4-1
2011	Dallas Mavericks (W) over Miami Heat (E)	4-2
2010	Los Angeles Lakers (W) over Boston Celtics (E)	4-3
2009	Los Angeles Lakers (W) over Orlando Magic (E)	4-1
2008	Boston Celtics (E) over Los Angeles Lakers (W)	4-2
2007	San Antonio Spurs (W) over Cleveland Cavaliers (E)	4-0
2006	Miami Heat (E) over Dallas Mavericks (W)	4-2
2005	San Antonio Spurs (W) over Detroit Pistons (E)	4-3
2004	Detroit Pistons (E) over Los Angeles Lakers (W)	4-1
2003	San Antonio Spurs (W) over New Jersey Nets (E)	4-2
2002	Los Angeles Lakers (W) over New Jersey Nets (E)	4-0
2001	Los Angeles Lakers (W) over Philadelphia 76ers (E)	4-1
2000	Los Angeles Lakers (W) over Indiana Pacers (E)	4-2
1999	San Antonio Spurs (W) over New York Knicks (E)	4-1
1998	Chicago Bulls (E) over Utah Jazz (W)	4-2
1997	Chicago Bulls (E) over Utah Jazz (W)	4-2
1996	Chicago Bulls (E) over Seattle SuperSonics (W)	4-2
1995	Houston Rockets (W) over Orlando Magic (E)	4-0
1994	Houston Rockets (W) over New York Knicks (E)	4-3
1993	Chicago Bulls (E) over Phoenix Suns (W)	4-2
1992	Chicago Bulls (E) over Portland Trail Blazers (W)	4-2
1991	Chicago Bulls (E) over Los Angeles Lakers (W)	4-1
1990	Detroit Pistons (E) over Portland Trail Blazers (W)	4-1
1989	Detroit Pistons (E) over Los Angeles Lakers (W)	4-0
1988	Los Angeles Lakers (W) over Detroit Pistons (E)	4-3
1987	Los Angeles Lakers (W) over Boston Celtics (E)	4-2
1986	Boston Celtics (E) over Houston Rockets (W)	4-2
1985	Los Angeles Lakers (W) over Boston Celtics (E)	4-2
1984	Boston Celtics (E) over Los Angeles Lakers (W)	4-3
1983	Philadelphia 76ers (E) over Los Angeles Lakers (W)	4-0
1982	Los Angeles Lakers (W) over Philadelphia 76ers (E)	4-2
1981	Boston Celtics (E) over Houston Rockets (W)	4-2
1980	Los Angeles Lakers (W) over Philadelphia 76ers (E)	4-2
1979	Seattle SuperSonics (W) over Washington Bullets (E)	4-1
1978	Washington Bullets (E) over Seattle SuperSonics (W)	4-3
1977	Portland Trail Blazers (W) over Philadelphia 76ers (E)	4-2
1976	Boston Celtics (E) over Phoenix Suns (W)	4-2
1975	Golden State Warriors (W) over Washington Bullets (E)	4-0
1974	Boston Celtics (E) over Milwaukee Bucks (W)	4-3
1973	New York Knicks (E) over Los Angeles Lakers (W)	4-1
1972	Los Angeles Lakers (W) over New York Knicks (E)	4-1
1971	Milwaukee Bucks (W) over Baltimore Bullets (E)	4-0
1970	New York Knicks (E) over Los Angeles Lakers (W)	4-3
1969	Boston Celtics (E) over Los Angeles Lakers (W)	4-3
1968	Boston Celtics (E) over Los Angeles Lakers (W)	4-2
1967	Philadelphia 76ers (E) over San Francisco Warriors (W)	4-2
1966	Boston Celtics (E) over Los Angeles Lakers (W)	4-3
1965	Boston Celtics (E) over Los Angeles Lakers (W)	4-1
1964	Boston Celtics (E) over San Francisco Warriors (W)	4-1
1963	Boston Celtics (E) over Los Angeles Lakers (W)	4-2
1962	Boston Celtics (E) over Los Angeles Lakers (W)	4-3
1961	Boston Celtics (E) over St. Louis Hawks (W)	4-1
1960	Boston Celtics (E) over St. Louis Hawks (W)	4-3
1959	Boston Celtics (E) over Minneapolis Lakers (W)	4-0
1958	St. Louis Hawks (W) over Boston Celtics (E)	4-2
1957	Boston Celtics (E) over St. Louis Hawks (W)	4-3
1956	Philadelphia Warriors (E) over Fort Wayne Pistons (W)	4-1
1955	Syracuse Nationals (E) over Fort Wayne Pistons (W)	4-3
1954	Minneapolis Lakers (W) over Syracuse Nationals (E)	4-3
1953	Minneapolis Lakers (W) over New York Knicks (E)	4-1
1952	Minneapolis Lakers (W) over New York Knicks (E)	4-3
1951	Rochester Royals (W) over New York Knicks (E)	4-3
1950	Minneapolis Lakers (W) over Syracuse Nationals (E)	4-2
1949	Minneapolis Lakers (W) over Washington Capitols (E)	4-2
1948	Baltimore Bullets (W) over Philadelphia Warriors (E)	4-2
1947	Philadelphia Warriors (E) over Chicago Stags (W)	4-1

GOLF MAJOR TOURNAMENTS

Year	Masters	US Open	PGA Championship
2019	Tiger Woods	Gary Woodland-Pebble Beach	Brooks Koepka-Bethpage Black
2018	Patrick Reed	Brooks Koepka-Shinnecock	Brooks Koepka-Bellerive
2017	Sergio Garcia*	Brooks Koepka-Erin Hills	Justin Thomas-Quail Hollow
2016	Danny Willett	Dustin Johnson-Oakmont	Jimmy Walker-Baltusrol
2015	Jordan Spieth	Jordan Spieth-Chambers Bay	Jason Day-Whistling Straits
2014	Bubba Watson	Martin Kaymer-Pinehurst	Rory McIlroy-Valhalla
2013	Adam Scott*	Justin Rose-Merion	Jason Dufner-Oak Hill
2012	Bubba Watson*	Webb Simpson-Olympic Club	Rory McIlroy-Kiawah Island
2011	Charl Schwartzel	Rory McIlroy-Congressional	Keegan Bradley-Atlanta Athletic*
2010	Phil Mickelson	Graeme McDowell-Pebble Beach	Martin Kaymer-Whistling Straits*
2009	Angel Cabrera*	Lucas Glover-Bethpage Black	Yang Yongeun-Hazeltine
2008	Trevor Immelman	Tiger Woods-Torrey Pines*	Padraig Harrington-Oakland Hills
2007	Zach Johnson	Angel Cabrera-Oakmont	Tiger Woods-Southern Hills
2006	Phil Mickelson	Geoff Ogilvy-Winged Foot	Tiger Woods-Medinah
2005	Tiger Woods*	Michael Campbell- Pinehurst	Phil Mickelson- Baltusrol
2004	Phil Mickelson	Retief Goosen- Shinnecock	Vijay Singh- Whistling Straits*
2003	Mike Weir*	Jim Furyk-Olympia Fields	Shaun Micheel-Oak Hill
2002	Tiger Woods	Tiger Woods-Bethpage Black	Rich Beem- Hazeltine
2001	Tiger Woods	Retief Goosen-Southern Hills*	David Toms- Atlanta Athletic
2000	Vijay Singh	Tiger Woods- Pebble Beach	Tiger Woods- Valhalla*
1999	Jose Maria Olazabal	Payne Stewart- Pinehurst	Tiger Woods- Medinah
1998	Mark O'Meara	Lee Janzen- Olympic Club	Vijay Singh-Sahalee
1997	Tiger Woods	Ernie Els- Congressional	Davis Love III-Winged Foot
1996	Nick Faldo	Steve Jones-Oakland Hills	Mark Brooks- Valhalla*
1995	Ben Crenshaw	Corey Pavin- Shinnecock	Steve Elkington-Riviera*
1994	Jose Maria Olazabal	Ernie Els- Oakmont*	Nick Price-Southern Hills
1993	Bernhard Langer	Lee Janzen-Baltusrol	Paul Azinger-Inverness*
1992	Fred Couples	Tom Kite- Pebble Beach	Nick Price-Bellerive
1991	Ian Woosnam	Payne Stewart-Hazeltine*	John Daley-Crooked Stick
1990	Nick Faldo*	Hale Irwin-Medinah*	Wayne Grady-Shoal Creek
1989	Nick Faldo*	Curtis Strange-Oak Hill	Payne Stewart-Kemper Lakes
1988	Sandy Lyle	Curtis Strange-The Country Club*	Jeff Sluman-Oak Tree
1987	Larry Mize*	Scott Simpson- Olympic Club	Larry Nelson-PGA Natl-PBG*
1986	Jack Nicklaus	Raymond Floyd- Shinnecock	Bob Tway-Inverness
1985	Bernhard Langer	Andy North- Oakland Hills	Hubert Green-Cherry Hill
1984	Ben Crenshaw	Fuzzy Zoeller- Winged Foot*	Lee Trevino-Shoal Creek
1983	Seve Ballesteros	Larry Nelson- Oakmont	Hal Sutton-Riviera
1982	Craig Stadler*	Tom Watson- Pebble Beach	Raymond Floyd-Southern Hills
1981	Tom Watson	David Graham- Merion	Larry Nelson-Atlanta Athletic
1980	Seve Ballesteros	Jack Nicklaus- Baltusrol	Jack Nicklaus-Oak Hill
1979	Fuzzy Zoeller*	Hale Irwin-Inverness	David Graham-Oakland Hills*
1978	Gary Player	Andy North-Cherry Hills	John Mahaffey-Oakmont*
1977	Tom Watson	Hubert Green-Southern Hills	Lanny Wadkins-Pebble Beach*

Land of the Free, Home of the Brave

GOLF MAJOR TOURNAMENTS

Year	Masters	US Open	PGA Championship
1976	Raymond Floyd	Jerry Pate-Atlanta Athletic	Dave Stockton-Congressional
1975	Jack Nicklaus	Lou Graham- Medinah*	Jack Nicklaus-Firestone
1974	Gary Player	Hale Irwin- Winged Foot	Lee Trevino-Tanglewood Park
1973	Tommy Aaron	Johnny Miller- Oakmont	Jack Nicklaus-Canterbury
1972	Jack Nicklaus	Jack Nicklaus- Pebble Beach	Gary Player-Oakland Hills
1971	Charles Coody	Lee Trevino- Merion*	Jack Nicklaus- PGA Natl-PBG
1970	Billy Casper*	Tony Jacklin- Hazeltine	Dave Stockton- Southern Hills
1969	George Archer	Orville Moody-Champions	Raymond Floyd-NCR CC
1968	Bob Goalby	Lee Trevino- Oak Hill	Julius Boros-Pecan Valley
1967	Gay Brewer	Jack Nicklaus- Baltusrol	Don January-Columbine*
1966	Jack Nicklaus*	Billy Casper- Olympic Club*	Al Geiberger- Firestone
1965	Jack Nicklaus	Gary Player-Bellerive*	Dave Marr-Laurel Valley
1964	Arnold Palmer	Ken Venturi- Congressional	Bobby Nichols-Columbus
1963	Jack Nicklaus	Julius Boros- The Country Club*	Jack Nicklaus-Dallas Athletic
1962	Arnold Palmer*	Jack Nicklaus- Oakmont*	Gary Player-Aronimink
1961	Gary Player	Gene Littler- Oakland Hills	Jerry Barber-Olympia Fields*
1960	Arnold Palmer	Arnold Palmer- Cherry Hills	Jay Hebert- Firestone
1959	Art Wall Jr	Billy Casper- Winged Foot	Bob Rosburg-Minneapolis GC
1958	Arnold Palmer	Tommy Bolt- Southern Hills	Dow Finsterwald-Llanerch
1957	Doug Ford	Dick Mayer- Inverness*	Lionel Hebert-Miami Valley
1956	Jack Burke Jr	Cary Middlecoff- Oak Hill	Jack Burke Jr-Blue Hill
1955	Cary Middlecoff	Jack Fleck- Olympic Club*	Doug Ford-Meadowbrook
1954	Sam Snead*	Ed Furgol- Baltusrol	Chick Harbert-Keller
1953	Ben Hogan	Ben Hogan- Oakmont	Walter Burkemo-Birmingham CC
1952	Sam Snead	Julius Boros-Northwood	Jim Turnesa-Big Spring CC
1951	Ben Hogan	Ben Hogan- Oakland Hills	Sam Snead-Oakmont
1950	Jimmy Demaret	Ben Hogan- Merion*	Chandler Harper-Scioto CC
1949	Sam Snead	Cary Middlecoff- Medinah	Sam Snead-Hermitage CC
1948	Claude Harmon	Ben Hogan-Riviera	Ben Hogan-Norwood Hills
1947	Jimmy Demaret	Lew Worsham-St. Louis CC*	Jim Ferrier-Plum Hollow
1946	Herman Keiser	Lloyd Mangrum-Canterbury*	Ben Hogan-Portland CC
1945	————	————	Byron Nelson-Moraine
1944	————	————	Bob Hamilton-Manito
1943	————	————	————
1942	Byron Nelson*	————	Sam Snead-Seaview
1941	Craig Wood	Craig Wood-Colonial	Vic Ghezzi-Cherry Hills
1940	Jimmy Demaret	Lawson Little-Canterbury*	Byron Nelson-Hershey CC
1939	Ralph Guldahl	Byron Nelson-Philadelphia CC*	Henry Picard-Pomonok
1938	Henry Picard	Ralph Guldahl- Cherry Hills	Paul Runyan-Shawnee Inn
1937	Byron Nelson	Ralph Guldahl- Oakland Hills	Denny Shute-Pittsburgh FC
1936	Horton Smith	Tony Manero- Baltusrol	Denny Shute-Pinehurst
1935	Gene Sarazen*	Sam Parks Jr- Oakmont	Johnny Revolta-Twin Hills
1934	Horton Smith	Olin Dutra- Merion	Paul Runyan-The Park

Land of the Free, Home of the Brave

GOLF MAJOR TOURNAMENTS

Year	Masters	US Open	PGA Championship
1933		Johnny Goodman (a)-North Shore	Gene Sarazen-Blue Mound
1932		Gene Sarazen-Fresh Meadow	Olin Dutra-Keller
1931		Billy Burke- Inverness*	Tom Creavy-Wannamoisett
1930		Bobby Jones (a)-Interlachen	Tommy Armour-Fresh Meadow
1929		Bobby Jones (a)- Winged Foot*	Leo Diegel-Hillcrest
1928		Johnny Farrell-Olympia Fields*	Leo Diegel-Baltimore CC
1927		Tommy Armour- Oakmont*	Walter Hagen-Cedar CC
1926		Bobby Jones (a)-Scioto	Walter Hagen-Salisbury
1925		Willie Macfarlane-Worcester*	Walter Hagen-Olympia Fields
1924		Cyril Walker- Oakland Hills	Walter Hagen-French Lick
1923		Bobby Jones (a)-Inwood*	Gene Sarazen-Pelham CC
1922		Gene Sarazen-Skokie	Gene Sarazen-Oakmont
1921		Jim Barnes-Columbia	Walter Hagen-Inwood
1920		Ted Ray- Inverness	Jock Hutchison-Flossmoor
1919		Walter Hagen-Brae Burn*	Jim Barnes-Engineers CC
1918		———	———
1917		———	———
1916		Chick Evans (a)-Minikahda	Jim Barnes-Siwanoy CC
1915		Jerome Travers (a)-Baltusrol	
1914		Walter Hagen-Midlothian	
1913		Francis Ouimet (a)- The Country Club*	
1912		John McDermott-County Club Buffalo	
1911		John McDermott-Chicago Golf Club*	
1910		Alex Smith-Philadelphia Cricket*	
1909		George Sargent-Englewood	
1908		Fred McLeod-Myopia*	
1907		Alec Ross- Philadelphia Cricket	
1906		Alex Smith-Onwentsia	
1905		Willie Anderson-Myopia	
1904		Willie Anderson-Glen View	
1903		Willie Anderson- Baltusrol*	
1902		Laurie Auchterlonie-Garden City	
1901		Willie Anderson-Myopia*	
1900		Harry Vardon-Chicago Golf Club	
1899		Willie Smith-Baltimore CC	
1898		Fred Herd-Myopia	
1897		Joe Lloyd-Chicago Golf Club	
1896		James Foulis- Shinnecock	
1895		Horace Rawlins-Newport CC	

*Won Playoff (a) Amateur
PGA Championship match play until 1958.
US Open 36 holes on Saturday until 1965.
Masters did not begin until 1934.

INDIANAPOLIS 500 RESULTS

Year	Winner	Ave Speed (mph)
2019	Simon Pagenaud	175.794
2018	Will Power	166.935
2017	Takuma Sato	155.395
2016	Alexander Rossi	166.634
2015	Juan Pablo Montoya	161.341
2014	Ryan Hunter-Reay	186.563
2013	Tony Kanaan	**187.433**
2012	Dario Franchitti	167.734
2011	Dan Wheldon	170.265
2010	Dario Franchitti	161.623
2009	Helio Castroneves	150.318
2008	Scott Dixon	143.567
2007	Dario Franchitti	151.774
2006	Sam Hornish Jr	157.085
2005	Dan Wheldon	157.603
2004	Buddy Rice	138.518
2003	Gil de Ferran	156.291
2002	Helio Castroneves	166.499
2001	Helio Castroneves	141.574
2000	Juan Pablo Montoya	167.607
1999	Kenny Brack	153.176
1998	Eddie Cheever	145.155
1997	Arie Luyendyk	145.827
1996	Buddy Lazier	147.956
1995	Jacques Villeneuve	153.616
1994	Al Unser Jr	160.872
1993	Emerson Fittipaldi	157.207
1992	Al Unser Jr	134.477
1991	Rick Mears	176.457
1990	Arie Luyendyk	185.981
1989	Emerson Fittipaldi	167.581
1988	Rick Mears	144.809
1987	Al Unser Sr	162.175
1986	Bobby Rahal	170.722
1985	Danny Sullivan	152.982
1984	Rick Mears	163.612
1983	Tom Sneva	162.117
1982	Gordon Johncock	162.029
1981	Bobby Unser	139.084
1980	Johnny Rutherford	142.862
1979	Rick Mears	158.899
1978	Al Unser Sr	161.363
1977	AJ Foyt	161.331
1976	Johnny Rutherford	148.725
1975	Bobby Unser	149.213
1974	Johnny Rutherford	158.589
1973	Gordon Johncock	159.036
1972	Mark Donohue	162.962
1971	Al Unser Sr	157.735
1970	Al Unser Sr	155.749
1969	Mario Andretti	156.867
1968	Bobby Unser	152.882
1967	AJ Foyt	151.207
1966	Graham Hill	144.317
1965	Jim Clark	150.686
1964	AJ Foyt	147.35
1963	Parnelli Jones	143.137
1962	Rodger Ward	140.293
1961	AJ Foyt	139.13
1960	Jim Rathmann	138.767
1959	Rodger Ward	135.857
1958	Jimmy Bryan	133.791
1957	Sam Hanks	135.601
1956	Pat Flaherty	128.49
1955	Bob Sweikert	128.213
1954	Bill Vukovich	130.84
1953	Bill Vukovich	128.74
1952	Troy Ruttman	128.922
1951	Lee Wallard	126.244
1950	Johnnie Parsons	124.002
1949	Bill Holland	121.327
1948	Mauri Rose	119.814
1947	Mauri Rose	116.338
1946	George Robson	114.82
1945	No race	
1944	No race	
1943	No race	
1942	No race	
1941	Mauri Rose/F Davis	115.117
1940	Wilbur Shaw	114.277
1939	Wilbur Shaw	115.035
1938	Floyd Roberts	117.20
1937	Wilbur Shaw	113.58
1936	Louis Meyer	109.069
1935	Kelly Petillo	106.24
1934	Bill Cummings	104.863
1933	Louis Meyer	104.162
1932	Fred Frame	104.144
1931	Louis Schneider	96.629
1930	Billy Arnold	100.448
1929	Ray Keech	97.585
1928	Louis Meyer	99.482
1927	George Souders	97.545
1926	Frank Lockhart	95.904
1925	Peter DePaolo	101.127
1924	Joe Boyer/Lora Corum	98.234
1923	Tommy Milton	90.545
1922	Jimmy Murphy	94.484
1921	Tommy Milton	89.621
1920	Gaston Chevrolet	88.618
1919	Howdy Wilcox	88.05
1918	No race	
1917	No race	
1916	Dario Resta	84.001
1915	Ralph DePalma	89.84
1914	Rene Thomas	82.474
1913	Jules Goux	75.933
1912	Joe Dawson	78.719
1911	Ray Harroun	74.59

— Land of the Free, Home of the Brave —

NASCAR CUP WINNERS

Season	Driver	Team	Manufacturer
2019	Kyle Busch	Joe Gibbs Racing	Toyota
2018	Joey Lagano	Team Penske	Ford
2017	Martin Truex Jr.	Furniture Row Racing	Toyota
2016	Jimmie Johnson	Hendrick Motorsports	Chevrolet
2015	Kyle Busch	Joe Gibbs Racing	Toyota
2014	Kevin Harvick	Stewart-Haas Racing	Chevrolet
2013	Jimmie Johnson	Hendrick Motorsports	Chevrolet
2012	Brad Keselowski	Team Penske	Dodge
2011	Tony Stewart	Stewart-Haas Racing	Chevrolet
2010	Jimmie Johnson	Hendrick Motorsports	Chevrolet
2009	Jimmie Johnson	Hendrick Motorsports	Chevrolet
2008	Jimmie Johnson	Hendrick Motorsports	Chevrolet
2007	Jimmie Johnson	Hendrick Motorsports	Chevrolet
2006	Jimmie Johnson	Hendrick Motorsports	Chevrolet
2005	Tony Stewart	Stewart-Haas Racing	Chevrolet
2004	Kurt Busch	Rousch Racing	Ford
2003	Matt Kensuth	Rousch Racing	Ford
2002	Tony Stewart	Joe Gibbs Racing	Pontiac
2001	Jeff Gordon	Hendrick Motorsports	Chevrolet
2000	Bobby Labonte	Joe Gibbs Racing	Pontiac
1999	Dale Jarrett	Robt Yates Racing	Ford
1998	Jeff Gordon	Hendrick Motorsports	Chevrolet
1997	Jeff Gordon	Hendrick Motorsports	Chevrolet
1996	Terry Labonte	Hendrick Motorsports	Chevrolet
1995	Jeff Gordon	Hendrick Motorsports	Chevrolet
1994	Dale Earnhardt	Richard Childress Racing	Chevrolet
1993	Dale Earnhardt	Richard Childress Racing	Chevrolet
1992	Alan Kulwicki	AK Racing	Ford
1991	Dale Earnhardt	Richard Childress Racing	Chevrolet
1990	Dale Earnhardt	Richard Childress Racing	Chevrolet
1989	Rusty Wallace	Blue Max Racing	Pontiac
1988	Bill Elliott	Melling Racing	Ford
1987	Dale Earnhardt	Richard Childress Racing	Chevrolet
1986	Dale Earnhardt	Richard Childress Racing	Chevrolet
1985	Darrell Waltrip	Junior Johnson & Assoc	Chevrolet
1984	Terry Labonte	Hagan Racing	Chevrolet
1983	Bobby Allison	DiGard Motorsports	Chevy, Buick
1982	Dale Earnhardt	Richard Childress Racing	Buick
1981	Dale Earnhardt	Richard Childress Racing	Chevy, Buick
1980	Dale Earnhardt	Osterlund Racing	Chevy, Olds
1979	Richard Petty	Petty Enterprises	Chevy, Olds
1978	Cale Yarborough	Junior Johnson & Assoc	Olds
1977	Cale Yarborough	Junior Johnson & Assoc	Chevrolet
1976	Cale Yarborough	Junior Johnson & Assoc	Chevrolet
1975	Richard Petty	Petty Enterprises	Dodge
1974	Richard Petty	Petty Enterprises	Dodge
1973	Benny Parsons	LG DeWitt	Chevy, Mercury
1972	Richard Petty	Petty Enterprises	Dodge, Plymouth

KENTUCKY DERBY RESULTS

Year	Winner	Jockey	Trainer	Time
2019	Country House	Flavien Prat	Bill Mott	2:03.93
2018	**Justify**	Mike E Smith	Bob Baffert	2:04.20
2017	Always Dreaming	John Valazquez	Todd Pletcher	2:03.59
2016	Nyquist	Mario Gutierrez	Doug O'Neill	2:01.31
2015	**American Pharoah**	Victor Espinoza	Bob Baffert	2:03.02
2014	California Chrome	Victor Espinoza	Art Sherman	2:03.66
2013	Orb	Joel Rosario	Claude McGaughey III	2:02.89
2012	I'll Have Another	Mario Gutierrez	Doug O'Neill	2:01.83
2011	Animal Kingdom	John Velazquez	H. Graham Motion	2:02.04
2010	Super Saver	Calvin Borel	Todd Pletcher	2:04.45
2009	Mine That Bird	Calvin Borel	Bennie L. Woolley, Jr.	2:02.66
2008	Big Brown	Kent Desormeaux	Richard E. Dutrow, Jr.	2:01.82
2007	Street Sense	Calvin Borel	Carl Nafzger	2:02.17
2006	Barbaro	Edgar Prado	Michael R. Matz	2:01.36
2005	Giacomo	Mike E. Smith	John Shirreffs	2:02.75
2004	Smarty Jones	Stewart Elliott	John Servis	2:04.06
2003	Funny Cide	José A. Santos	Barclay Tagg	2:01.19
2002	War Emblem	Victor Espinoza	Bob Baffert	2:01.13
2001	Monarchos	Jorge F. Chavez	John T. Ward, Jr.	1:59.97
2000	Fusaichi Pegasus	Kent Desormeaux	Neil Drysdale	2:01.0
1999	Charismatic	Chris Antley	D. Wayne Lukas	2:03.2
1998	Real Quiet	Kent Desormeaux	Bob Baffert	2:02.2
1997	Silver Charm	Gary Stevens	Bob Baffert	2:02.4
1996	Grindstone	Jerry Bailey	D. Wayne Lukas	2:01.0
1995	Thunder Gulch	Gary Stevens	D. Wayne Lukas	2:01.2
1994	Go for Gin	Chris McCarron	Nick Zito	2:03.6
1993	Sea Hero	Jerry Bailey	MacKenzie Miller	2:02.4
1992	Lil E. Tee	Pat Day	Lynn S. Whiting	2:03.0
1991	Strike the Gold	Chris Antley	Nick Zito	2:03.0
1990	Unbridled	Craig Perret	Carl Nafzger	2:02.0
1989	Sunday Silence	Pat Valenzuela	Charlie Whittingham	2:05.0
1988	Winning Colors *	Gary Stevens	D. Wayne Lukas	2:02.2
1987	Alysheba	Chris McCarron	Jack Van Berg	2:03.4
1986	Ferdinand	Bill Shoemaker	Charlie Whittingham	2:02.8
1985	Spend A Buck	Angel Cordero, Jr.	Cam Gambolati	2:00.2
1984	Swale	Laffit Pincay, Jr.	Woody Stephens	2:02.4
1983	Sunny's Halo	Eddie Delahoussaye	David C. Cross Jr.	2:02.2
1982	Gato Del Sol	Eddie Delahoussaye	Edwin J. Gregson	2:02.4
1981	Pleasant Colony	Jorge Velasquez	John P. Campo	2:02.0
1980	Genuine Risk *	Jacinto Vasquez	LeRoy Jolley	2:02.0

KENTUCKY DERBY RESULTS

Year	Winner	Jockey	Trainer	Time
1979	Spectacular Bid	Ronnie Franklin	Bud Delp	2:02.4
1978	**Affirmed**	Steve Cauthen	Laz Barrera	2:01.2
1977	**Seattle Slew**	Jean Cruguet	William H. Turner, Jr.	2:02.2
1976	Bold Forbes	Angel Cordero, Jr.	Laz Barrera	2:01.6
1975	Foolish Pleasure	Jacinto Vasquez	LeRoy Jolley	2:02.0
1974	Cannonade	Angel Cordero, Jr.	Woody Stephens	2:04.0
1973	**Secretariat**	Ron Turcotte	Lucien Laurin	**1:59.4**
1972	Riva Ridge	Ron Turcotte	Lucien Laurin	2:01.8
1971	Canonero II	Gustavo Avila	Juan Arias	2:03.2
1970	Dust Commander	Mike Manganello	Don Combs	2:03.4
1969	Majestic Prince	Bill Hartack	Johnny Longden	2:01.8
1968	Forward Pass	Ismael Valenzuela	Henry Forrest	2:02.2
1967	Proud Clarion	Bobby Ussery	Loyd Gentry, Jr.	2:00.6
1966	Kauai King	Don Brumfield	Henry Forrest	2:02.0
1965	Lucky Debonair	Bill Shoemaker	Frank Catrone	2:01.2
1964	Northern Dancer	Bill Hartack	Horatio Luro	2:00.0
1963	Chateaugay	Braulio Baeza	James P. Conway	2:01.8
1962	Decidedly	Bill Hartack	Horatio Luro	2:00.4
1961	Carry Back	Johnny Sellers	Jack A. Price	2:04.0
1960	Venetian Way	Bill Hartack	Victor J. Sovinski	2:02.4
1959	Tomy Lee	Bill Shoemaker	Frank E. Childs	2:02.2
1958	Tim Tam	Ismael Valenzuela	Jimmy Jones	2:05.0
1957	Iron Liege	Bill Hartack	Jimmy Jones	2:02.2
1956	Needles	David Erb	Hugh L. Fontaine	2:03.4
1955	Swaps	Bill Shoemaker	Mesh Tenney	2:01.8
1954	Determine	Raymond York	William Molter	2:03.0
1953	Dark Star	Henry E. Moreno	Eddie Hayward	2:02.0
1952	Hill Gail	Eddie Arcaro	Ben A. Jones	2:01.6
1951	Count Turf	Conn McCreary	Sol Rutchick	2:02.6
1950	Middleground	William Boland	Max Hirsch	2:01.6
1949	Ponder	Steve Brooks	Ben A. Jones	2:04.2
1948	**Citation**	Eddie Arcaro	Ben A. Jones	2:05.4
1947	Jet Pilot	Eric Guerin	Tom Smith	2:06.8
1946	**Assault**	Warren Mehrtens	Max Hirsch	2:06.6
1945	Hoop Jr.	Eddie Arcaro	Ivan H. Parke	2:07.0
1944	Pensive	Conn McCreary	Ben A. Jones	2:04.2
1943	**Count Fleet**	Johnny Longden	Don Cameron	2:04.0
1942	Shut Out	Wayne D. Wright	John M. Gaver, Sr.	2:04.4
1941	**Whirlaway**	Eddie Arcaro	Ben A. Jones	2:01.4
1940	Gallahadion	Carroll Bierman	Roy Waldron	2:05.0

KENTUCKY DERBY RESULTS

Year	Winner	Jockey	Trainer	Time
1939	Johnstown	James Stout	Jim Fitzsimmons	2:03.4
1938	Lawrin	Eddie Arcaro	Ben A. Jones	2:04.8
1937	**War Admiral**	Charley Kurtsinger	George Conway	2:03.2
1936	Bold Venture	Ira Hanford	Max Hirsch	2:03.6
1935	**Omaha**	Willie Saunders	Jim Fitzsimmons	2:05.0
1934	Cavalcade	Mack Garner	Bob Smith	2:04.0
1933	Brokers Tip	Don Meade	Herbert J. Thompson	2:06.8
1932	Burgoo King	Eugene James	Herbert J. Thompson	2:05.2
1931	Twenty Grand	Charley Kurtsinger	James G. Rowe, Jr.	2:01.8
1930	**Gallant Fox**	Earl Sande	Jim Fitzsimmons	2:07.6
1929	Clyde Van Dusen	Linus McAtee	Clyde Van Dusen	2:10.8
1928	Reigh Count	Chick Lang	Bert S. Michell	2:10.4
1927	Whiskery	Linus McAtee	Fred Hopkins	2:06.0
1926	Bubbling Over	Albert Johnson	Herbert J. Thompson	2:03.8
1925	Flying Ebony	Earl Sande	William B. Duke	2:07.6
1924	Black Gold	J. D. Mooney	Hanley Webb	2:05.2
1923	Zev	Earl Sande	David J. Leary	2:05.4
1922	Morvich	Albert Johnson	Fred Burlew	2:04.6
1921	Behave Yourself	Charles Thompson	Herbert J. Thompson	2:04.2
1920	Paul Jones	Ted Rice	William M. Garth	2:09.0
1919	**Sir Barton**	Johnny Loftus	H. Guy Bedwell	2:09.8
1918	Exterminator	Willie Knapp	Henry McDaniel	2:10.8
1917	Omar Khayyam	Charles Borel	Charles T. Patterson	2:04.6
1916	George Smith	Johnny Loftus	Hollie Hughes	2:04.0
1915	Regret*	Joe Notter	James G. Rowe, Sr.	2:05.4
1914	Old Rosebud	John McCabe	Frank D. Weir	2:03.40
1913	Donerail	Roscoe Goose	Thomas P. Hayes	2:04.8
1912	Worth	Carroll H. Shilling	Frank M. Taylor	2:09.4
1911	Meridian	George Archibald	Albert Ewing	2:05.0
1910	Donau	Frederick Herbert	George Ham	2:06.4
1909	Wintergreen	Vincent Powers	Charles Mack	2:08.2
1908	Stone Street	Arthur Pickens	J. W. Hall	2:15.2
1907	Pink Star	Andy Minder	William H. Fizer	2:12.6
1906	Sir Huon	Roscoe Troxler	Pete Coyne	2:08.8
1905	Agile	Jack Martin	Robert Tucker	2:10.75
1904	Elwood	Shorty Prior	Charles E. Durnell	2:08.5
1903	Judge Himes	Harold Booker	John P. Mayberry	2:09.0
1902	Alan-a-Dale	Jimmy Winkfield	Thomas C. McDowell	2:08.75
1901	His Eminence	Jimmy Winkfield	Frank B. Van Meter	2:07.75
1900	Lieut. Gibson	Jimmy Boland	Charles Hughes	2:06.25

KENTUCKY DERBY RESULTS

Year	Winner	Jockey	Trainer	Time
1899	Manuel	Fred Taral	Robert J. Walden	2:12.0
1898	Plaudit	Willie Simms	John E. Madden	2:09.0
1897	Typhoon II	Buttons Garner	Julius C. Cahn	2:12.5
1896	Ben Brush	Willie Simms	Hardy Campbell, Jr.	2:07.75
1895	Halma	James Perkins	Byron McClelland	2:37.5
1894	Chant	Frank Goodale	H. Eugene Leigh	2:41.0
1893	Lookout	Eddie Kunze	William McDaniel	2:39.25
1892	Azra	Alonzo Clayton	John H. Morris	2:41.5
1891	Kingman	Isaac Murphy	Dud Allen	2:52.25
1890	Riley	Isaac Murphy	Edward Corrigan	2:45.0
1889	Spokane	Thomas Kiley	John Rodegap	2:34.5
1888	Macbeth II	George Covington	John Campbell	2:38.25
1887	Montrose	Isaac Lewis	John McGinty	2:39.25
1886	Ben Ali	Paul Duffy	Jim Murphy	2:36.5
1885	Joe Cotton	Erskine Henderson	Abraham Perry	2:37.25
1884	Buchanan	Isaac Murphy	William Bird	2:40.25
1883	Leonatus	Billy Donohue	Raleigh Colston Sr.	2:43.0
1882	Apollo	Babe Hurd	Green B. Morris	2:40.25
1881	Hindoo	Jim McLaughlin	James G. Rowe, Sr.	2:40.0
1880	Fonso	George Lewis	Tice Hutsell	2:37.50
1879	Lord Murphy	Charlie Shauer	George Rice	2:37.00
1878	Day Star	Jimmy Carter	Lee Paul	2:37.25
1877	Baden-Baden	Billy Walker	Edward D. Brown	2:38.0
1876	Vagrant	Robert Swim	James Williams	2:38.25
1875	Aristides	Oliver Lewis	Ansel Williamson	2:37.75

Triple Crown Winner

* Filly

COLLEGE NCAA FOOTBALL CHAMPIONS

Year	Team	Selector
2019	LSU	College Football Playoff
2018	Clemson	CFP
2017	Alabama	CFP
2016	Clemson	CFP
2015	Alabama	CFP
2014	Ohio State	CFP
2013	Florida State	Bowl Championship Series
2012	Alabama	BCS
2011	Alabama	BCS
2010	Auburn	BCS
2009	Alabama	BCS
2008	Florida	BCS
2007	LSU	BCS
2006	Florida	BCS
2005	Texas	BCS
2004	Southern California	BCS
2003	LSU, Southern California	BCS, AP, FWAA
2002	Ohio State	BCS
2001	Miami (Fla.)	BCS
2000	Oklahoma	BCS
1999	Florida State	BCS
1998	Tennessee	BCS
1997	Michigan, Nebraska	AP, FWAA, NFF, USA/ESPN
1996	Florida	AP, FWAA, NFF, USA/CNN
1995	Nebraska	AP, FWAA, NFF, USA/CNN, UPI
1994	Nebraska	AP, FWAA, NFF, USA/CNN, UPI
1993	Florida St.	AP, FWAA, NFF, USA/CNN, UPI
1992	Alabama	AP, FWAA, NFF, USA/CNN, UPI
1991	Washington, Miami (Fla.)	FWAA, NFF, USA/CNN, UPI, AP
1990	Colorado, Georgia Tech	FWAA, NFF, USA/CNN, AP, UPI
1989	Miami (Fla.)	AP, FWAA, NFF, USA/CNN, UPI
1988	Notre Dame	AP, FWAA, NFF, USA/CNN, UPI
1987	Miami (Fla.)	AP, FWAA, NFF, USA/CNN, UPI
1986	Penn State	AP, FWAA, NFF, USA/CNN, UPI
1985	Oklahoma	AP, FWAA, NFF, USA/CNN, UPI
1984	Brigham Young	AP, FWAA, NFF, USA/CNN, UPI
1983	Miami (Fla.)	AP, FWAA, NFF, USA/CNN, UPI
1982	Penn State	AP, FWAA, NFF, USA/CNN, UPI
1981	Clemson	AP, FWAA, NFF, UPI
1980	Georgia	AP, FWAA, NFF, UPI
1979	Alabama	AP, FWAA, NFF, UPI

COLLEGE NCAA FOOTBALL CHAMPIONS

Year	Champion(s)	Selectors
1978	Alabama, Southern California	AP, FWAA, NFF, UPI
1977	Notre Dame	AP, FWAA, NFF, UPI
1976	Pittsburgh	AP, FWAA, NFF, UPI
1975	Oklahoma	AP, FWAA, NFF, UPI
1974	Southern California, Oklahoma	FWAA, NFF, UPI, AP
1973	Notre Dame, Alabama	AP, FWAA, NFF, UPI
1972	Southern California	AP, FWAA, NFF, UPI
1971	Nebraska	AP, FWAA, NFF, UPI
1970	Nebraska, Texas, Ohio State	AP, FWAA, NFF, UPI, NFF
1969	Texas	AP, FWAA, NFF, UPI
1968	Ohio State	AP, FWAA, NFF, UPI
1967	Southern California	AP, FWAA, NFF, UPI
1966	Notre Dame, Michigan State	AP, FWAA, NFF, UPI, NFF
1965	Michigan State, Alabama	FWAA, NFF, UPI, AP
1964	Alabama, Arkansas, Notre Dame	AP, UPI, FWAA, NFF
1963	Texas	AP, FWAA, NFF, UPI
1962	Southern California	AP, FWAA, NFF, UPI
1961	Alabama, Ohio State	AP, NFF, UPI, FWAA
1960	Minnesota, Mississippi	AP, NFF, UPI, FWAA
1959	Syracuse	AP, FWAA, NFF, UPI
1958	LSU, Iowa	AP, UPI, FWAA
1957	Ohio State, Auburn	FWAA, UPI, AP
1956	Oklahoma	AP, FWAA, UPI
1955	Oklahoma	AP, FWAA, UPI
1954	UCLA, Ohio State	FWAA, UPI, AP
1953	Maryland	AP, UPI
1952	Michigan State	AP, UPI
1951	Tennessee	AP, UPI
1950	Oklahoma	AP, UPI
1949	Notre Dame	AP
1948	Michigan	AP
1947	Notre Dame	AP
1946	Notre Dame	AP
1945	Army	AP
1944	Army	AP
1943	Notre Dame	AP
1942	Ohio State	AP
1941	Minnesota	AP
1940	Minnesota	AP
1939	Texas A&M	AP
1938	Texas Christian	AP

COLLEGE NCAA FOOTBALL CHAMPIONS

Year	Champion	Selectors
1937	Pittsburgh	AP
1936	Minnesota	AP
1935	Minnesota	CFRA, HAF, NCF
1934	Minnesota	CFRA, HAF, NCF
1933	Michigan	CFRA, HAF, NCF
1932	Southern California	CFRA, HAF, NCF
1931	Southern California	CFRA, HAF, NCF
1930	Alabama, Notre Dame	CFRA, HAF, NCF
1929	Notre Dame	CFRA, HAF, NCF
1928	Georgia Tech	CFRA, HAF, NCF
1927	Illinois, Yale	HAF, NCF, CFRA
1926	Alabama, Stanford	CFRA, HAF, NCF, HAF
1925	Alabama	CFRA, HAF, NCF
1924	Notre Dame	CFRA, HAF, NCF
1923	Illinois, Michigan	CFRA, HAF, NCF, NCF
1922	California, Cornell, Princeton	NCF, HAF, CFRA, NCF
1921	California, Cornell	CFRA, NCF, HAF
1920	California	CFRA, HAF, NCF
1919	Harvard, Illinois, Notre Dame, Texas A&M	CFRA, HAF, NCF, CFRA, NCF, NCF
1918	Michigan, Pittsburgh	NCF, HAF, NCF
1917	Georgia Tech	HAF, NCF
1916	Pittsburgh	HAF, NCF
1915	Cornell	HAF, NCF
1914	Army	HAF, NCF
1913	Harvard	HAF, NCF
1912	Harvard, Penn State	HAF, NCF, NCF
1911	Penn State, Princeton	NCF, HAF, NCF
1910	Harvard, Pittsburgh	HAF, NCF, NCF
1909	Yale	HAF, NCF
1908	LSU, Pennsylvania	NCF, HAF, NCF
1907	Yale	HAF, NCF
1906	Princeton	HAF, NCF
1905	Chicago	HAF, NCF
1904	Michigan, Pennsylvania	NCF, HAF, NCF
1903	Michigan, Princeton	NCF, HAF, NCF
1902	Michigan	HAF, NCF
1901	Michigan	HAF, NCF
1900	Yale	HAF, NCF
1899	Harvard	HAF, NCF
1898	Harvard	HAF, NCF
1897	Pennsylvania	HAF, NCF

COLLEGE NCAA FOOTBALL CHAMPIONS

Year	Champion	Selector
1896	Lafayette, Princeton	NCF, HAF, NCF
1895	Pennsylvania	HAF, NCF
1894	Yale	HAF, NCF
1893	Princeton	HAF, NCF
1892	Yale	HAF, NCF
1891	Yale	HAF, NCF
1890	Harvard	HAF, NCF
1889	Princeton	HAF, NCF
1888	Yale	HAF, NCF
1887	Yale	HAF, NCF
1886	Yale	HAF, NCF
1885	Princeton	HAF, NCF
1884	Yale	HAF, NCF
1883	Yale	HAF, NCF
1882	Yale	NCF
1881	Yale	NCF
1880	Princeton, Yale	NCF, NCF
1879	Princeton	NCF
1878	Princeton	NCF
1877	Yale	NCF
1876	Yale	NCF
1875	Harvard	NCF
1874	Yale	NCF
1873	Princeton	NCF
1872	Princeton	NCF
1871	None selected	NCF
1870	Princeton	NCF
1869	Princeton, Rutgers	NCF

Largest Football Stadiums

Rank	Stadium	Capacity	Location	Built
1	Michigan Stadium	107,601	Ann Arbor, MI	1927
2	Beaver Stadium	106,572	University Park, PA	1960
3	Ohio Stadium	102,780	Columbus, OH	1922
4	Kyle Field	102,733	College Station, TX	1927
5	Neyland Stadium	102,455	Knoxville, TN	1921
6	Tiger Stadium	102,321	Baton Rouge, LA	1924
7	Bryant-Denny Stadium	101,821	Tuscaloosa, AL	1929
8	Royal-Texas Mem. Stadium	101,821	Austin, TX	1924
9	Sanford Stadium	95,723	Athens, GA	1924
10	Cotton Bowl	92,100	Dallas, TX	1930
11	Rose Bowl	90,888	Pasadena, CA	1922
12	Ben Hill Griffin Stadium	88,548	Gainesville, FL	1930
13	Jordan-Hare Stadium	87,451	Auburn, AL	1939
14	Gaylord Memorial Stadium	86,112	Norman, OK	1925
15	Memorial Stadium	86,047	Lincoln, NE	1923
16	MetLife Stadium	82,500	E Rutherford, NJ	2010
17	FedEx Field	82,000	Landover, MD	1997
18	Memorial Stadium	81,500	Clemson, SC	1942
19	Lambeau Field	81,435	Green Bay, WI	1957
20	Notre Dame Stadium	80,795	Notre Dame, IN	1930

NCAA-National Collegiate Athletic Association

USA/ESPN-USA Today/Entertainment and Sports Programming Network

USA/CNN-USA Today/Cable News Network

AP-Associated Press

UPI-United Press International

NCF-National Championship Foundation

HAF-Helms Athletic Foundation

NFF-National Football Foundation

FWAA-Football Writers Association of America

CFRA-College Football Researchers Association

COLLEGE NCAA BASKETBALL CHAMPIONS

Year	Champion (Record)	Coach	Score	Runner-Up	Site
2019	Virginia (35-3)	Tony Bennett	85-77 (OT)	Texas Tech	Minneapolis, Minn.
2018	Villanova (36-4)	Jay Wright	79-62	Michigan	San Antonio, Texas
2017	North Carolina (33-7)	Roy Williams	71-65	Gonzaga	Phoenix, Ariz.
2016	Villanova (35-5)	Jay Wright	77-74	North Carolina	Houston, Texas
2015	Duke (35-4)	Mike Krzyzewski	68-63	Wisconsin	Indianapolis, Ind.
2014	Connecticut (32-8)	Kevin Ollie	60-54	Kentucky	Arlington, Texas
2013	Louisville (35-5)*	Rick Pitino	82-76	Michigan	Atlanta, Ga.
2012	Kentucky (38-2)	John Calipari	67-59	Kansas	New Orleans, La.
2011	Connecticut (32-9)	Jim Calhoun	53-41	Butler	Houston, Texas
2010	Duke (35-5)	Mike Krzyzewski	61-59	Butler	Indianapolis, Ind.
2009	North Carolina (34-4)	Roy Williams	89-72	Michigan State	Detroit, Mich.
2008	Kansas (37-3)	Bill Self	75-68 (OT)	Memphis	San Antonio, Texas
2007	Florida (35-5)	Billy Donovan	84-75	Ohio State	Atlanta, Ga.
2006	Florida (33-6)	Billy Donovan	73-57	UCLA	Indianapolis, Ind.
2005	North Carolina (33-4)	Roy Williams	75-70	Illinois	St. Louis, Mo.
2004	Connecticut (33-6)	Jim Calhoun	82-73	Georgia Tech	San Antonio, Texas
2003	Syracuse (30-5)	Jim Boeheim	81-78	Kansas	New Orleans, La.
2002	Maryland (32-4)	Gary Williams	64-52	Indiana	Atlanta, Ga.
2001	Duke (35-4)	Mike Krzyzewski	82-72	Arizona	Minneapolis, Minn.
2000	Michigan State (32-7)	Tom Izzo	89-76	Florida	Indianapolis, Ind.
1999	Connecticut (34-2)	Jim Calhoun	77-74	Duke	St. Petersburg, Fla.
1998	Kentucky (35-4)	Tubby Smith	78-69	Utah	San Antonio, Texas
1997	Arizona (25-9)	Lute Olson	84-79 (OT)	Kentucky	Indianapolis, Ind.
1996	Kentucky (34-2)	Rick Pitino	76-67	Syracuse	East Rutherford, N.J.
1995	UCLA (31-2)	Jim Harrick	89-78	Arkansas	Seattle, Wash.
1994	Arkansas (31-3)	Nolan Richardson	76-72	Duke	Charlotte, N.C.
1993	North Carolina (34-4)	Dean Smith	77-71	Michigan	New Orleans, La.
1992	Duke (34-2)	Mike Krzyzewski	71-51	Michigan	Minneapolis, Minn.
1991	Duke (32-7)	Mike Krzyzewski	72-65	Kansas	Indianapolis, Ind.
1990	UNLV (35-5)	Jerry Tarkanian	103-73	Duke	Denver, Colo.
1989	Michigan (30-7)	Steve Fisher	80-79 (OT)	Seton Hall	Seattle, Wash.
1988	Kansas (27-11)	Larry Brown	83-79	Oklahoma	Kansas City, Mo.
1987	Indiana (30-4)	Bob Knight	74-73	Syracuse	New Orleans, La.
1986	Louisville (32-7)	Denny Crum	72-69	Duke	Dallas, Texas
1985	Villanova (25-10)	Rollie Massimino	66-64	Georgetown	Lexington, Ky.
1984	Georgetown (34-3)	John Thompson	84-75	Houston	Seattle, Wash.
1983	N Carolina State (26-10)	Jim Valvano	54-52	Houston	Albuquerque, N.M.
1982	North Carolina (32-2)	Dean Smith	63-62	Georgetown	New Orleans, La.
1981	Indiana (26-9)	Bob Knight	63-50	North Carolina	Philadelphia, Pa.
1980	Louisville (33-3)	Denny Crum	59-54	UCLA	Indianapolis, Ind.
1979	Michigan State (26-6)	Jud Heathcote	75-64	Indiana State	Salt Lake City, Utah

Land of the Free, Home of the Brave

COLLEGE NCAA BASKETBALL CHAMPIONS

Year	Champion (Record)	Coach	Score	Runner-Up	Site
1978	Kentucky (30-2)	Joe Hall	94-88	Duke	St. Louis, Mo.
1977	Marquette (25-7)	Al McGuire	67-59	North Carolina	Atlanta, Ga.
1976	Indiana (32-0)	Bob Knight	86-68	Michigan	Philadelphia, Pa.
1975	UCLA (28-3)	John Wooden	92-85	Kentucky	San Diego, Calif.
1974	N Carolina State (30-1)	Norm Sloan	76-64	Marquette	Greensboro, N.C.
1973	UCLA (30-0)	John Wooden	87-66	Memphis State	St. Louis, Mo.
1972	UCLA (30-0)	John Wooden	81-76	Florida State	Los Angeles, Calif.
1971	UCLA (29-1)	John Wooden	68-62	Villanova	Houston, Texas
1970	UCLA (28-2)	John Wooden	80-69	Jacksonville	College Park, Md.
1969	UCLA (29-1)	John Wooden	92-72	Purdue	Louisville, Ky.
1968	UCLA (29-1)	John Wooden	78-55	North Carolina	Los Angeles, Calif.
1967	UCLA (30-0)	John Wooden	79-64	Dayton	Louisville, Ky.
1966	UTEP (28-1)	Don Haskins	72-65	Kentucky	College Park, Md.
1965	UCLA (28-2)	John Wooden	91-80	Michigan	Portland, Ore.
1964	UCLA (30-0)	John Wooden	98-83	Duke	Kansas City, Mo.
1963	Loyola (Ill.) (29-2)	George Ireland	60-58 (OT)	Cincinnati	Louisville, Ky.
1962	Cincinnati (29-2)	Ed Jucker	71-59	Ohio State	Louisville, Ky.
1961	Cincinnati (27-3)	Ed Jucker	70-65 (OT)	Ohio State	Kansas City, Mo.
1960	Ohio State (25-3)	Fred Taylor	75-55	California	Daly City, Calif.
1959	California (25-4)	Pete Newell	71-70	West Virginia	Louisville, Ky.
1958	Kentucky (23-6)	Adolph Rupp	84-72	Seattle	Louisville, Ky.
1957	North Carolina (32-0)	Frank McGuire	54-53 (3OT)	Kansas	Kansas City, Mo.
1956	San Francisco (29-0)	Phil Woolpert	83-71	Iowa	Evanston, Ill.
1955	San Francisco (28-1)	Phil Woolpert	77-63	LaSalle	Kansas City, Mo.
1954	La Salle (26-4)	Ken Loeffler	92-76	Bradley	Kansas City, Mo.
1953	Indiana (23-3)	Branch McCracken	69-68	Kansas	Kansas City, Mo.
1952	Kansas (28-3)	Phog Allen	80-63	St. John's	Seattle, Wash.
1951	Kentucky (32-2)	Adolph Rupp	68-58	Kansas State	Minneapolis, Minn.
1950	CCNY (24-5)	Nat Holman	71-68	Bradley	New York, N.Y.
1949	Kentucky (32-2)	Adolph Rupp	46-36	Oklahoma A&M	Seattle, Wash.
1948	Kentucky (36-3)	Adolph Rupp	58-42	Baylor	New York, N.Y.
1947	Holy Cross (27-3)	Doggie Julian	58-47	Oklahoma	New York, N.Y.
1946	Oklahoma State (31-2)	Henry Iba	43-40	North Carolina	New York, N.Y.
1945	Oklahoma State (27-4)	Henry Iba	49-45	NYU	New York, N.Y.
1944	Utah (21-4)	Vadal Peterson	42-40 (OT)	Dartmouth	New York, N.Y.
1943	Wyoming (31-2)	Everett Shelton	46-34	Georgetown	New York, N.Y.
1942	Stanford (28-4)	Everett Dean	53-38	Dartmouth	Kansas City, Mo.
1941	Wisconsin (20-3)	Bud Foster	39-34	Washington State	Kansas City, Mo.
1940	Indiana (20-3)	Branch McCracken	60-42	Kansas	Kansas City, Mo.
1939	Oregon (29-5)	Howard Hobson	46-33	Ohio State	Evanston, Ill.

*Louisville's participation in the 2013 tournament was later vacated by the Committee on Infractions.

COLLEGE NCAA WOMEN'S BASKETBALL CHAMPIONS

Year	Champion (Record)	Coach	Score	Runner-Up	Site
2019	Baylor (37-1)	Kim Mulkey	82-81	Notre Dame	Tampa, Fla.
2018	Notre Dame (34-3)	Muffet McGraw	61-58	Mississippi State	Columbus, Ohio
2017	South Carolina (33-4)	Dawn Staley	67-55	Mississippi State	Dallas, Texas
2016	Connecticut (38-0)	Gino Auriemma	82-51	Syracuse	Indianapolis, Ind.
2015	Connecticut (38-1)	Gino Auriemma	63-53	Notre Dame	Tampa, Fla.
2014	Connecticut (40-0)	Gino Auriemma	79-58	Notre Dame	Nashville, Tenn.
2013	Connecticut (35-4)	Gino Auriemma	93-60	Louisville	New Orleans, La.
2012	Baylor (40-0)	Kim Mulkey	80-61	Notre Dame	Denver, Colo.
2011	Texas A&M (33-5)	Gary Blair	76-70	Notre Dame	Indianapolis, Ind.
2010	Connecticut (39-0)	Gino Auriemma	53-47	Stanford	San Antonio, Texas
2009	Connecticut (39-0)	Gino Auriemma	76-54	Louisville	St. Louis, Mo.
2008	Tennessee (36-2)	Pat Summitt	64-48	Stanford	Tampa, Fla.
2007	Tennessee (34-3)	Pat Summitt	59-46	Rutgers	Cleveland, Ohio
2006	Maryland (34-4)	Brenda Frese	78-75(OT)	Duke	Boston, Mass.
2005	Baylor (33-3)	Kim Mulkey	84-62	Michigan State	Indianapolis, Ind.
2004	Connecticut (31-4)	Gino Auriemma	70-61	Tennessee	New Orleans, La.
2003	Connecticut (37-1)	Gino Auriemma	73-68	Tennessee	Atlanta, Ga.
2002	Connecticut (39-0)	Gino Auriemma	82-70	Oklahoma	San Antonio, Texas
2001	Notre Dame (34-2)	Muffet McGraw	68-66	Purdue	St. Louis, Mo.
2000	Connecticut (36-1)	Gino Auriemma	71-52	Tennessee	Philadelphia, Pa.
1999	Purdue (34-1)	Carolyn Peck	62-45	Duke	San Jose, Calif.
1998	Tennessee (39-0)	Pat Summitt	93-75	Louisiana Tech	Kansas City, Mo.
1997	Tennessee (29-10)	Pat Summitt	68-59	Old Dominion	Cincinnati, Ohio
1996	Tennessee (32-4)	Pat Summitt	83-65	Georgia	Charlotte, N.C.
1995	Connecticut (35-0)	Gino Auriemma	70-64	Tennessee	Minneapolis, Minn.
1994	North Carolina (33-2)	Sylvia Hatchell	60-59	Louisiana Tech	Richmond, Va.
1993	Texas Tech (31-3)	Marsha Sharp	84-82	Ohio State	Atlanta, Ga.
1992	Stanford (30-3)	Tara VanDerveer	78-62	Western Kentucky	Los Angeles, Calif.
1991	Tennessee (30-5)	Pat Summitt	70-67(OT)	Virginia	New Orleans, La.
1990	Stanford (32-1)	Tara VanDerveer	88-81	Auburn	Knoxville, Tenn.
1989	Tennessee (35-2)	Pat Summitt	76-60	Auburn	Tacoma, Wash.
1988	Louisiana Tech (32-2)	Leon Barmore	56-54	Auburn	Tacoma, Wash.
1987	Tennessee (28-6)	Pat Summitt	67-44	Louisiana Tech	Austin, Texas
1986	Texas (34-0)	Jody Conradt	97-81	USouthern California	Lexington, Ky.
1985	Old Dominion (31-3)	Marianne Stanley	70-65	Georgia	Austin, Texas
1984	USouthern California (29-4)	Linda Sharp	72-61	Tennessee	Los Angeles, Calif.
1983	USouthern California (31-2)	Linda Sharp	69-67	Louisiana Tech	Norfolk, Va.
1982	Louisiana Tech (35-1)	Sonja Hogg	76-62	Cheney State	Norfolk, Va.

OLYMPIC GAMES IN THE USA

Games		Host city	Nations	Participants	Events
1904	Summer Olympics	St. Louis, Mo.	12	651	91
1932	Winter Olympics	Lake Placid, N.Y.	17	252	14
1932	Summer Olympics	Los Angeles, Calif.	37	1,332	117
1960	Winter Olympics	Squaw Valley, Calif.	30	665	27
1980	Winter Olympics	Lake Placid, N.Y.	37	1,072	38
1984	Summer Olympics	Los Angeles, Calif.	140	6,829	221
1996	Summer Olympics	Atlanta, Ga.	197	10,318	271
2002	Winter Olympics	Salt Lake City, Utah	77	2,399	78
2028	Summer Olympics	Los Angeles, Calif.	TBA	TBA	TBA

Medal Count-USA

Games	Gold	Silver	Bronze	Total	Rank
1904 S	78	82	79	239	1
1932 W	6	4	2	12	1
1932 S	41	32	30	103	1
1960 W	3	4	3	10	3
1980 W	6	4	2	12	3
1984 S	83	61	30	174	1
1996 S	44	32	25	101	1
2002 W	10	13	11	34	3

Learning More ~ Suggested Readings

Albion's Seed: Four British Folkways in America, David Hackett Fischer, Oxford University Press, 1989.

Battle Cry of Freedom, James McPherson, Oxford University Press, 2003.

The Civil War: A Narrative, Shelby Foote, Vintage, 1986.

Washington: A Life, Ron Chernow, Penguin Press, 2010.

Grant, Ron Chernow, Penguin Press, 2017.

Founding Brothers: The Revolutionary Generation, Joseph Ellis, Vintage, 2002.

The Glorious Cause: The American Revolution, 1763-1789, Robert Middlekauff, Oxford University Press, 2005.

The British Are Coming: The War for America, Lexington to Princeton, 1775-1777, Rick Atkinson, Henry Holt & Co., 2019.

The Blood of Heroes: The 13-Day Struggle for the Alamo and the Sacrifice That Forged a Nation, James Donovan, Little, Brown and Co., 2012.

Freedom's Forge: How American Business Produced Victory in World War II, Arthur Herman, Random House, 2012.

The Admirals: Nimitz, Halsey, Leahy, and King–The Five-Star Admirals Who Won the War at Sea, Walter R. Borneman, Little, Brown and Co., 2012.

The French and Indian War: Deciding the Fate of North America, Walter R. Borneman, Harper Perennial, 2007.

American Caesar: Douglas MacArthur 1880-1964, William Manchester, Back Bay Books, 2008.

The Great Bridge: The Epic Story of the Building of the Brooklyn Bridge, David McCullough, Simon & Schuster, 1983.

Vietnam: A History, Stanley Karnow, Viking Adult, 1983.

America's Living History: The Early Years, Suzanne and Craig Sheumaker, Red Corral Publishing, 2007.

John Adams, David McCullough, Simon & Schuster, 2001.

1776, David McCullough, Simon & Schuster, 2005.

A Grand Old Flag: A History of the United States Through its Flags, Kevin and Peter Keim, DK Adult, 2007.

The First American: The Life and Times of Benjamin Franklin, H.W. Brands, Doubleday, 2000.

Andrew Jackson: His Life and Times, H.W. Brands, Anchor Books, 2006.

The War of 1812: A Forgotten Conflict, Bicentennial Edition, Donald R. Hickey, University of Illinois Press, 2012.

Mayflower: Voyage, Community, War, Nathaniel Philbrick, Penguin Books, 2007.

The Last Stand: Custer, Sitting Bull, and the Battle of the Little Bighorn, Nathaniel Philbrick, Penguin Books, 2010.

The Earth Is Weeping: The Epic Story of the Indian Wars for the American West, Peter Cozzens, Vintage, 2017.

Patriotic Fire: Andrew Jackson and Jean Laffite at the Battle of New Orleans, Winston Groom, Knopf, 2006.

The Battle of New Orleans: Andrew Jackson and America's First Military Victory, Robert Remini, Penguin Books, 2001.

Learning More ~ Suggested Readings

The House: The History of the House of Representatives, Robert Remini, Smithsonian Books, 2006.

The Victory with No Name: The Native American Defeat of the First American Army, Colin G. Calloway, Oxford University Press, 2014.

Eisenhower: A Life, Paul Johnson, Viking, 2014.

Six Frigates: The Epic History of the Founding of the U.S. Navy, Ian W. Toll, W.W. Norton & Co., 2008.

The Making of the Atomic Bomb, Richard Rhodes, Simon & Schuster, 1986.

Hue 1968: A Turning Point of the American War in Vietnam, Mark Bowden, Atlantic Monthly Press, 2017.

Lindbergh, A. Scott Berg, Berkley, 1999.

Traitor to His Class: The Privileged Life and Radical Presidency of Franklin Delano Roosevelt, H.W. Brands, Anchor, 2009.

On Desperate Ground: The Marines at The Reservoir, the Korean War's Greatest Battle, Hampton Sides, Doubleday, 2018.

Undaunted Courage: Meriwether Lewis, Thomas Jefferson, and the Opening of the American West, Stephen E. Ambrose, Simon & Schuster, 1997.

Nothing Like It In the World: The Men Who Built the Transcontinental Railroad 1863-1869, Stephen E. Ambrose, Simon & Schuster, 2001.

Edison, Edmund Morris, Random House, 2019.

Titan: The Life of John D. Rockefeller, Sr., Ron Chernow, Random House, 1998.

Where Valor Rests: Arlington National Cemetery, Rick Atkinson, National Geographic, 2015.

The Worst Hard Time: The Untold Story of Those Who Survived the Great American Dust Bowl, Timothy Egan, Mariner Books, 2006.

The Right Stuff, Tom Wolfe, Picador, 2008.

The Mound Builders, Robert Silverberg, Ohio University Press, 1986.

American Creation: Triumphs and Tragedies in the Founding of the Republic, Joseph Ellis, Vintage, 2008.

Monuments: America's History in Art and Memory, Judith Dupre, Random House, 2007.

The Americans Trilogy, Daniel J. Boorstin, Random House, 2002.

The American Heritage Illustrated History of the Presidents, Michael Beschloss, Crown, 2000.

Books for the Historically Curious

Website: zimcopubs.com

Contact: info @ zimcopubs.com

Available on Amazon.com

Bookstore owners, gift shop managers, and other retailers order online from Ingram at the standard 55% discount/returnable.

Takes a fresh look, with 16 maps, at the unprecedented pursuit of the Army of Tennessee by Federal troops following the Battle of Nashville. The non-stop action begins at Compton's Hill and surges 120 miles in ten days over rugged terrain and horrendous winter conditions to the final showdown between blue troopers and gray rearguard. Paperback. 192 pages. ISBN 978-0-9858692-6-7.

Tells the fascinating story of the Federal naval invasion of Middle Tennessee on the Tennessee and Cumberland rivers and the Confederate response via river gun batteries and cavalry armed with artillery. The paperback is well-illustrated and features 26 maps, including 14 battle maps. 184 pages. ISBN 978-0-9858692-5-0.

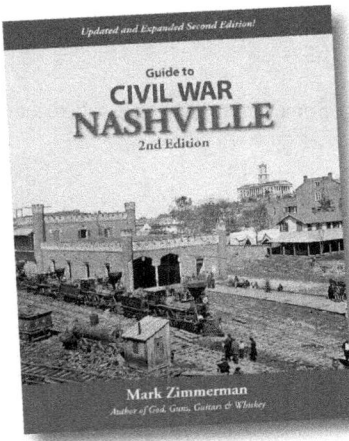

The definitive illustrated guidebook to Nashville during the Civil War—its capture and conversion to the huge Federal depot and transportation hub, and the decisive 1864 Battle of Nashville. Dozens of photos and maps. Paperback. 96 pages.
ISBN 978-0-9858692-2-9

An illustrated guidebook spotlighting more than 170 historic sites and artifacts of Nashville, the capital of Tennessee and Music City USA. Includes downtown walking tour. 265 photographs and 17 maps. Paperback. 164 pages.
ISBN 978-0-9858692-3-6

An illustrated guide to the gravesites of the famous personages in Nashville history, including Presidents Jackson and Polk, famous pioneers and generals, and Nashville country music and Grand Ole Opry stars! 140 photos and maps. Paperback. 68 pages.
ISBN 978-0-9858692-4-3

www.ingramcontent.com/pod-product-compliance
Lightning Source LLC
Chambersburg PA
CBHW060513300426

44112CB00017B/2653